Kyoto

SPATIAL HABITUS

MAKING AND MEANING IN ASIA'S ARCHITECTURE

edited by Ronald G. Knapp and Xing Ruan

House Home Family: Living and Being Chinese
EDITED BY RONALD G. KNAPP AND KAI-YIN LO

Allegorical Architecture: Living Myth and Architectonics in Southern China
XING RUAN

Chinese Architecture and the Beaux-Arts
EDITED BY JEFFREY W. CODY, NANCY S. STEINHARDT, AND TONY ATKIN

Chinese Architecture and Metaphor: Song Culture in the Yingzao Fashi *Building Manual*
JIREN FENG

Original Copies: Architectural Mimicry in Contemporary China
BIANCA BOSKER

China's Contested Capital: Architecture, Ritual, and Response in Nanjing
CHARLES D. MUSGROVE

Architecture and Urbanism in Modern Korea
INHA JUNG

The Hermit's Hut: Architecture and Asceticism in India
KAZI K. ASHRAF

Architecturalized Asia: Mapping a Continent through History
EDITED BY VIMALIN RUJIVACHARAKUL, H. HAZEL HAHN, KEN TADASHI OSHIMA, AND PETER CHRISTENSEN

Chinese Architecture in an Age of Turmoil, 200–600
NANCY SHATZMAN STEINHARDT

Kyoto: An Urban History of Japan's Premodern Capital
MATTHEW STAVROS

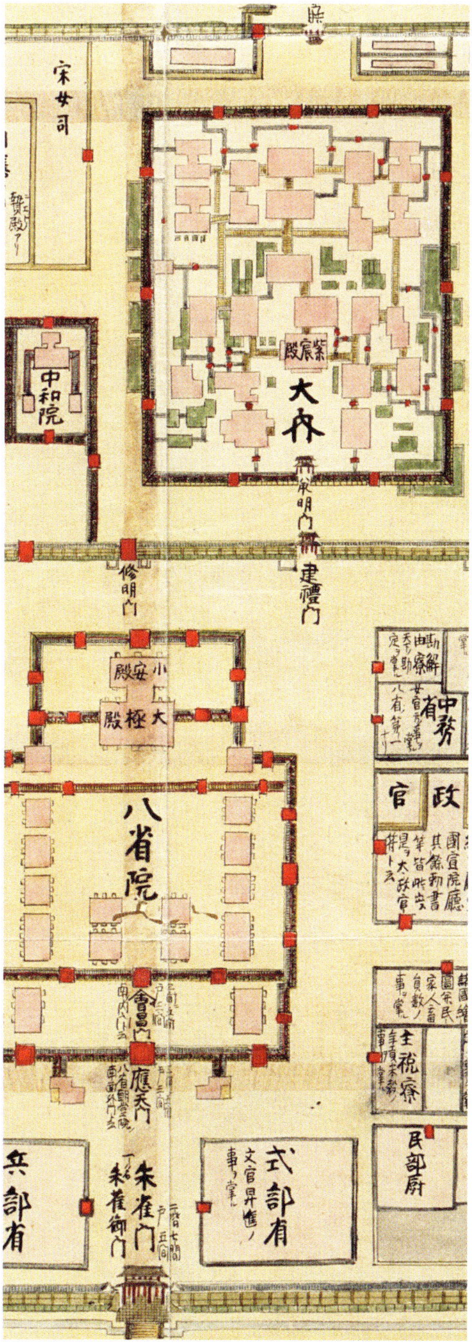

Kyoto

An Urban History of Japan's Premodern Capital

MATTHEW STAVROS

UNIVERSITY OF HAWAI'I PRESS

HONOLULU

Paperback edition 2016

Printed in the United States of America

21 20 19 18 17 16 6 5 4 3 2 1

The Australian Academy of the Humanities and the Japan Foundation provided generous funding to support this publication.

Library of Congress Cataloging-in-Publication Data

Stavros, Matthew Gerald, author.

Kyoto : an urban history of Japan's premodern capital / Matthew Stavros.

pages cm—(Spatial habitus: making and meaning in Asia's architecture)

Includes bibliographical references and index.

ISBN 978-0-8248-3879-9 (cloth : alk. paper)

1. Kyoto (Japan)—History. I. Title. II. Series: Spatial habitus (Series)

DS897.K857S73 2014 952'.1864—dc23 2014005899

ISBN 978-0-8248-6788-1 (pbk).

University of Hawai'i Press books are printed on acid-free paper and meet the guidelines for permanence and durability of the Council on Library Resources.

Designed by Julie Matsuo-Chun

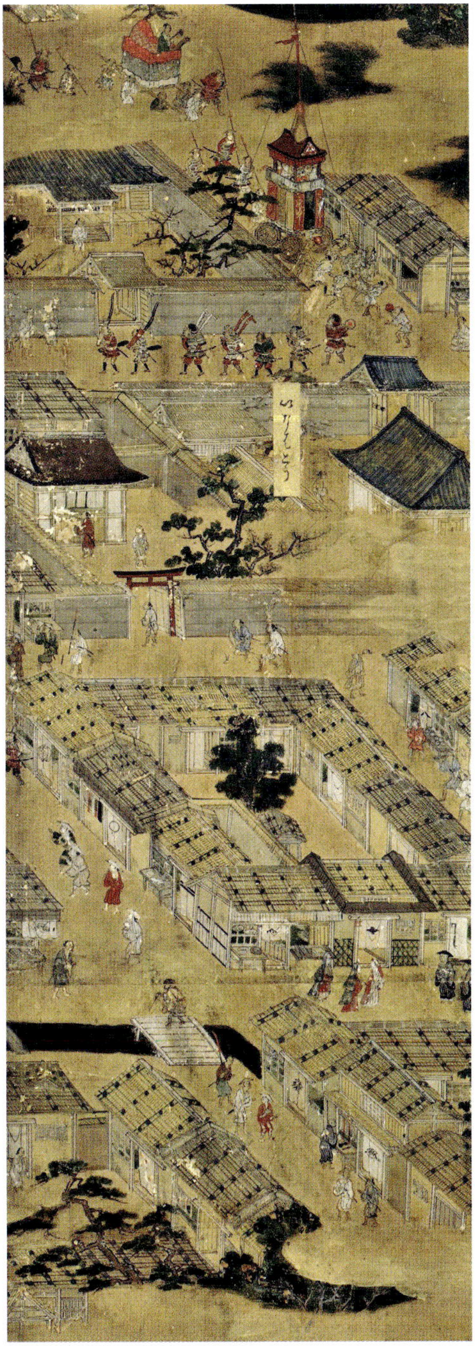

Contents

Supplementary materials are available at www.kyotohistory.com

for **Kyoko**

Illustrations

Acknowledgments

From the beginning of my research on Kyoto, Takahashi Yasuo has been a wise and generous mentor. While under his supervision during two extended periods of research at Kyoto University, I also benefited from the guidance and friendship of Yamagishi Tsuneto, Tomishima Yoshiyuki, Kishi Yasuko, and Toya Nobuhiro. At Princeton University, Martin Collcutt and David Howell were outstanding advisors, perfectly blending strong academic training with personal warmth and support. Thomas Hare and Jacqueline Stone inspired my research and Yasuko Makino provided practical assistance with library materials. As reliable sources of counsel and good humor, my peers in the Vicus Lusorum that was Princeton's graduate program also deserve recognition. They include Reggie Jackson, Stacy Nakamura, Eric Dinmore, Hans Bjarne Thomsen, Sakurako Handa, Micah Auerbach, Alexander Vesey, Aaron Moore, Robert Cross, Jonathan Abel, Xiaojin Wu, Young-Ah Chung, Mark Rowe, Lori Meeks, and Rick Berger. I will always feel a special sense of fraternity toward Morgan Pitelka. He first nudged me onto my current path while we were living, quite coincidentally, as neighbors in Kyoto in 1998. I am grateful he did.

Several extended periods of research at the University of Tokyo's Historiographical Institute were facilitated by Ishigami Eiichi and Takahashi Shin'ichirō. Professor Takahashi continues to be a source of tremendous guidance and friendship. Haruko Wakabayashi welcomed me to the Institute's Japan Memory Project and arranged for my ongoing access to the archives. In Tokyo, I also benefited from regular contact with Itō Takeshi and Yoshida Nobuyuki. Ellen Van Goethem generously hosted me at Hōsei University and was an outstanding source of advice and support.

The manuscript for this book was finalized at Kyoto University during a visiting professorship arranged by Nakajima Setsuko. I feel a profound sense of gratitude to Professor Nakajima and her colleagues, Iyori Tsutomu and Noboru Ogata.

At the University of Sydney, I am surrounded by admirable colleagues who support my work and help keep me sane. For their institutional leadership and good counsel, Elise Tipton and Olivier Ansart are foremost among them. Adrian Vickers and Robert Aldrich are inspirational for their balance of scholarly achievement and humanity. It is a special pleasure to work side by side with Michael Lewis at Sydney. It was he who, at Michigan State University many years ago, first introduced me to the professional study of history. His influence on my career has been long-standing, diverse, and always positive.

There are several people who deserve recognition for their constant—albeit often virtual—presence as mentors and friends. They include Suzanne Gay, Yukio Lippit, Kawamoto Shigeo, Thomas Conlan, Yoshimura Takahiko, Royall Tyler, Michael Watson, Mikael Bauer, and Brian Ruppert. Kuniko McVey of the Harvard-Yenching Library generously found, scanned, and sent to me a large number of sources. Stephen Parker provided invaluable advice on the final manuscript that both refined and clarified.

I am indebted to many institutions that facilitated and funded my research over the years. Although they are mentioned only in passing here, I would like express my most sincere sentiment that the work of each is critical to the continued advancement of knowledge. This book is only one modest result. The Japanese Ministry of Education (Monbushō) funded two long stays in Japan, first at Hiroshima University (1995–1996) and then at Kyoto University (1998–2000). The Graduate School at Princeton University fully endowed my five years of doctoral study, including summers in Japan. A dissertation fellowship from J. William Fulbright-IIE, which was underwritten by the Mitsubishi Kinyōkai, allowed me to conduct another year of research at Kyoto University in 2002. A sabbatical spent at the University of Tokyo in 2009 was made possible by the Japan Foundation, which, mainly through its office in Sydney, has supported my work in countless other ways as well. Koike Wakao and Tokuman Sayuri have made sure of that, and to them both I am deeply grateful. The University of Sydney's Faculty of Arts and Social Sciences gave me several grants for materials and travel, as did the School of Languages and Culture and the Department of Japanese Studies. The latter also supplied a generous publishing subsidy for this book. Additional publishing support was received from the Australian Academy of the Humanities and the Japan Foundation.

I am grateful to the several institutions that provided images and image permissions for this book. They are acknowledged individually in the captions. At the Kyoto City Library of Historical Documents, Matsunaka Hiroshi graciously gave me access to illustrations, maps, and a stunning 1/1000 model of Heian-kyō. The Kyoto Prefectural Archives in Kitayama deserves special mention. It is one of the best libraries I have used, staffed by professionals who facilitated my research in many ways. Yoriko Igari and Umatani Osamu provided illustrations for this book and advice on presenting visual materials.

My impulse to thank the editor is by no means a mere courtesy. I have found Patricia Crosby's near legendary status in the field well deserved. For her extraordinary professionalism and grace, I record here my most sincere thanks. Managing editor Ann Ludeman was equally as helpful, and Drew Bryan was an excellent copy editor. David Kelly stepped in at the last minute to assist with key editorial decisions.

This book is dedicated to Kyoko, my wife and companion throughout. Quality time spent with her and our children, Miyako and Kent, kept me from finishing this book sooner, and I would never have had it any other way.

Matthew Stavros
CAMPERDOWN

Conventions and Abbreviations

All Japanese names are written in the customary Japanese manner, family name followed by given name. Months and days are given according to the lunar calendar, although years are rounded to the closest equivalent in the Western calendar. For example, Enbun 3/8/22 refers to the twenty-second day of the eighth month of 1358. For Japanese imperial years (*nengō*) between 1336 and 1392, those of the Northern Court are used throughout.

In this study, all of Kyoto's thoroughfares are called "roads." Calling them "avenues," "boulevards," "lanes," or anything else based on relative size or location can invite confusion because each of these words can mean something different in different cultural contexts. The only exception is the use of the word "street" in reference to a social phenomenon, as in "the street as the center of daily life." The names of all roads, locations, and buildings are indicated using the current consensus on their contemporaneous readings. The homes of elite members of Kyoto society are referred to as "palaces." This is a rough equivalent of the Japanese suffix "*dono*," customarily attached to the names of such properties. It is not an implication about opulence or grandeur. Indeed, during long stretches of the city's history, these "palaces" were often not particularly palatial.

"Heian-kyō" is used to refer to the capital during the classical era, up to about the eleventh century. Beyond that, "Kyoto" is used primarily. The reason for this linguistic shift has nothing to do with historical naming practices. In fact, as far as we can tell, the proper noun "Heian-kyō" was almost never used, not even during the Heian period. It appears in an eighth-century poem composed around the time of the city's establishment and then only sporadically thereafter, and almost always in literary ways. Instead, throughout the premodern era, contemporaries tended to signify their city using one of several common (rather than proper) nouns that meant plainly "the capital." Written using a variety of ideographs and character combinations, we read the most common among these today as “Kyōto,” “Miyako,” or “Kyō,” and use each as a proper noun. How each of these words was read contemporaneously, however, and whether or not they were used as proper nouns is not known and is most likely unknowable. Readings and usages notwithstanding, it is important to note that, contrary to popular understanding, no substantial change in the city’s name, formal or otherwise, occurred during the transition from the classical to medieval eras. The naming distinction made in this study (from Heian-kyō to Kyoto) leverages popular conventions to emphasize the dramatic material and political changes that took place in about the eleventh century. While the conventions are discursive, the changes were most certainly real.

Unless otherwise noted, all figures and photographs in this book have been produced by the author. More are available at www.kyotohistory.com.

Abbreviations used in notes:

AHK	Nicolas Fiévé, ed., *Atlas historieque de Kyoto*
CHJ	*Cambridge History of Japan*
CYK(i)	Fujiwara Munetada, *Chūyūki* (Iwanami shoten)
CYK(r)	Fujiwara Munetada, *Chūyūki* (Rinsen shoten)
DNS	*Dai Nihon shiryō*
GMK	Sanjō Kintada, *Gogumaiki*
GR	*Gunsho ruijū*
KR	Kyōto-shi, ed., *Kyōto no rekishi*
KST	*Kokushi taikei (shintei zōho)*
MMK	Nakahara Moromori, *Moromoriki*
SKR	Kyōto-shi, ed., *Shiryō Kyōto no rekishi*

Introduction

Kyoto was Japan's political and cultural capital for more than a millennium before the dawn of the modern era. Throughout most of that period, it was home and ritual center to the emperor and the civil aristocracy, the focal point of both sectarian and warrior politics, and the seat of the country's most successful industries. Until about the fifteenth century, it was also among the world's largest cities and, as the eastern terminus of the Silk Road, it was a place where the political, artistic, and religious currents of Asia coalesced and flourished. Despite these and many other traits that make Kyoto a place of both Japanese and world historical significance, the physical appearance of the premodern city remains largely unknown. What makes this problem significant is that there existed in premodern Kyoto a strong relationship between space, place, and authority. As an imperial city planned according to Chinese geomantic models and embedded with status-specific architectural codes, the cityscape itself can be read as a text rich in information on politics, religion, and daily life. Understanding the built environment, therefore, reveals a great deal about the structures of power and social organization in early Japan. Through a synthesis of textual, pictorial, and archeological sources, this book explores that environment with the aim of opening up new vistas for thinking about key aspects of premodern Japanese history.

In 1974, John W. Hall published a brief essay titled "Kyoto as Historical Background." While in some respects this book is a dramatic expansion and updating of that early work, its refusal to see the city as mere "background" is novel. This is a history of architecture and space that examines how the city changed over time, from a classical imperial capital in the eighth century, first into a thriving medieval metropolis in the twelfth, and then finally—after a devastating age of war and lawlessness—into an early modern castle-town. While the policies and personalities of various leaders, institutions, and commoners who shaped the city over time figure prominently in the narrative, the focus returns time and again to the city itself, its homes and temples, roads, markets, and monuments. In this respect, this is an urban history in the purest sense. The city *is* the topic, not merely the setting or backdrop of what is otherwise a social, cultural, or institutional history.

Architecture and urban planning have been closely tied to influence and authority in virtually any city of any age. In Europe, the very act of establishing a city was itself key to political expansion from as early as classical antiquity. In Sicily, for example, Hellenistic road plans and thickly columned city halls bespoke of the ideals of egalitarianism and democracy just as much as they did Athenian dominion. Across the Iberian peninsula and Germanic countryside, Rome imposed order and spread centralized control by superimposing grids upon native settlements. Urban grids in Korea, Japan, and Vietnam were unmistakable signs of Sinification and, as such, civilization. At the height of Western colonial expansion, imperial powers created "new towns" next to native antecedents in Delhi, Casablanca, Saigon, New Orleans, and elsewhere. Once independent, former colonies created entirely new, purpose-built capitals in Washington D.C., Canberra, and Brasilia. In each of these cases, grand urban plans and public buildings served to instill confidence in the citizens of a fledgling nation while projecting strength abroad. Their locations reflected an impulse to settle yet unsettled frontiers.

For its role in inspiring awe and confidence in public authority, monumentalism is another virtually universal trait of great historical cities. The Arc de Triomphe and the Washington Monument are only two among many famous structures that serve no function other than to symbolize the power embodied in the state, be it authoritarian or democratic. Dual-function structures such as the Château de Versailles or the Great Wall of China were just as potent. Urban monuments need not always be physical objects, however. The breathtaking vistas of Beijing and Philadelphia harness the visual magic of perspective to inspire awe and instill foreboding.

In premodern Kyoto, the relationships between form, function, and influence were particularly strong due to the city's special status. The classical capital was established for the express purpose of serving as an inert venue of imperial government and ritual, a place to accommodate the emperor, state institutions, the lives of its officials, and little else. Notions about functional purity informed taboos proscribing the existence of religious institutions, violence, warriors, and burial. These and other ideals made Kyoto and its architecture powerful symbols and constant reminders of the authority of the state and the emperor. For those who sought to possess the kind of public authority the city was created to symbolize and functionally accommodate, the capital's founding spatial and architectural ideals impacted their interactions with the cityscape, what they built, where, and how.

Despite profound changes to both the city and its polity over time, Kyoto's ruling elite continued to reinforce notions about the capital being an exclusive domain where the state remained not merely relevant, but supreme. The impulse for such a view—which rapidly became anachronistic—was similar to that which motivated the almost universal coveting of imperial ranks and posts: Reinforcing and respecting the classical state in both its abstract and material forms remained elemental to claims of legitimacy. Long after the weakening of public institutions and the rise of temple and warrior power from about the twelfth century, the traditional imperial hierarchy continued to be the universal benchmark of elite status while the capital remained the formal venue of imperial ritual and statecraft. Working to maintain the integrity of both, however imperfect, was a marker of membership in the traditional order, a membership that power holders of all stripes—including courtiers, monks, and warriors—sought to attain and maintain with unflagging enthusiasm throughout most of the premodern age. Central to this discussion is the complex interplay of "public authority" and "private power." In this study, the former refers to the formal, statutory, and ultimately abstract efficacy of the state (or emperor) while the latter signifies the real-world influence of individuals or institutions with access to massive wealth and vast networks of personal allegiance. As we shall see, focus on the built environment sheds new light on this old dichotomy, which runs like a topical thread through the entire book.

This study begins by exploring Kyoto's highly idealized urban plan as adapted from Chinese models in the eighth century. First described in literary sources as "Heian-kyō," meaning the "capital of peace and tranquility," emperor Kanmu's new city was meant to be a monument to a strong, centralized, Chinese-style polity. Land was divided systematically into identical blocks, and roads were laid out according to a symmetrical grid pattern. The emperor and his bureaucratic offices occupied a large, exclusive enclosure at the top-center of the city, while the civil aristocracy built official residences that were symbols of formal status and prescribed venues of ritualized statecraft. Wide, level roads facilitated efficient transportation as well as choreographed imperial processions. Heian-kyō was meant to be a mononuclear capital: the imperial institution was the political, economic, and social center of gravity, and every constituent element of the city was oriented around a single, unified, public core. A panoply of formal codes and indelible social customs dictated everything from the location of the city itself to the width of its roads and the styles of aristocratic palaces. Where people lived, what they built, and how they interacted with the cityscape were guided by principles of status, propriety, and precedent. At least that was the ideal.

The second chapter reveals how the classical urban model failed to be realized or, even in cases where it was, the results were often short-lived. For example, not only does it appear that Heian-kyō's hallmark urban grid was never finished as planned, but the way its blocks were defined and used in practice also departed significantly from the original, and ultimately unrealistic, top-down planning scheme. We also discover how evolving politics, financial problems, and natural disasters conspired to almost entirely eviscerate the primary venues of imperial government by as early as the eleventh century. The Imperial Palace, government bureaus, and diplomatic compounds disappeared at an alarming rate while the western half of the city was promptly converted into farmland. Finally, elite palaces never quite lived up to their structural and functional ideals as the rarified venues of ritualized statecraft.

Over time, influence became increasingly privatized. By the tenth century, due in large part to the expansion of tax-free landed estates (*shōen*) and hereditary control of government offices, the location of real-world influence had shifted from the Imperial Palace to the residences of court aristocrats, religious institutions, and, in time, the headquarters of retired emperors and warriors. The third chapter examines how these nodes of private political and economic influence became the nuclei of dense clusters of urban development. The advent of nodal urban development, it is argued, constituted a profound spatial transformation whereby Kyoto evolved from a state- and emperor-centric city into a composite of semi-autonomous urban islands associated more by proximity than by a unified urban identity. The structure of the medieval city became a homology of the sociopolitical conditions of the era: space, like power, was fractured, privatized, and pluralistic.

Thinking in terms of nodes of privatized power helps explain the appearance of several premodern urban phenomena that, although well known, remain unappreciated for their historical significance. First among these are the suburbs of Kamigyō and Shimogyō. Chapter 3 begins by explaining what led to the formation of these areas in early medieval Kyoto and how they acquired their distinct social characteristics, with Kamigyō as the elite district and Shimogyō as a thriving hub of commoners and commerce. Also examined is the appearance of numerous temporary imperial palaces that, over time, became increasingly less temporary. Known as *sato-dairi*, these compounds themselves, as centers of private wealth and sexual politics, played key roles in the process by which state institutions were weakened through privatization. A similar description can be applied to many of the large sectarian temples that came to virtually surround the city, as well as three temple-palace complexes built by retired emperors in the eleventh and twelfth centuries. The latter, including Shirakawa, Toba, and Hōjūji, are of particular significance because their synthesis of administrative, religious, and military facilities embodied an attempt by members of the imperial family to reassert influence through private channels. And as we shall see, their doing so from bases located outside the formal boundaries of the imperial capital was of profound significance.

During the medieval era, heightened attention was given to questions about what should and should not be built within the city, who should be excluded, and who was allowed to enter. Chapter 4 explores the emergence of a medieval discourse on capital exclusivity that conveys an impulse to insulate Kyoto from the growing influence of temples and warriors. In this context, precisely where the city's boundaries were drawn became an important question, and a difficult one to answer due to physical change having rendered the classical grid obsolete. The geopolitical dilemma, I argue, led to the articulation of the notion of "Rakuchū-Rakugai," meaning "the capital and its surroundings." Coming into currency in the thirteenth century, this well-known term and its eventual discursive mainstreaming indicated a powerful impulse among the traditional capital elite to revive classical notions of an inviolable realm, however small, where state authority remained unchallenged. Such an interpretation is reinforced by a discovery that the dichotomy of medieval power mapped neatly onto the geographic binary of "Rakuchū-Rakugai." Readers familiar with early Japanese history will be well aware of the tendency for men of great influence—noble and warrior alike—to enjoy a sort of dual identity: one as public servants and another as possessors of great private power and wealth. Inside the capital, within Rakuchū, these men maintained official residences (*honjo*) that in terms of their sizes and styles generally adhered to status-based building conventions. Outside, they created lavish temple-palace complexes (*betsugyō* or *bessō*) that reflected vast private wealth and influence, as well as personal religious convictions. The most powerful figures in Kyoto's premodern history consistently built and used Rakugai complexes as bases from which to rule from behind the scenes. It was this trend that led to the creation of many of the most important architectural monuments that stand on Kyoto's outskirts today, including Byōdōin, Sanjūsangendō, Kinkakuji, and Ginkakuji.

Established in 1336, the Ashikaga shogunate was the first and only warrior regime to make its headquarters in Kyoto. Chapter 5 begins by exploring the ways Ashikaga leaders interacted with Kyoto's urban landscape, particularly in terms of what they built and where. The findings uncover a striking level of shogunal deference toward classical spatial paradigms, indicative of a reluctance to violate age-old capital customs. The second part of the chapter shows that successive Ashikaga leaders consistently built capital residences in the same styles as their aristocratic counterparts, *shinden* style. Doing so endowed them with the architectural infrastructure necessary to conduct rituals that authenticated their membership in the imperial hierarchy. In sum, the urban record supports a growing body of evidence suggesting that the Ashikaga shogunate's success in Kyoto was due in large part to the regime's adherence to the behavior and language of traditional authority rather than (merely) forceful coercion.

The last part of this long chapter outlines the recent discovery that Ashikaga Yoshimitsu, the third and most powerful of the regime's shoguns, had a master plan for medieval Kyoto that entailed a fundamental reorganization of capital space. All of Yoshimitsu's major building projects—including several major temples, the Imperial Palace, and his own shogunal headquarters—lined up along a series of axes that overlapped to form a complex and highly contrived urban matrix. The evidence suggests that the shogun was constructing a cityscape in which each of the most powerful bodies of interest (the imperial estate, warriors, and monks) was assigned a clearly defined place within the greater order, an order that he himself was constructing in the process. Yoshimitsu's well-organized urban plan was the material manifestation of a political unifier capable of reversing the medieval trend toward ever greater degrees of political and urban fragmentation.

The dramatic physical and social changes that took place during the Age of Warring States (1467–1680s) are the topic of chapter 6. While the findings of earlier research are echoed strongly, the discussion is novel in terms of its focus on how the violence, fires, and lawlessness of the age conspired to decisively sever the physical and philosophical tendrils that anchored Kyoto to its classical past. The Ōnin War (1467–1477) and the conflicts that followed destroyed the urban grid and key venues of aristocratic pageantry. *Shinden* style and the formalized activities it facilitated became unsustainable while the ubiquitous presence of warriors and temples erased all traditional notions about capital exclusivity. Commoners and soldiers of the most base origins began buying, selling, and controlling land within the old city as the boundaries of that space came to be defined by walls and moats instead of laws and customs. The classical city and all it was meant to represent were finally and truly wiped away during the late fifteenth and early sixteenth centuries.

The final chapter explores Kyoto's postwar reconstruction under the successive leadership of Oda Nobunaga and Toyotomi Hideyoshi. The first section examines Nobunaga's impact on the urban landscape through the construction of the castle of Nijō in 1569. Besides transforming Kyoto into a castle-town (*jōka-machi*), Nijō's creation—as well as its eventual destruction—contributed to the city's postwar revitalization. The second section of this chapter explores even more substantial changes under Hideyoshi. Through either his creation or rehabilitation of several major architectural projects, Hideyoshi sought to use monumentalism as a means of co-opting and leveraging the authority of Kyoto's traditional institutions. By accepting imperial honors, moving to Kyoto, and then taking up residence within a courtly palace, he signaled that his legitimacy was tied to public authority, not just military might. This chapter also explores several large-scale zoning projects and the creation of a wall around the city. Throughout, a case is made that Nobunaga and Hideyoshi's impact on sixteenth-century Kyoto both established the basic framework of the modern city and became the prototype for the many castle-towns that proliferated throughout the archipelago during the succeeding era.

The book ends with an epilogue that briefly introduces some of the most important architectural and urban projects of the early modern era (1600–1868).

A project of this nature cannot begin without some qualifying remarks. First, this is by no means a comprehensive history of premodern Kyoto. Such an endeavor would be well beyond the scope of a single volume and, most likely, the capacity of any single author. To be sure, a great many details about the city's almost countless historic temples, palaces, and monuments have been reluctantly abbreviated for the sake of providing a largely panoramic overview of the entire premodern age. Coverage, however, is admittedly uneven. The medieval era receives the greatest attention, with chapters 3 through 6 containing the most original findings. Earlier and later sections draw liberally upon the research of others. Throughout, commoners, who always made up the largest segment of Kyoto's population, receive far less attention than they deserve. Alas, despite archeological findings that have mitigated the perennial problem of investigating an almost universally illiterate demographic, the profound material impacts of Kyoto's commoners prior to the sixteenth century remain mostly and tragically ellusive.

This book touches on a wide range of academic debates, including several that continue to occupy scholars of Japan at home and abroad. While the findings reinforce some interpretations and challenge others, this study seeks to overthrow none. It is simply not that kind of project. Instead, the overarching aim is to demonstrate how careful attention to space, place, and the built environment can reveal novel facets of old problems, enriching complexity and opening up new avenues of interpretation. If the book succeeds in achieving this method-based objective, its value will surely outlive any single argument that might otherwise have been advanced.

A final comment relates to sentiment and sentimentality. Kyoto is a place that evokes tremendous fascination and admiration. It is a city of great natural beauty and virtually countless architectural treasures. In Japanese literature, no other single location has been celebrated as frequently or as floridly as Kyoto. The city has one of the highest concentrations of Buddhist temples in the world and boasts as many as seventeen UNESCO World Heritage sites. Because it was the only major Japanese city not subjected to aerial bombardment during the Second World War, its many wooden houses, narrow byways, and shops give it a distinctly traditional flavor that visitors tend to find appealing. The author is equally fond of Kyoto, enough so to have conceived of a book-length project aimed, in part, at maximizing his time there. Nevertheless, this work is decidedly unromantic. Readers seeking effusive descriptions of the architectural and cultural glories of Japan's "eternal capital" may be disappointed. The images of early Kyoto that come from literary works such as *The Tale of Genji* or *The Pillow Book of Sei Shōnagon* are not reinforced. This is not to suggest that these images are inaccurate. They are simply not useful in the context of a study of this nature, where urban forms and the premodern cityscape are examined as historical artifacts, not cultural treasures. Readers may instead notice a marked ambivalence toward the use of subjective terms altogether. References, for example, to architectural "opulence" or "grandiosity" are limited primarily to cases where such traits were unambiguous, sometimes even codified, markers of status or influence. Otherwise, they are generally (although not entirely) avoided. This principle notwithstanding, the hope is that readers will find that even when stripped of romance and effusion, Kyoto remains an attractive city of unquestionable historical and cultural significance.

1

Heian-kyō

The Ideal

When Emperor Kanmu (737–806) founded Heian-kyō in 794, the new capital was meant to be the permanent bureaucratic and ritual seat of a strong, centralized, Chinese-style state. The scale and opulence of the plan was grand and ambitious, in fact probably too much so. Some of the key traits meant to define Heian-kyō's appearance were never entirely realized, while many of those that were rapidly disintegrated. Not only did the Japanese polity function very differently from its Chinese prototype, real power, even from the outset, rested more with private political actors than the state. Before examining how these factors contributed to Heian-kyō's failure to materialize as planned, we must begin by exploring the plan itself as well as its founding principles and prescriptions. As we shall see, these principles retained their relevance with remarkable resilience well into the succeeding eras, long after the city and its polity had changed dramatically. To be sure, for those who sought to possess the kind of orthodox authority the capital was meant to represent, Heian-kyō's founding ideals remained more than relevant. They were elemental to their engagement in the pageantry of legitimized power.

Heian-kyō's urban plan and architecture have been examined previously in English, and Japanese scholarship on the topic is vast.[1] While some detail can therefore be abbreviated, the broad outlines need to be drawn in order to set the stage for the narrative of change that follows.

The statutory government that Heian-kyō was built to accommodate was based on a body of criminal (*ritsu*) and administrative (*ryō*) codes adapted from Tang China in stages leading up to formal codification in the eighth century. The so-called "Ritsuryō" system defined the institutions of imperial government and created an official hierarchy composed of formal status ranks (*kurai*) and bureaucratic posts (*kanshoku*). As a supreme sacerdotal ruler, the emperor was at the top of the Ritsuryō system, but it was a narrow population of high-ranking civil aristocrats who administered the institutional organs of the statutory state. Access to high office was a matter of rank, and in Japan (unlike China), rank was a matter of birth rather than merit. In striking detail, Ritsuryō codes advised on a sweeping repertoire of elite customs, practices, and rituals, as well as the material infrastructure necessary to realize them. The numerous events that punctuated the official calendar—including such things as the bestowal of ranks and posts, new year's celebrations, ablutions, prayers for the protection of the body of the emperor and state, and a plethora of additional "annual observances"—were all carefully scripted affairs, following a strict regime of codes, customs, and precedents that dictated what people did, how, and in what setting. It was the strong relationship between function and form as first codified in Ritsuryō laws that made the capital and its official architecture elemental to the infrastructure of the classical state system.

Heian-kyō was conceived as an inert venue of Ritsuryō statecraft. It was to be a capital in the purest sense of the word: the seat of the statutory government, home and ritual center of the emperor and the civil aristocracy, and the location of numerous official buildings and monuments that facilitated imperial pageantry, bureaucratic administration, and diplomacy. Buddhist temples and shrines were excluded, and the presence of warriors in the city was, in principle, taboo. Due to their polluting effects, killing and burial were also formally proscribed.[2] Commercial activity was limited, while farming was generally not allowed. All land within the capital's formal boundaries was planned for urbanization. Heian-kyō was meant to be a mononuclear capital: the imperial institution was the political, economic, and social center of gravity, and every constituent element of the city was oriented—physically and philosophically—around a single, unified, public core embodied in the emperor and his palace compound. Formal codes and indelible social customs dictated everything from the location of the city itself to the width of its roads and the styles of official architecture. Where people lived, what they built, and how they interacted with the cityscape were guided by principles of status, propriety, and precedent.

As the seat of a large and complex government bureaucracy, Heian-kyō became home to a diverse population of officials numbering between five and seven thousand. Estimated allowances for their families and household servants put the number of people whose full-time presence was justified through an affiliation with the state near seventy thousand.[3] For the dozen or so individuals who constituted the highest echelon of the civil aristocracy, residence in Heian-kyō was more than a convenience; it was an obligation. From the foundation of the Japanese imperial polity, a key objective of those seeking to make the state and emperor the sole sources of political legitimacy was to sever the ties that bound the regional, landed elites to their provincial bases of private wealth and familial influence. Nationalizing all land through the Taika reforms of 646 was one important step. Physically removing those regional elites from the provinces, endowing them with public ranks and posts, then compelling them to live permanently in the capital were others.[4] It was because of this basic principle of mandatory residence that, for much of Kyoto's premodern history, a sudden and unsanctioned departure from the city was interpreted as an unambiguous act of rebellion. In sum, housing the aristocracy was not just one of Heian-kyō's functions, it was one of the primary reasons for establishing a permanent capital in the first place.[5]

And yet residence in the capital city was also a privilege. As Spiro Kostof has shown, throughout history and in various settings, the "luck of first ownership" served to reinforce aristocracy through the concentration of property rights.[6] The relationship between physical space and the aristocracy was on ubiquitous display in Heian-kyō because the aristocracy—who were the only ones initially permitted to engage in a real estate market—frequently took family names from the locations of their first official urban residences. It is for this reason that the documentary record is replete with mention of such people as the "Lord of Sanjō" (Sanjō-dono) or the "Lord of Kyōgoku" (Kyōgoku-dono). While the Japanese aristocracy was not unlike its European counterparts in this respect (the Duke of Orange Nassau or the Prince of Wales are just two of many examples), it is unique that in the Japanese case so many family names come from the names of roads in the classical capital.

The Location

Emperor Kanmu's decision to establish Heian-kyō might have appeared rash and impulsive to contemporaries. Just ten years earlier, he had undertaken the monumental task of moving the capital from Heijō-kyō (contemporary Nara) to Nagaoka-kyō (see Figure 1.1). That costly endeavor was justified, in part, on the grounds that it was to be the last time such a transfer took place. Nagaoka-kyō, indeed, was supposed to be Japan's "eternal capital" (*eien no miyako*).[7] Not only was the move to Heian-kyō soon, it was rapid. Only a few months separate Kanmu's decision and the move itself. Scholars have sought to explain why Nagaoka-kyō failed or why the Heian transfer became necessary. Some cite malevolent spirits haunting Nagaoka-kyō; others write of political and material incentives pulling Kanmu and his court to Heian. The most recent scholarship, however, finds that the single most important factor was Nagaoka-kyō's perennial and catastrophic problem with flooding.[8] The site, which construction had rendered a steep and badly denuded slope, was simply not viable as the venue of a densely built environment, let alone a capital with eternal ambitions.

The site of Heian-kyō, the Uta basin located immediately northwest of Nagaoka-kyō, was a vast improvement over its predecessor, not only in terms of topography but also matters of defense, transportation, and geomancy (see Figures 1.1 and 1.2). The cultivated fields of Uta were broad and flat with only a gentle slope from north to south. Low mountains that surrounded the greater basin in the north, east, and west supplied the land below with abundant fresh water via two major rivers, the Katsura in the west and the Kamo in the east. Due to these favorable circumstances and in contrast to Nagaoka-kyō, the whole of the new capital could be planned and constructed without any major hydraulic undertakings. Besides supplying water, the surrounding mountains were rich sources of timber. They also functioned as a natural line of defense against potential assailants. Despite the relative peace enjoyed by the region where Heian-kyō and earlier capitals stood, imperial campaigns against the "barbarian" tribes of the Emishi in the archipelago's northeast were common prior to the tenth century. Such circumstances might help explain not only the attention given to defense but also the impulse to embed peaceful aspirations into the new capital's sobriquet. The following verse, the first text to mention Heian-kyō by name, conveys this impulse precisely:

1.1. Map of central Japan indicating locations of Chinese-style capitals established during the sixth through eighth centuries.

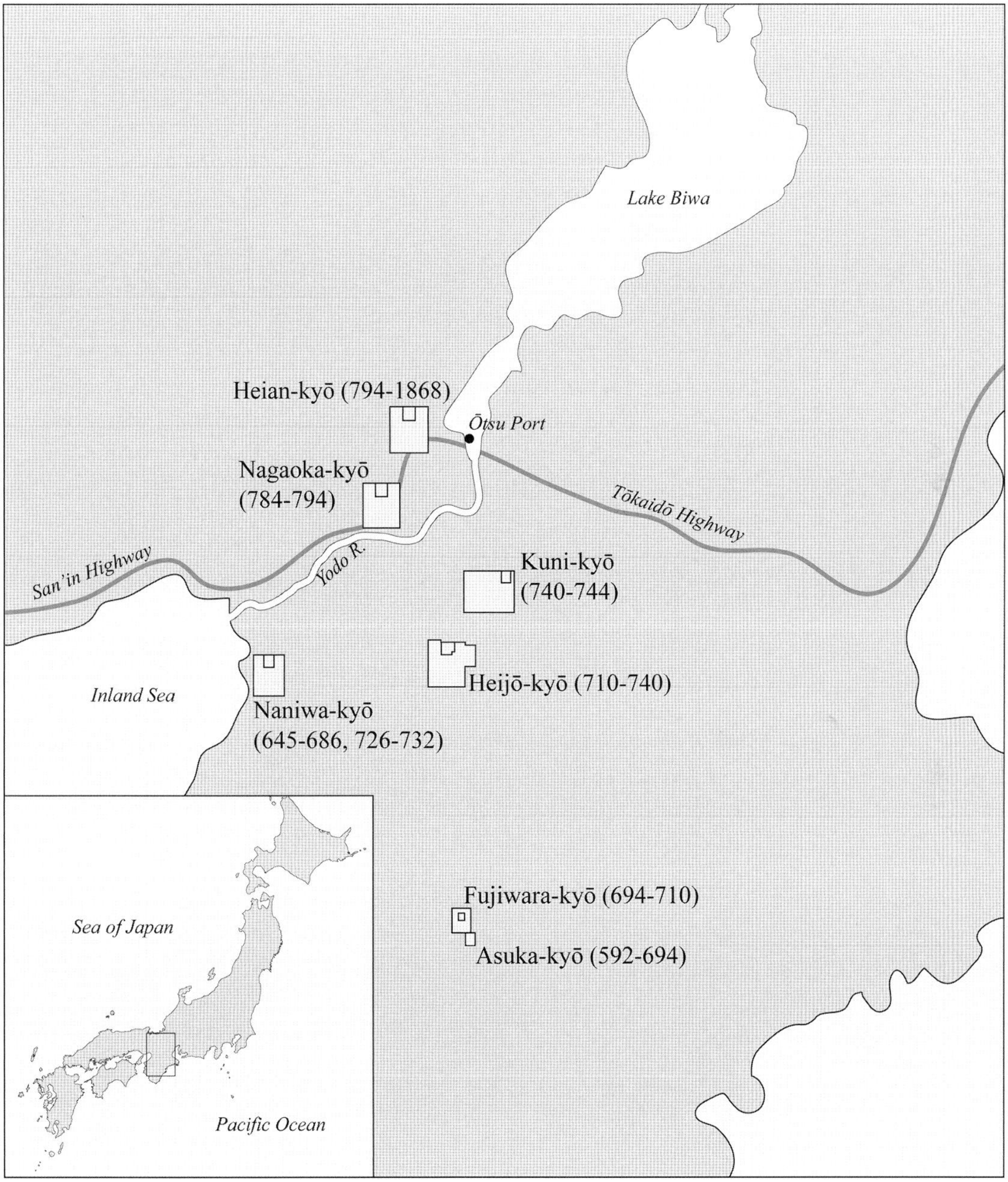
Lake Biwa
Heian-kyō (794-1868)
Ōtsu Port
Nagaoka-kyō
(784-794)
Tōkaidō Highway
San'in Highway
Yodo R.
Kuni-kyō
(740-744)
Heijō-kyō (710-740)
Inland Sea
Naniwa-kyō
(645-686, 726-732)
Fujiwara-kyō (694-710)
Asuka-kyō (592-694)
Sea of Japan
Pacific Ocean

> Enclosed collar-and-sash by mountains and rivers, the province here makes a natural citadel. Because of that configuration, we devise a new designation for it: let this Postmontaine Province [Yamashiro 山背] be renamed the Province of Mountain Citadel [Yamashiro 山城]. Moreover, the joyfully flocking people and singers of praise raise their different voices in identical words, naming this "Heian-kyō," The Capital of Peace and Tranquility.[9]

Kanmu's government during this period was seeking to exert greater centralized control over the provinces, even those not occupied by Emishi. Being based at Heian helped facilitate this goal because the site was located at a key transportation crossroads near the intersection of the Tōkaidō and San'in highways, the major overland routes connecting the eastern and western parts of the country. The Yodo River, immediately to the south, provided easy access to the Inland Sea

1.2. Heian-kyō bird's-eye representation from the south. Illustration by Yoriko Igari

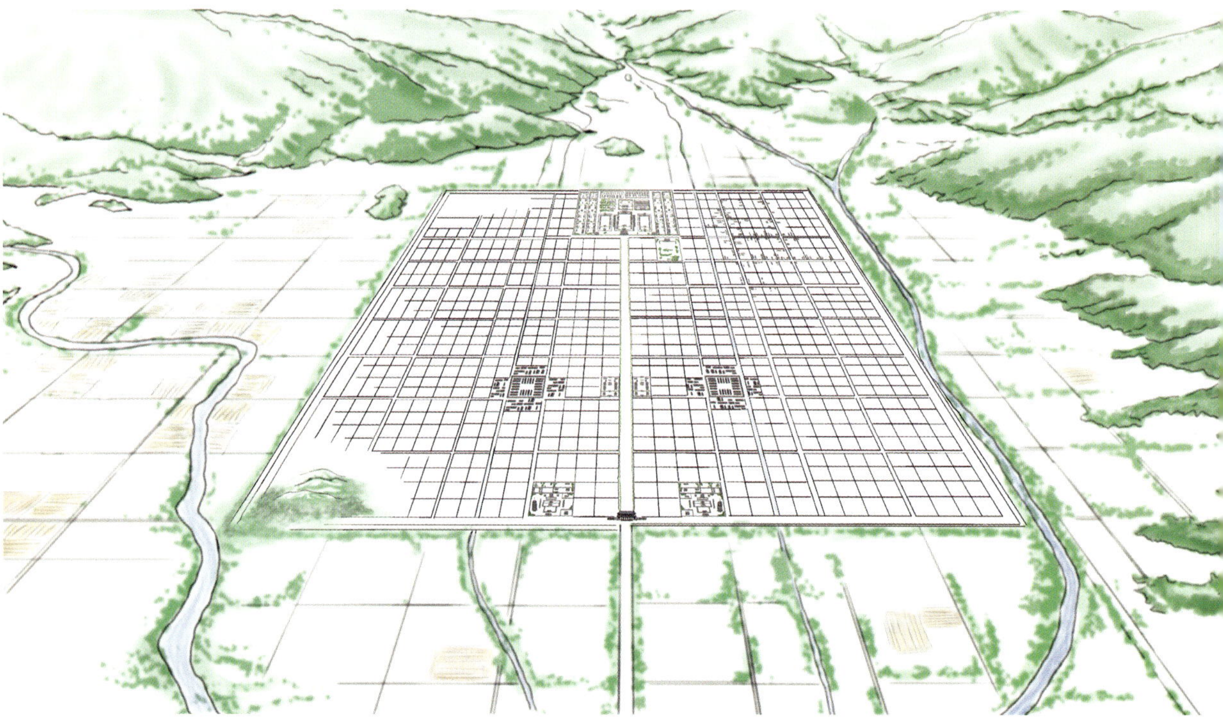

while the freshwater port at Ōtsu connected the capital to several key provinces to the north and east. Finally, Heian-kyō's location had certain metaphysical significance. According to geomantic theories imported from China, a site considered favorable for capital construction needed to meet specific topographic criteria indicative of harmonious coexistence with the forces of nature and the universe (Jp. *ki*, Ch. *chi*). To ensure good government, a capital was to be guarded in the cardinal directions by four gods whose presence was represented in the topographic landscape by three mountains encircling the site in an inverted "U" formation. A fourth mountain was to be well removed to the south.[10] Heian-kyō met these criteria perfectly, a condition cited by many over the centuries as the reason the city endured and flourished.

The Plan

The simple rationality of Heian-kyō's urban grid belies the complexities involved in creating a master-planned city that looked and functioned as intended. Before examining the details, let us begin with some broad brushstrokes and a disclaimer that, due to early deviations from the idealized plan and a paucity of reliable historical sources, postulating on Heian-kyō's "original" appearance is problematic. Scholars who collaborated to create a one one-thousandth scale model of Heian-Kyoto to mark the twelve hundredth anniversary of the capital's establishment in 1994 compressed accounts from the city's first four hundred years to manufacture a composite historical profile. Such a method might be the only effective way to create a viable picture of the classical city.[11]

The basic structural plan upon which Heian-kyō was based was, like the Ritsuryō codes, imported from the continent in the seventh century as part of a multifaceted campaign to adopt the technologies, institutions, and ideas indicative of a modern, "civilized" society. Adopting the Chinese capital model was important to the emerging Japanese imperial state because it provided the material infrastructure necessary to engage in "proper"—meaning Chinese-style—government, ritual, and international diplomacy. There is debate on the extent to which certain continental elements were adopted and adapted, but most scholars agree that the Japanese sought to mimic the majestic imperial cityscapes of Chang'an and Luoyang, the dual capitals of the Sui (581–618) and Tang (618–907) dynasties.[12]

Just like other cultural imports, once in Japan, the Chinese model changed significantly, not only to accommodate domestic circumstances, but also because frequent relocations during this early period might have accelerated material evolution. When Heian-kyō was founded in 794, it was the sixth Chinese-style city built in Japan in just over a century (see Figure 1.1).[13] Despite adaptations and evolution, most of the basic continental attributes remained intact. Among these, the most defining was the geometric grid plan (Figure 1.3). Oriented from north to south, Heian-kyō's grid covered a rectangular area 4.4 kilometers wide and 5.2 kilometers tall.[14] A massive, walled imperial enclosure, called the Daidairi, was located at the top center of the cityscape, a position indicative of the emperor's place at the top of the polity and the center of society. Extending south from the Daidairi and connecting that enclosure to the capital's formal entrance gate of Rajō (Rajōmon) to the south was Suzaku Road. At a staggering eighty-five meters in width and lined on both sides by lush willow trees spaced at exact intervals along the 3.8-kilometer-long route, Suzaku was monumental in scope and design. It served to inspire awe among visiting foreign dignitaries, many of whom would see the capital, its great gates, and official buildings as tangible evidence of Sinification.[15] Suzaku also partitioned the city into two symmetrical halves: Sakyō, meaning the "Left Capital," in the east, and Ukyō, meaning the "Right Capital," in the west. From the perspective of the emperor—which was the only perspective that really mattered—this "left" and "right" distinction was not backward because the sovereign looked down on the city from his palace located in the north. To him, east was left and west was right. Sakyō and Ukyō were considered discrete institutional units and each possessed its own executive officers (*kyōshiki*).

1.3. Heian-kyō grid plan, depicted after a two-block expansion to the north created the "northern zone" (*kitanohe*) in the ninth century.

In stark contrast to its continental forebears, Heian-kyō possessed no city wall. There is early textual and archeological evidence of an earthen bulwark that extended out from both sides of the Rajō Gate, but the rest of the city was surrounded by little more than a low embankment and shallow drainage ditch, perhaps only vaguely resembling a moat. These apparatuses appear infrequently in early texts, but their complete disappearance from the documentary record by the tenth century suggests none were particularly important nor functionally significant.[16] Traditionally, historians have pointed to Heian-kyō's lack of defenses as proof of the era's relative stability and the absence of domestic threats. It was, after all, the "Capital of Peace and Tranquility." This view, however, is unsustainable.[17] While it is true that the

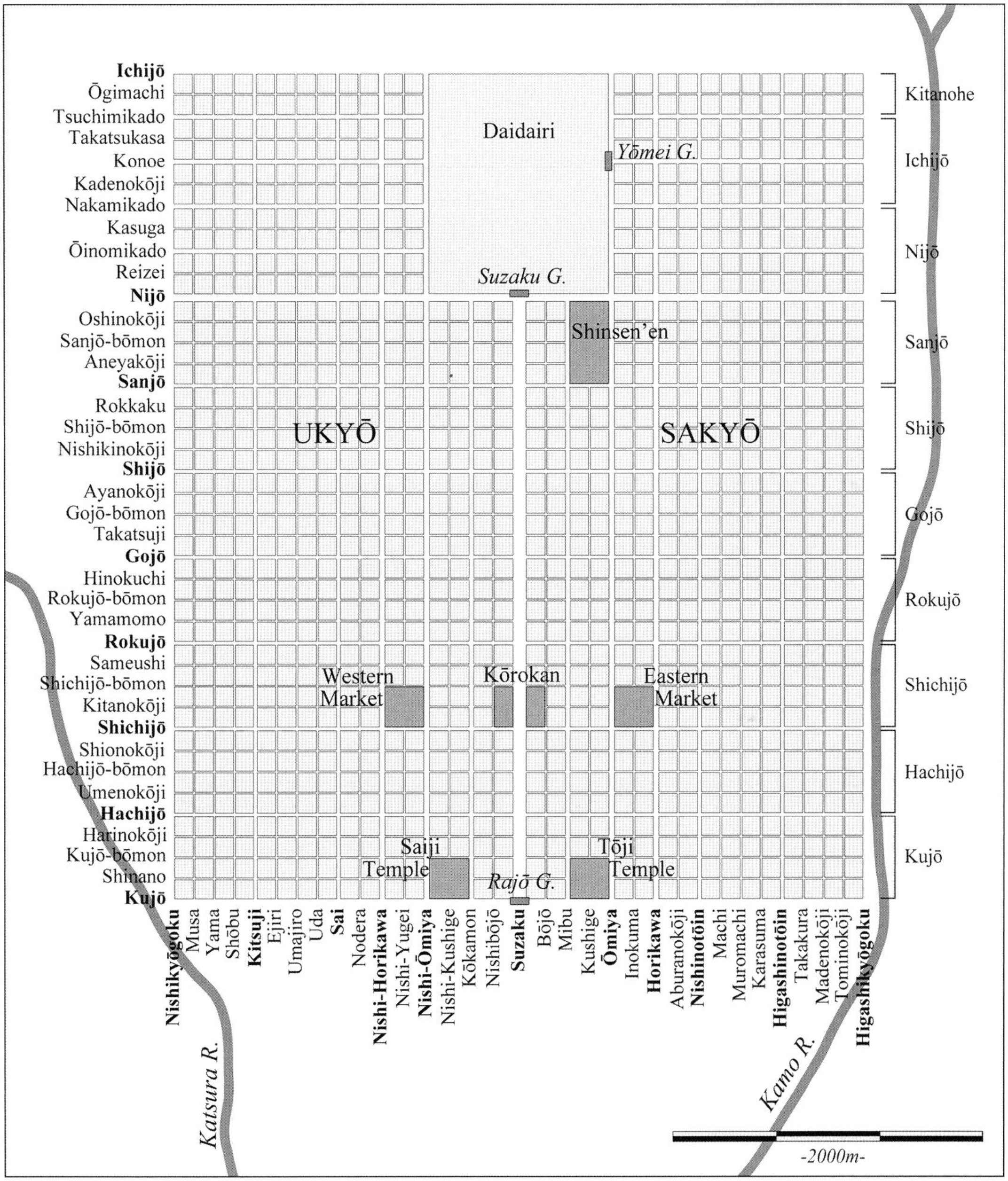
Ichijō
Ōgimachi
Tsuchimikado
Takatsukasa
Konoe
Kadenokōji
Nakamikado
Kasuga
Ōinomikado
Reizei
Nijō
Oshinokōji
Sanjō-bōmon
Aneyakōji
Sanjō
Rokkaku
Shijō-bōmon
Nishikinokōji
Shijō
Ayanokōji
Gojō-bōmon
Takatsuji
Gojō
Hinokuchi
Rokujō-bōmon
Yamamomo
Rokujō
Sameushi
Shichijō-bōmon
Kitanokōji
Shichijō
Shionokōji
Hachijō-bōmon
Umenokōji
Hachijō
Harinokōji
Kujō-bōmon
Shinano
Kujō
Kitanohe
Ichijō
Nijō
Sanjō
Shijō
Gojō
Rokujō
Shichijō
Hachijō
Kujō
Daidairi
Yōmei G.
Suzaku G.
Shinsen'en
UKYŌ
SAKYŌ
Western Market
Kōrokan
Eastern Market
Saiji Temple
Tōji Temple
Rajō G.
Nishikyōgoku
Musa
Yama
Shōbu
Kitsuji
Ejiri
Umajiro
Uda
Sai
Nodera
Nishi-Horikawa
Nishi-Yugei
Nishi-Ōmiya
Nishi-Kushige
Kōkamon
Nishibōjō
Suzaku
Bōjō
Mibu
Kushige
Ōmiya
Inokuma
Horikawa
Aburanokōji
Nishinotōin
Machi
Muromachi
Karasuma
Higashinotōin
Takakura
Madenokōji
Tominokōji
Higashikyōgoku
Katsura R.
Kamo R.
-2000m-

immediate capital region was tranquil during most of the early Heian period (794–1180s), the same cannot be said of previous Japanese capitals built in the Chinese style, which, despite being plagued by intermittent warfare, likewise possessed no city walls. Most noteworthy about the omission, besides the apparent necessity, is that a wall was the defining material trait of the Chinese capital model, a model the Japanese sought so vociferously to mimic in other respects.[18] They were clearly aware of the convention, even going so far as to use the word "*tojō*" in reference to their own capitals, the term similar to that used in China to signify a walled environment.[19]

In the final analysis, the construction of a city wall was probably not feasible in Japan. Circumstances surrounding the creation of Heian-kyō offer a possible explanation for why. At the end of the eighth century, the failure of imperial troops to vanquish the Emishi cast a pall over central politics and, in the end, stymied progress on the new capital's completion. The central government was forced to exact high taxes from the provinces and conscript people for both the war effort and the capital's construction.[20] Petitions complaining of overwork and overtaxation poured in from all directions; even members of the aristocracy, who had private provincial interests themselves, began lobbying the emperor for relief. Forced to make a decision between completing the capital and continuing the war, Kanmu chose the war, dissolving the Office of Palace Construction (*zōgū-shiki*) in 805, thereby formally halting, albeit only temporarily, Heian-kyō's construction. What is most striking about this turn of events is that they came to pass during a time when the power of the central government was expanding dramatically under the rulership of a powerful and charismatic emperor. Presumably, if Kanmu was unable to rally resources and political support sufficient to complete a Chinese-style capital even while waging a protracted war, then none of his predecessors would have either. Perhaps from the outset, the bar on capital construction was set lower in Japan than in China. After all, building a city wall on the scale of those that surrounded Chang'an and Luoyang—standing over eight meters high, made of stone and rammed earth and wide enough to allow troops to move about freely atop—would have required a level of sustained resource and labor management we have no reason to believe existed in Japan until perhaps the late sixteenth century, when warlords began building early modern castles and castle-towns. Maybe the Japanese never tried, instead excluding that particular trait from their own capital plans from the outset in the name of expediency. This argument, if correct, also helps explain why Japanese capitals were substantially smaller than their continental counterparts, instead of assuming that the salient factor was a smaller population.

More important than the reasons behind why no wall was built is consideration of the long-term ramifications of there never having been a wall. As we shall see in later chapters, it was, in part, the capital's inextricable connection to the surrounding hinterland that fueled the rapid and dramatic urban expansion of the succeeding era.

Machi: The Essential Urban Building Block

Heian-kyō's most immediately recognizable physical trait was its supremely rational and geometrically symmetrical grid pattern. Indicative of a strong, centralized, and Sinicized polity that ruled the city (and the state) from the top down, the capital's urban grid possessed certain symbolic significance. The roads that made up the grid, however, also fulfilled an important practical, albeit performative, function as the venues of highly scripted and grandly orchestrated public processions carried out by the emperor, the court aristocracy, and other members of elite society. In a theater state such as the Heian polity, capital roads sometimes served as the stage.

When discussing the grid, it is critical to avoid the impulse to characterize the creation of city blocks, first called *machi*, as the incidental result of laying roads perpendicularly in a crisscross pattern.[21] In the case of Heian-kyō, such a description would not only be incorrect, it would misrepresent a critical spatial trait that not only made this Japanese capital essentially different from its predecessors but likely contributed to the city's long-term viability. Fatal flaws in earlier urban plans resulted in the creation of blocks of various sizes, a circumstance that had led to elite infighting over residential land. To understand this problem and explain how it was solved in Heian-kyō, let us first explore how earlier Japanese capitals were planned and how residential land was distributed.

When the Japanese first attempted to mimic the Chinese urban model in places such as Fujiwara-kyō and Heijō-kyō, planners privileged the core significance of an idealized grid pattern. They most likely began the planning process by marking out a site using long strands of cord

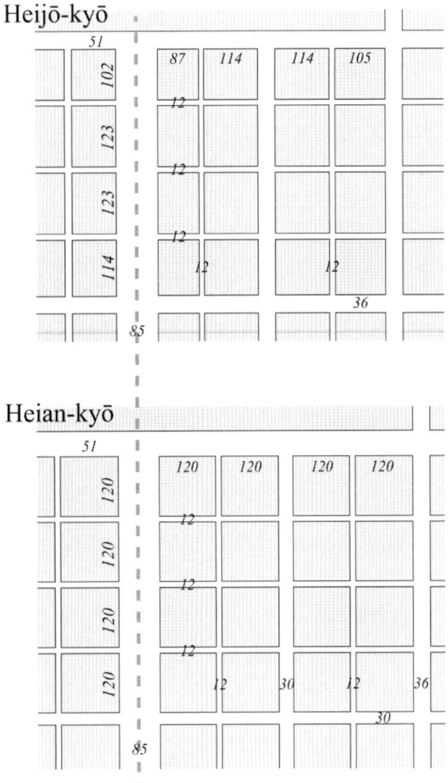

1.4. Grid plans of Heijō-kyō (Nara) and Heian-kyō compared. Note cases of irregular blocks in the former. Numbers indicate widths of blocks and roads in meters.

that, through their intersection at equal intervals, created a grid pattern of perfect equilateral squares.[22] A problem emerged, however, when roads were subsequently superimposed over this ideal grid, because the creation of roads itself required the shaving away of land on all four sides of nascent blocks. Since roads had various widths, the blocks, or *machi*, that took shape around them ended up having various sizes (see the case of Heijō-kyō illustrated in Figure 1.4).

This physical complication led to social strife due to the nature of the land allocation system. Lower-ranking members of the aristocracy, sixth rank and below, were allocated one-fourth of a *machi*, upon which they were expected to built an official residence. Mid-ranking aristocrats, those of fourth and fifth rank, were given a half *machi*. And finally, whole *machi* were allocated to the highest members of the court aristocracy, third rank and above. As straightforward as this scheme was, problems arose prior to the Heian period because the sizes of *machi* were not tied to an absolute geometric measurement and, as a result, ended up being all different sizes. And due to an elite preference for residential land along major (and wider) roads, those with higher formal statuses often ended up with plots significantly smaller than those of their social inferiors. The resulting inverse relationship between status and residential land size was a grave social problem; the highest elites railed against a system that seemed unquestionably inappropriate.

Heian-kyō's planners sought to correct the flawed *machi* system by reversing the planning process. They started not with the master grid plan but rather with the single unit of the *machi*, making it the essential urban building block. They first set the specific size of *machi* at 40 *jō* to a side, a length of about 120 meters. This made every block a perfect square with an inviolable area of about 14,400 square meters, or 3.6 acres. Planners then arranged those blocks into rows and columns, leaving set spaces between each to create roads of different widths. It should be understood, therefore, that Heian-kyō's roads materialized incidentally, through the strategic arrangement of *machi*, not the other way around.[23] As mentioned, members of the aristocracy were granted residential plots ranging in size from one-fourth to a whole city block (see Figure 1.5). The majority of the capital's residents, however, were not so fortunate. *Machi* were partitioned into much smaller administrative units for allocation to low-ranking officials and eventually to commoners. Arranged into a system called "four columns–eight rows" (*shigyō-hachimon*), each unit, called *henushi*, was just less than thirty meters from east to west and fifteen meters from north to south (see Figure 1.6). At 450 square meters, a plot such as this would be large by modern Japanese urban standards, but in Heian-kyō it was the paltry allotment of the lowest members of capital society.

In yet another departure from the continental model, Heian-kyō's planners did not create walls around each individual *machi*. While aristocrats certainly did use walls to surround their homes, some of which covered a whole block, the Japanese capital was not a "container city," which, as defined by Lewis Mumford, exhibits a series of nested

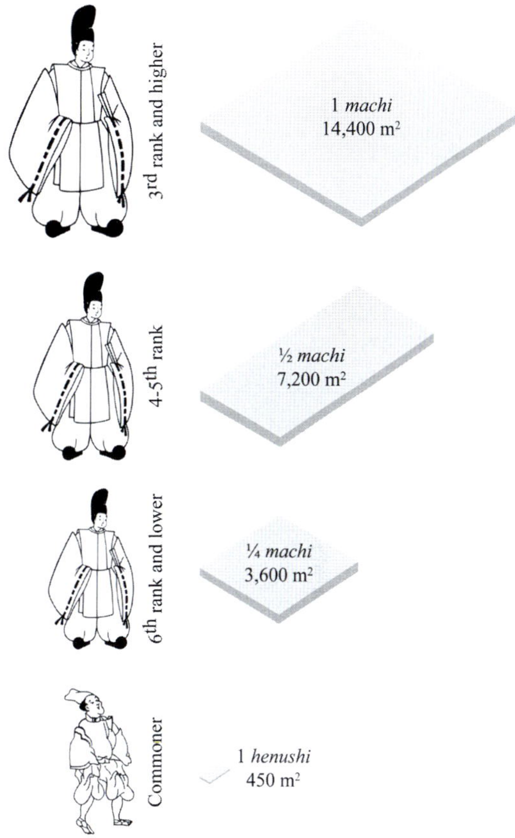

1.5. Heian-kyō residential land allocation.

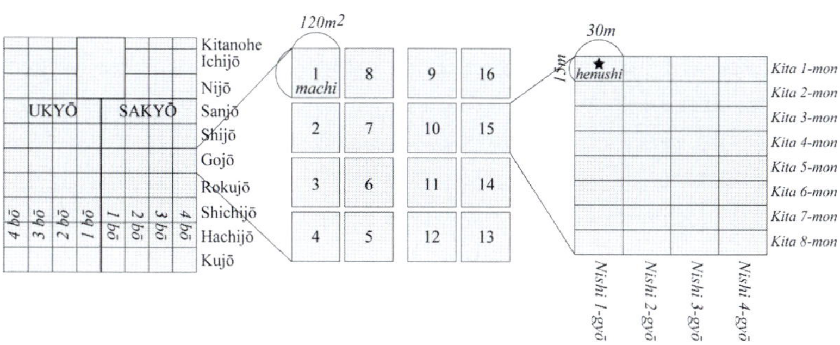

1.6. Heian-kyō block division and organization.

enclosures.[24] As we shall see, the generally open relationship between blocks and the roads that surrounded them was to have a profound impact on Kyoto's history, both materially and socially.

Roads and Addresses

The planning of *machi* took priority over roads in the construction of Heian-kyō, but roads were no less important. In addition to facilitating movement around the city, including the elite processions mentioned above, they divided the capital into a rational matrix of formal and informal zones. The names of each indicated their locations and their locations became functions of status (in the discussion that follows, refer to Figure 1.3).

In the broadest terms, there were two distinct types of roads in Heian-kyō: "great roads," called *ōji*, and "minor roads," called *kōji*.[25] The most important of the great roads, and by far the capital's widest thoroughfare, was Suzaku. As the formal approach to the Daidairi imperial enclosure, its use was reserved exclusively for the emperor, the highest members of the imperial court, and official emissaries visiting from abroad. As mentioned, Suzaku also divided the capital into the symmetrical left-right administrative zones of Sakyō and Ukyō.

Nijō, meaning something akin to "Second Road," was the one other "great road" that deserves special mention. It ran east-west along the southern face of the Daidairi, providing another passage to and from the imperial enclosure. At fifty-one meters in width, Nijō was significantly narrower than Suzaku, yet still much wider than all other Heian-kyō roads, which measured, on average, about eighteen meters.[26]

In addition to Nijō, there were eight other sequentially numbered east-west "great roads" that together divided the city into nine laterally oriented administrative zones, called *jō*. Some confusion is possible because the east-west great roads and the zones immediately north of each shared the same names. For example, the "ninth zone," called Kujō, included all the land from Kujō Road, north to Hachijō Road. The "eighth zone," called Hachijō, included all the land from Hachijō Road, north to Shichijō Road, and so on, up the grid. Because of the similarities in names, there can sometimes be ambiguity in the documentary record about such things as, for example, whether someone lived *in* Sanjō (the zone) or *on* Sanjō (the road).

There were also longitudinal "great roads" that divided the capital into columnar zones called *bō*. Sakyō and Ukyō had four *bō* each that were numbered from inside out, the first being closest to Suzaku and the fourth being closest to the capital's eastern or western boundaries respectively (see Figure 1.6).

Using these overlapping zone names together with a system for numbering and subdividing *machi*, it was possible to pinpoint specific locations within the capital grid with extraordinary accuracy. Figure 1.6 illustrates how groups of sixteen *machi* were numbered boustrophedonically (as in the route of an ox plow) and how blocks themselves were divided into thirty-two smaller *henushi* units, each existing within a matrix of row and column coordinates. Using this system, administrators could, for example, signify the single *henushi* plot indicated with a star in Figure 1.6 as follows:

> ORIGINAL: 左京五条四坊十五町西一行北一門
> TRANSLITERATION: Sakyō, Gojō, Shibō, Jūgo-machi, Nishi-ichi-gyō, Kita-ichi-mon
> TRANSLATION: Left capital, fifth lateral zone, fourth columnar zone (of Sakyō), fifteenth block, first column from the west, first north row

Location in Heian-kyō was determined in absolute terms and each institutionally recognized unit of space had a name indicative of its place within the whole. The addressing system illustrates well the strength of the top-down planning regime and, more important, the capital's physical and philosophical organization under a strong, centralized polity.

In the classical city, not unlike today, one's address said something about who they were. While we know of no explicitly codified system, empirical evidence suggests there was a relationship between residential location and status. In general, the further north one lived, the higher one's status. Some scholars have argued that the northeast in particular, where the highest concentration of development occurred in the succeeding era, was favorable because it was higher, cooler, and drier than the rest of the city. Others have suggested that proximity to the emperor was the most cogent factor. Chapter 3 will explore this topic in depth, but for now it should suffice to say that whatever the guiding principle, the relationship between location and status seems to have been reflected in land prices. A low-ranking official writing in his diary in about the year 1000, for example, lamented that, after a long and distinguished career serving the palace, he was only able to afford his maximum allowed residential plot of one-fourth of a *machi* within the area of Rokujō, well removed from the upscale district north of Nijō where he had worked most of his life.[27]

The Daidairi Imperial Enclosure

The Daidairi was a large, walled compound that housed the ministries, bureaus, and offices of the imperial government, the most important venues of state ritual, and the Imperial Palace. The word Daidairi is customarily rendered in English as the "Greater Imperial Enclosure." The literal meaning, however, "Great Penetralia," better exemplifies both the physical and political centrality of the imperial state and the emperor's status as a sacerdotal ruler.

Unlike the capital itself, the Daidairi was surrounded by a formidable wall punctuated by fourteen gates.[28] The most important of these was Suzaku in the south, which, like the great road onto which it opened and with which it shared a name, was reserved for use by the emperor and only the most special of guests on rare occasions. The second most important gate, located on the eastern face of the Daidairi, was called Yōmei (Yōmeimon). It was the exclusive egress used by government officials when commuting to their palace offices from their homes, which were located on the outside. It was also the gate closest to the Imperial Palace (see Figure 1.7).

1.7. Daidairi imperial enclosure. The Jōsai and Jōtō Gates were created in the ninth century. Translations from McCullough, "The Capital and its Society," 110

Inside the Daidairi stood eight ministries (*shō*), ten bureaus (*ryō*), six offices (*shiki*), and a handful of other specialized institutions such as the imperial police (*kebiishi*) and chamberlains' office (*kurōdo-dokoro*).[29] These imperial organs were staffed by seven to eight thousand employees who together conducted the day-to-day business of national and capital administration. Despite their critical functions, these institutions were overshadowed by the symbolic importance and material opulence of the Daidairi's two main venues of state ritual, the Chōdō-in (Imperial Court Compound) and the Buraku-in (Court of Abundant Pleasures) (see Figure 1.11). The latter, located just inside the Suzaku Gate and oriented along the capital's central axis, was the formal venue of imperial statecraft, a highly ritualized kind of political pageantry that drew heavily on the emperor's sacred status. Early in the morning, six days a week, court noblemen would file ceremoniously into the Chōdō-in's vast courtyard. There, each would take up a

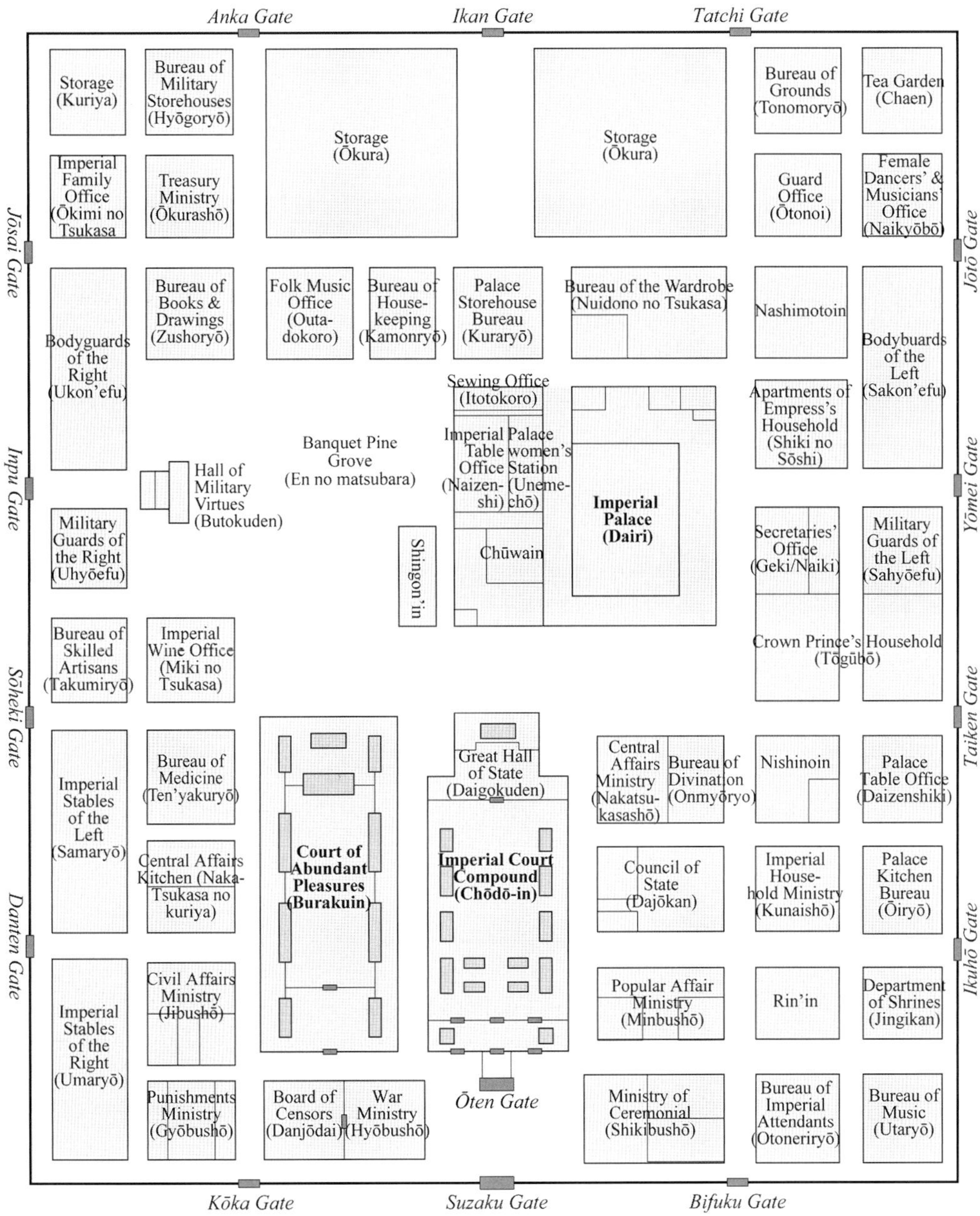

Anka Gate
Ikan Gate
Tatchi Gate
Storage (Kuriya)
Bureau of Military Storehouses (Hyōgoryō)
Storage (Ōkura)
Storage (Ōkura)
Bureau of Grounds (Tonomoryō)
Tea Garden (Chaen)
Imperial Family Office (Ōkimi no Tsukasa)
Treasury Ministry (Ōkurashō)
Guard Office (Ōtonoi)
Female Dancers' & Musicians' Office (Naikyōbō)
Jōsai Gate
Jōtō Gate
Bodyguards of the Right (Ukon'efu)
Bureau of Books & Drawings (Zushoryō)
Folk Music Office (Outa-dokoro)
Bureau of House-keeping (Kamonryō)
Palace Storehouse Bureau (Kuraryō)
Bureau of the Wardrobe (Nuidono no Tsukasa)
Nashimotoin
Bodybuards of the Left (Sakon'efu)
Sewing Office (Itotokoro)
Apartments of Empress's Household (Shiki no Sōshi)
Banquet Pine Grove (En no matsubara)
Hall of Military Virtues (Butokuden)
Imperial Table Office (Naizen-shi)
Palace women's Station (Uneme-chō)
Imperial Palace (Dairi)
Inpu Gate
Yōmei Gate
Military Guards of the Right (Uhyōefu)
Shingon'in
Chūwain
Secretaries' Office (Geki/Naiki)
Military Guards of the Left (Sahyōefu)
Bureau of Skilled Artisans (Takumiryō)
Imperial Wine Office (Miki no Tsukasa)
Crown Prince's Household (Tōgūbō)
Sōheki Gate
Taiken Gate
Imperial Stables of the Left (Samaryō)
Bureau of Medicine (Ten'yakuryō)
Great Hall of State (Daigokuden)
Central Affairs Ministry (Nakatsu-kasashō)
Bureau of Divination (Onmyōryo)
Nishinoin
Palace Table Office (Daizenshiki)
Central Affairs Kitchen (Naka-Tsukasa no kuriya)
Court of Abundant Pleasures (Burakuin)
Imperial Court Compound (Chōdō-in)
Council of State (Dajōkan)
Imperial House-hold Ministry (Kunaishō)
Palace Kitchen Bureau (Ōiryō)
Danten Gate
Ikuhō Gate
Imperial Stables of the Right (Umaryō)
Civil Affairs Ministry (Jibushō)
Popular Affair Ministry (Minbushō)
Rin'in
Department of Shrines (Jingikan)
Punishments Ministry (Gyōbushō)
Board of Censors (Danjōdai)
War Ministry (Hyōbushō)
Ōten Gate
Ministry of Ceremonial (Shikibushō)
Bureau of Imperial Attendants (Otoneriryō)
Bureau of Music (Utaryō)
Kōka Gate
Suzaku Gate
Bifuku Gate

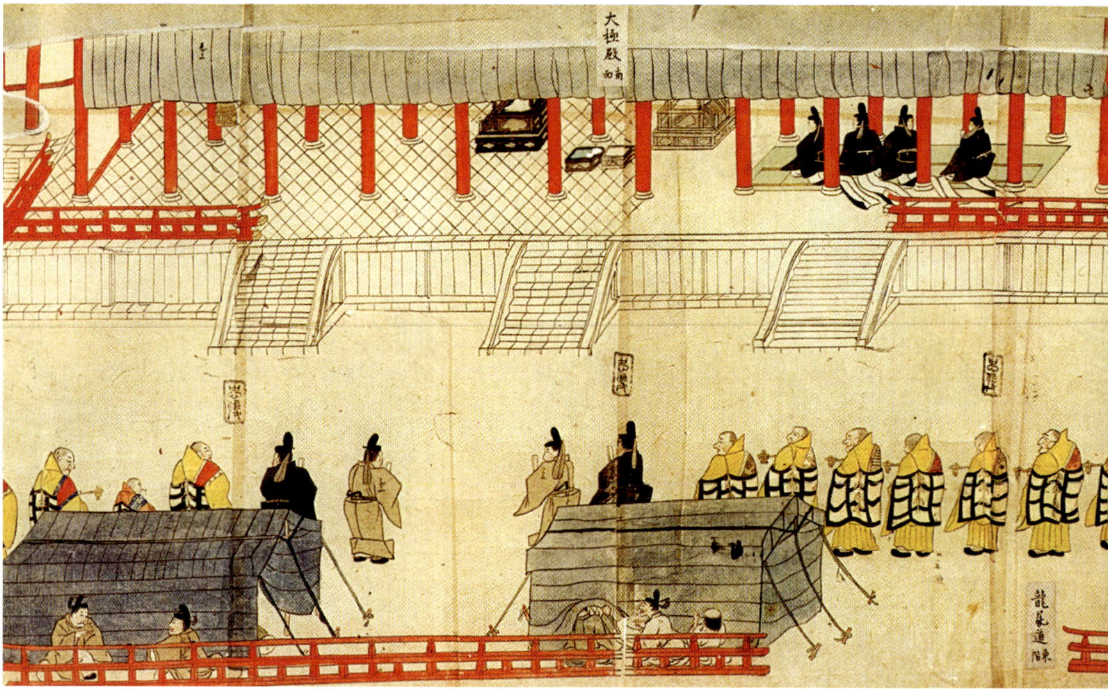

1.8. Great Hall of State (Daigokuden) during a new year's ceremony (*gosai-e*), in *Nenjūgyōji emaki*. Courtesy of Kyoto University Faculty of Letters

spot in front of the Great Hall of State (Daigokuden) corresponding to his—and it was always "his"—court post and rank. The emperor would sit upon a raised dais within the Great Hall, facing his courtiers to the south. From there, he would issue decrees, promotions, and public pronouncements, all while remaining concealed from direct view by a rolled bamboo blind. An occasion such as this is depicted in an illustration of the Great Hall reproduced in Figure 1.8. The stone staircases and liberal use of vermillion paint are indicative of strong Chinese influence. As remains the case in Beijing's Forbidden City, the greenish celadon tiles symbolized imperial status. Although the original no longer exists, visitors to Kyoto today can see a five-eighths replica of the Chōdo-in in the form of the Heian Shrine (Heian Jingū, pictured in Figure 1.9). Built in 1894 on the occasion of the city's eleven hundredth anniversary, the Shinto complex enshrines the spirit of Heian-kyō's founder, Emperor Kanmu.

The Court of Abundant Pleasures, or Buraku-in, which stood to the east of the Chōdō-in, was the principal imperial banquet venue. It was the setting of numerous festivals and many of the annual observances

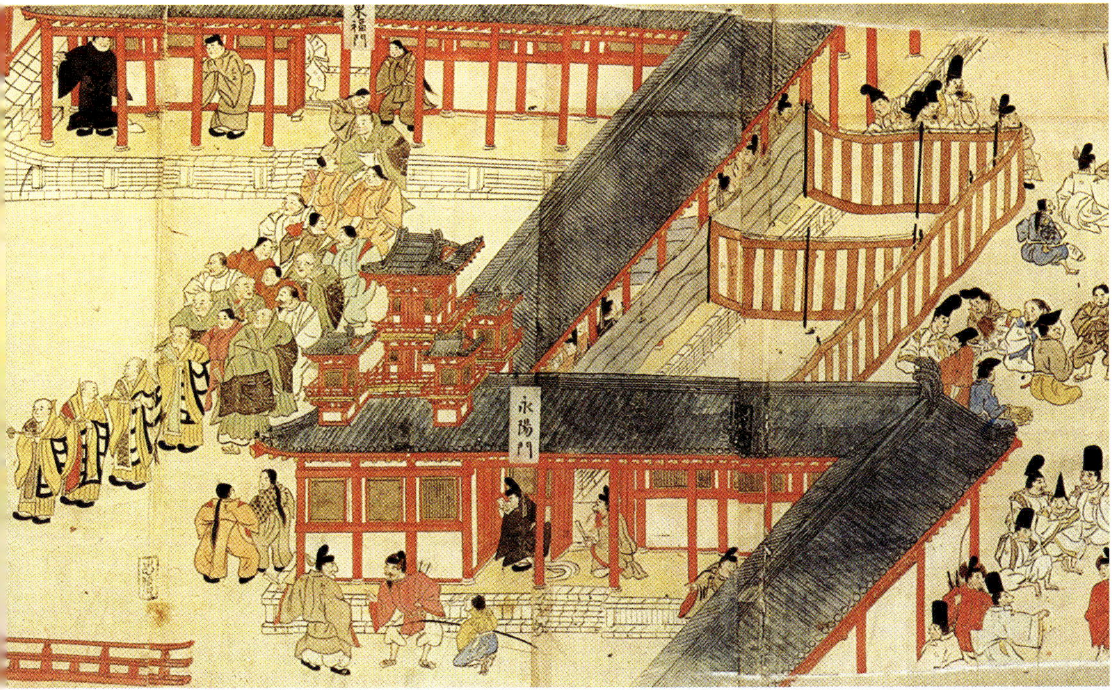

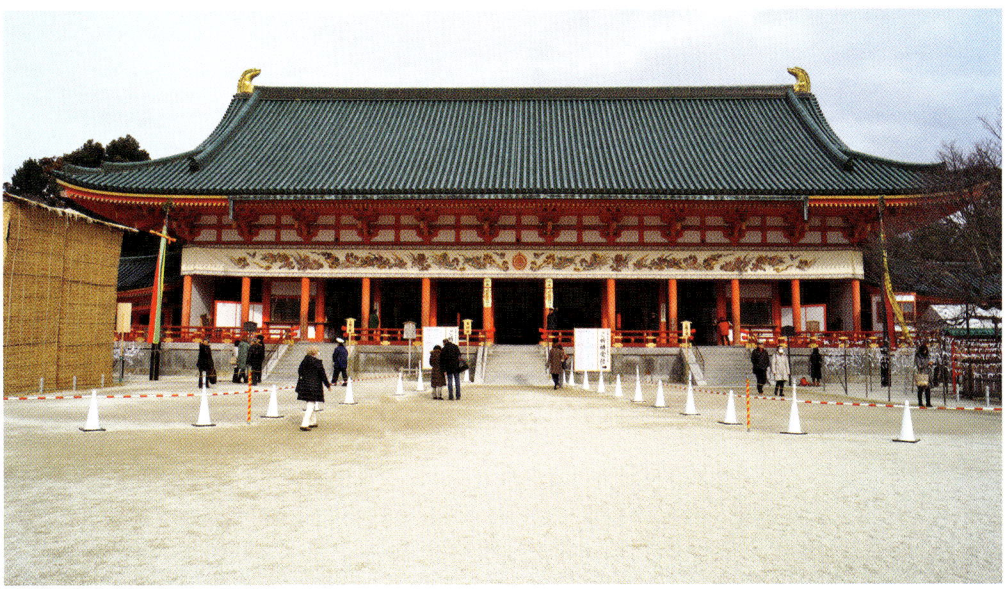

1.9. Heian Shrine (Heian Jingū), a five-eighths replica of the Chōdō-in, built in 1894.

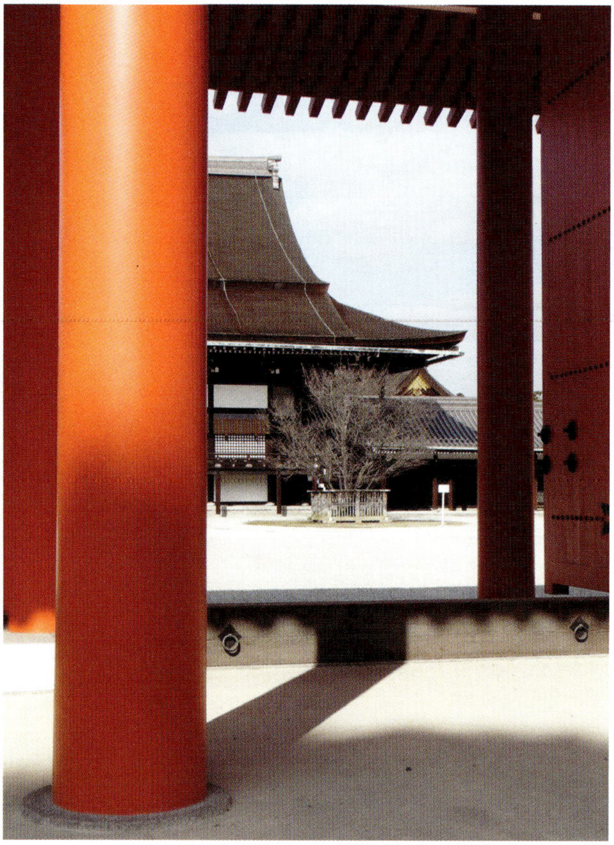

1.10. Kyoto Imperial Palace today, showing juxtaposition of Chinese and Japanese styles.

that punctuated the official calendar. The little information we have on this compound suggests that it too followed a fundamentally Chinese model.

The Imperial Palace, located just east of the very center of the greater enclosure, was called Dairi, or, literally, "Penetralia." While functioning primarily as the official residence to the emperor, the compound was also an important venue of imperial pageantry and ceremony. The buildings that faced the south, in fact, were dedicated exclusively for ritualized public events. Over time, the ritual repertoire expanded, eventually inheriting many of those activities native to the Chōdō-in and Buraku-in. The structures that occupied the "back" or northern side of the compound were more private in nature, used mainly to house the emperor, his family, and a usually large retinue of chamberlains and ladies-in-waiting. Textual and pictorial evidence confirms that the Dairi departed from continental styles in several key ways.[30] Cypress-bark roofing and the scant use of paint throughout gave the compound a distinctly subtle, earthtone complexion. Retrospectively, the appearance has been called more "Japanese." If, therefore, we back up to think of the Dairi as the physical and political center of the much larger imperial enclosure, we notice what might be described as a Japanese nucleus surrounded by a Chinese shell. In this respect, the Daidairi enclosure was a potent metaphor for the early Japanese polity itself: a large and complex institution that, while taking cosmetic cues from China, was different on a fundamental level (see Figures 1.10 and 1.11).[31]

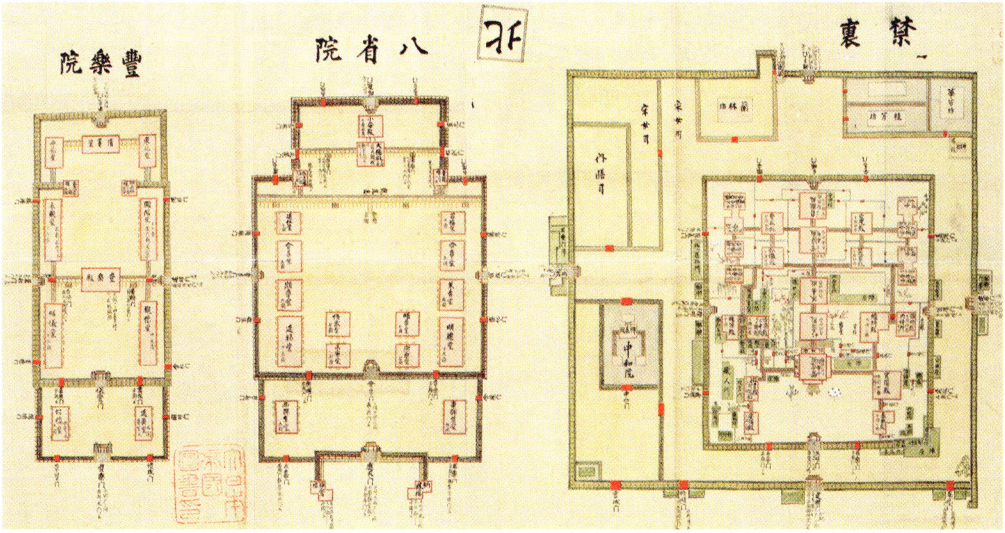

1.11. Dairi, Chōdō-in, and Buraku-in (from right to left), illustrated by Mori Kōan, 1750. The absence of symmetry in the Dairi is itself a departure from the continental model. National Archives of Japan

Corridor of Public Pageantry

Not all venues of government activity were secluded behind the walls of the Daidairi. Almost all that were not, however, shared a basic functional similarity in that they facilitated some form of direct and usually ostentatious interaction between the imperial institution and the outside world, including foreign dignitaries, members of the Buddhist establishment, and, usually only incidentally, commoners. These several sites were primarily located within a strip of land that extended south from the Daidairi toward the capital's southern boundary (between the roads of Nishi-Ōmiya and Ōmiya). This thick band of space on either side of the great Suzaku Road might be considered a sort of "corridor of public pageantry" (see Figure 1.3).

Because of the strong relationship between status and the built environment in Heian-kyō, some of these external venues can be considered as functional sets. For example, we might treat as a single set the capital's formal entrance gate of Rajō, Suzaku Road, and the Daidairi's main gate of Suzaku. Each was reserved for use by the emperor, the highest members of the court, and foreign ambassadors who, traveling in long processions—sometimes stately, sometimes festive—would pass through each on their way to or from the palace.[32] Together they provided for the public display of elite pageantry while, in a material sense, making a statement about Japanese imperial efficacy through their close adherence to Sinocentric models. The two great gates and the format of the city itself would have been immediately familiar to visitors from China and Korea, reminiscent of corresponding features in their own capitals. Two other facilities that might be added to this set are the twin Eastern and Western Kōrokan, diplomatic compounds built to receive, entertain, and lodge foreign visitors.[33] Located on either side of Suzaku Road, just north of Shichijō, these compounds were also part of the infrastructure of imperial pageantry in that they, through their use of Chinese-style architecture and gardens, provided a venue for the Japanese to demonstrate their attainment of continental-style civilization.

Just south of the Daidairi, but removed by several blocks from Suzaku Road to the east, was Shinsen'en. Covering eight city blocks, this sprawling, walled garden was the emperor's exclusive nature reserve. A natural spring irrigated a large pond around which stood palatial structures built in a continental style. What little we know about Shinsen'en suggests that while it may not initially have had a public function, it soon became a venue for high-profile divination rituals, particularly those related to rainfall.[34]

All commercial activity in Heian-kyō was meant to take place within two publicly sanctioned markets planned symmetrically on either side of the city between Rokujō and Shichijō Roads. Walled and gated, the Eastern and Western Markets operated on an alternating basis, and what took place within each was under the close scrutiny of imperial administrators and police.[35] Besides being a place where goods were bartered, bought, and sold, the markets also served as the capital's execution grounds.[36] On set days of the month, criminals were marched into the market en masse. After being publicly condemned for their crimes, they were either taken away to meet their ends or—in an apparently sanctioned exception to the rule against killing within the capital—executed on the spot.[37] The markets also fulfilled some of the functions of a modern town square or public park. They were, for example, choice locations for the activities of proselytizers and prostitutes. Among the former, the most famous is the monk Kūya (903–972). Referred to as the "market saint" (*ichi no hijiri*), Kūya gained notoriety for preaching the principles of Amida worship to commoners and later founding the temple of Rokuhara Mitsuji southeast of the city.[38] Although these sites were closely controlled, it appears that urban planners were keenly aware of their importance to the city's long-term viability. The official markets were among the earliest institutions transferred from Nagaoka-kyō when the new capital was founded.[39]

Perhaps the most important of the public institutions located outside the Daidairi were the two great temples of Tōji and Saiji.[40] Their names, meaning East and West Temple respectively, were informal appellations ascribed to each based on their locations vis-à-vis the Rajō Gate. Tōji and Saiji were built at government expense and placed under direct court supervision. The monks were charged with the task of ensuring divine protection for the state, the capital, and the body of the emperor. Besides standing as grand symbols of imperial wealth and moral veracity astride the capital's "front door," the physical infrastructure of the two temples themselves might have had cosmological implications. Geomancy experts have argued that contemporaries envisioned the five-storied pagodas adorning each of the temple grounds as serving to trap positive celestial energy (*ki*), thereby preventing it from leaking out of the city to the south.[41] Such a capacity would have been important to the overall geomantic fitness of a capital built to harness the forces of the universe and apply them to the execution of virtuous government.

Tōji and Saiji were exceptional because they were the only two temples that stood within Heian-kyō's official boundaries. It is a widely repeated notion that Emperor Kanmu banned temples from the capital because he sought to divorce imperial politics from the influence of the powerful Buddhist sects, such as those whose temples dominated the landscape of the earlier Heijō-kyō. But not only has the notion that Kanmu had an aversion to Buddhism been successfully challenged in recent scholarship, we actually have no historical evidence that temples were formally banned from Heian-kyō during Kanmu's lifetime. A paucity of textual evidence, of course, does not mean there was no ban and, to be sure, the extreme rarity of temples within the city remained real and conspicuous well into the fifteenth century.[42] Nevertheless, the many textual sources that refer to temple proscriptions use language that suggests a "custom" or "tradition" rather than a law. It is likely that this particular taboo belonged to a distinct repertoire of capital customs that, although perhaps never inscribed into law, were nevertheless followed assiduously and remained valid over time. Because of its importance, this theme will be discussed in much greater detail later in this study.

The most important government offices and ministries maintained detached facilities outside the Daidairi. With a name that might be rendered in English as "dormitory blocks of the various offices" (*shoshi-kuriya-machi*), these numerous yet unremarkable compounds occupied blocks throughout Heian-kyō's urban landscape.[43] Each employed and housed hundreds of workers who, conscripted from the provinces on a rotating basis, performed duties related to the functions of the ministries or offices to which their respective compounds were affiliated. Some were highly skilled tradesmen such as architects, accountants, potters, weavers, and metalworkers. Most, however, fulfilled more menial tasks as guards and laborers. Almost all their "dorms" were located north of Nijō in close proximity to the Daidairi, and a majority were clustered on the enclosure's eastern side, an area that would eventually become, for reasons not unrelated to the dorms themselves, the center of elite society.

Shinden Style: The Residential Architecture of the Ruling Elite

The residential architecture of Heian-kyō's ruling elite was based on the ritual state shrines of the Tang capital. Referred to today as *shinden* style (*shinden-zukuri*), its adoption by the Japanese imperial family from about the eighth century was part of the broader project of importing Chinese things and ideas. The style was initially implemented in the building of the imperial palace in Heijō-kyō as well as state-sponsored Buddhist temples.[44] Despite *shinden* style being poorly suited to residential uses, its adoption was related to the ruling elite's objective of reifying a ritualized form of statecraft based on the Ritsuryō codes. It was envisioned that the emperor would justify and perpetuate his virtuous rule through an almost continuous repertoire of carefully scripted rights and rituals, all of which adhered to strict codes of precedent and pageantry. Everything from clothing and gestures to architecture and interior décor (*shitsurai*) were meticulously prescribed. Starting with the Imperial Palace, *shinden*-style complexes were a key part of the formalized paraphernalia of classical authority. This fundamental correspondence between form and function, according to William Coaldrake, "reveals the adoption of an official architectural vocabulary based on Tang usage, and makes an equation between government by virtue, a fundamental Confucian tenant, and appropriate physical form." On the relationship between Ritsuryō government and *shinden* style, Coaldrake observes that "it is the same type of equation that we accept exists between democratic governments and Greek Classical architecture."[45]

"*Shinden-zukuri*" refers both to a prescribed grounds plan and building style.[46] In terms of the former, the earliest fully mature *shinden*-style palaces consisted of a conglomeration of as many as fifteen discrete structures arranged symmetrically along a north-south axis and enclosed within a rectangular earthen wall (see Figure 1.12). At the center, traditionally standing to the north of a garden or pond, was the compound's most important structure, the central *shinden* (lit. "sleeping palace"). Serving both as the primary ritual venue and the main residential quarters of the master of the house, the south-facing *shinden* was connected to surrounding subsidiary structures via a network of covered corridors (*rō*).

Perhaps the most noticeable structural trait of *shinden*-style architecture was the almost complete absence of fixed interior walls and, as a result, the nonexistence of discrete rooms (see Figure 1.13). Reticulating wooden shutters (*shitomido*) served to close buildings off from the outside, but inner chambers remained open, partitioned only by folding screens, curtains, or bamboo blinds. Such temporary

1.12. Typical *shinden*-style complex, bird's-eye representation from the south. Courtesy of Richard Bowring

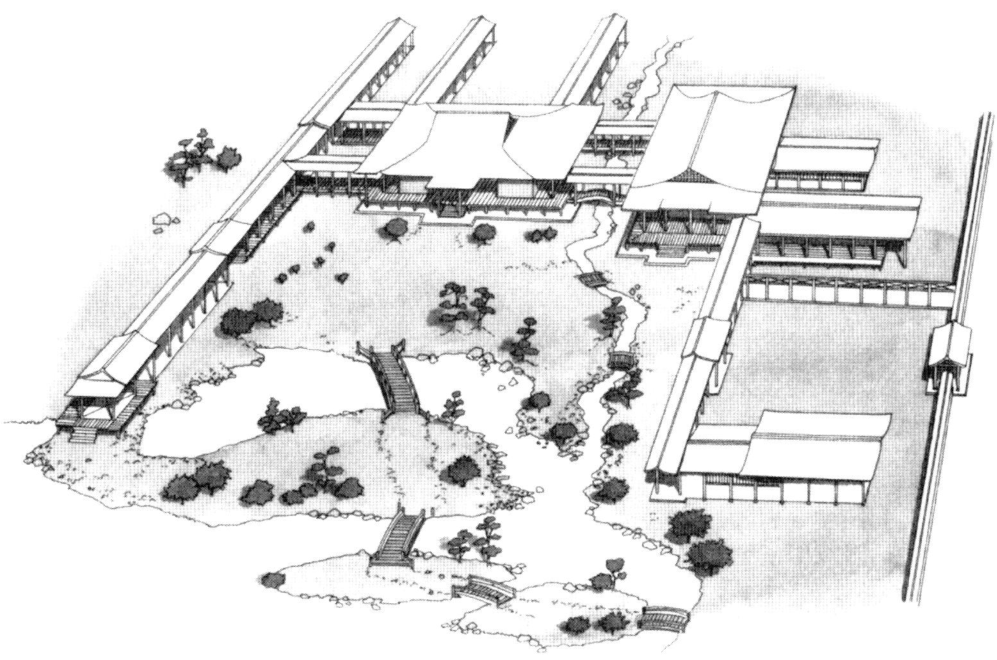

fixtures were used on an occasional basis to accommodate specific activities such as eating, sleeping, or the holding of particular events or rituals. Once their purpose was served, they were generally either rearranged or stowed.[47] It would be incorrect, therefore, to think in terms of the existence of "living rooms" or "bedrooms" within early *shinden*-style palaces. Interior space was definitively non-function-specific. This key characteristic was related to an impulse to preserve the original architectural ideal to the point where any alterations made to accommodate non-Ritsuryō functions (including daily life) were to be minimal and, most important, temporary. This tendency helps explain the overall austerity of *shinden*-style interiors. Straw mats known as *tatami* were used on occasion to facilitate sitting or reclining, but otherwise the wooden plank floors remained bare throughout. Without walls or any variations in floor level, large wooden pillars were the only permanent structural elements that interrupted interior space.[48]

Shinden-style palaces (or their prototypes) began to proliferate from about the late eighth century when members of the aristocracy started mimicking the forms of the Imperial Palace when building their own official urban residences. The broad adoption of the style was related to the aristocracy's increased employment of rituals based on the imperial model as a means of demonstrating their membership in the Ritsuryō hierarchy. Possessing the necessary architectural components endowed the elite with the physical infrastructure to hold those rituals. As time went by, a definitive grammar of architectural comportment emerged in which building elements and décors were, like the sizes of residential plots, closely mapped to formal statuses. The style of a nobleman's primary gate, for example, was a function of his rank and imperial post, as were his roofing tiles and the patterns and colors used in the edgings of his *tatami* mats.[49] Even the orientation of an entire complex became a function of status, with only those of the third rank or higher permitted to build primary gates that opened onto "great" roads (*ōji*).[50]

Conclusion

Heian-kyō might be characterized as a physical metaphor for a strong, centralized, Chinese-style government, organized around a supreme sacerdotal ruler, governed by laws and a rigid status system. Land was divided up systematically, roads were laid out rationally, and a top-down addressing scheme defined every fragment of the urban

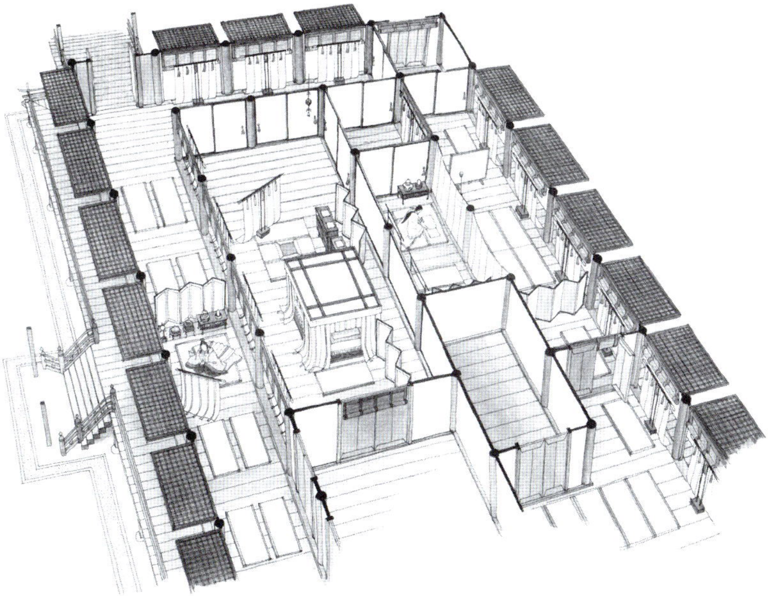

1.13. Typical central *shinden*, cutaway illustration.

landscape as an elemental part of the whole. The emperor and his governmental offices occupied a large, exclusive enclosure at the top center of the city, but also employed facilities on the outside to put imperial pageantry on regular public display. The elite lived in homes that, while generally large and luxuriant, were first and foremost symbols of formal status. As the power of central authority grew during the ninth century, it became increasingly clear that, through Heian-kyō's success, Emperor Kanmu would achieve his lifelong dream of establishing an eternal capital. When a challenge emerged shortly after the emperor's death in 806, the suggestion to move the capital yet again was summarily dismissed on the grounds that Heian was geographically ideal and, as a place to live, left its residents "wanting for nothing."[51]

In closing, it should be emphasized that the narrative thus far has described how Heian-kyō was *meant* to be; how it was planned; how it was idealized. The reality, however, is that the city never lived up to the grand vision of its founders. The area was too broad for convenience. Roads were too wide and too far apart for practicality. Public facilities were inordinately grand and numerous. And finally, the system for distributing land was simply incompatible with material necessities. Heian-kyō did indeed become Japan's eternal capital, but the city envisioned by Kanmu never fully materialized.

2

Heian-kyō

The Real

As TIME PASSED, an increasing number of entirely new urban phenomena emerged that together altered Heian-kyō's appearance as well as its social, political, and economic conditions. These new phenomena are the topic of chapter 3. Here the focus is on several key ways the classical urban ideal either failed to be realized or, even in cases where it was realized, how the material results were frequently short-lived. It is possible to argue that Heian-kyō's decay was synonymous with the medieval city's rise. Nevertheless, focusing initially and specifically on how the classical city declined, rather than on the emergence of medieval elements, helps bring into relief the extent to which the image we have of the original capital might be an artifact more of literature and historical imagination than of history.

The Unrealized Grid

According to the original urban grid plan, Heian-kyō would have possessed about 1,136 blocks, or *machi*, not including the large area occupied by the Daidairi imperial enclosure. Take away the various areas used by other public facilities—such as the two official markets and temples, Shinsen'en, the two Kōrokan, and the numerous "dormitory blocks"—and there would have remained about a thousand blocks reserved for residential use. This accounting notwithstanding, a court document from 819 describes "an abundance of empty land."[1] Another from 828 indicates that the "total number of *machi* within the capital . . . is a little more than 580."[2] Three decades after the city's establishment, just over half the planned area was being used as intended. Rather than allow unused blocks to remain vacant, authorities offered them to people willing to engage in farming, thereby formally, and in an apparent contravention of early codes, creating agricultural land within city limits. Cultivated land was apparently most common in Ukyō, the western half. In 1086, officers from the imperial police were dispatched to cut grass growing wild on "over 300 *machi* of farm land" in Ukyō.[3] The extent to which Ukyō had been given over to agriculture at an even earlier time is evident in records documenting food aid distributed following a flood that devastated the capital basin in 871. Households that received state aid in the western half of the city were much larger than their eastern counterparts. Such a demographic profile suggests extended-family structures typical of agrarian households.[4]

While these and other textual sources provide circumstantial evidence suggesting Heian-kyō did not develop as planned, the following excerpt from a literary memoir dated to 959 is explicit:

> Over the past twenty years, I have observed the situation throughout the eastern and western sections of the capital. In Ukyō, the houses have become fewer and fewer until it is almost a deserted wasteland. People move out but no one moves in. Houses fall to ruin but no new ones are built. Those who do not have any other place to move to, or who are not ashamed to be poor and lowly, live there . . .
>
> In years past, there was one palace [in Ukyō] with painted halls and vermilion doors, groves of bamboo and trees, rocks and fountains . . . But the owner was sent into exile because of some affair, and fire broke out and burned the buildings down. There were thirty or forty families of retainers living nearby, but one after another they moved away. Later, the owner of the house returned [to Kyoto], but he never tried to rebuild. . . . Thorns and brambles grew till they covered the gate, and foxes and raccoon dogs dug their burrows there in peace. From all this, it is clear that it is Heaven that is destroying Ukyō and no fault of men.[5]

This entry in Yoshishige Yasutane's (d. 1002) *Chiteiki* has been widely interpreted as an account of Ukyō's disintegration. Along with evidence that land in the west was boggy and prone to flooding, the standard narrative depicts a protracted but steady migration of capital residents from Ukyō to Sakyō, an exodus that eventually left the west largely vacant and open to conversion into agricultural land. Recent archeological research suggests, however, that *Chiteiki* might just as readily be interpreted as a testament to the extent to which large portions of Heian-kyō never materialized in the first place. Excavations carried out at dozens of sites within the city's original boundaries have failed to uncover any trace of the grid-road system or blocks dating to the Heian period (see Figure 2.1).[6] There can be little doubt that the great roads of Suzaku, Nijō, and several others, as well as their adjacent blocks, were completed during the early stages of capital construction. Many others, however, might have been delayed indefinitely due to the same lack of resources that led to the disbanding of the Office of Palace Construction in 805. It seems possible that authorities only went through the process of actually marking off blocks, grading roads, and digging drainage ditches in those areas where there existed immediate demand for residential development. Incidentally, such demand was highest in the city's northeast, near important state facilities, and along major roads, but sparse elsewhere. As a result, large swaths of Heian-kyō, particularly in Ukyō, were never initially developed for urbanization. Instead, they were allowed to become farmland before becoming anything else.

The shaded areas in Figure 2.1 indicate where artifacts indicative of urbanization during several periods have been unearthed. Note how much of the planned grid area is entirely devoid of development during the early period, including all four corners and a large chunk of land surrounding the Rajō Gate. This kind of evidence makes it possible to conclude that the Heian grid was likely never completed as planned.

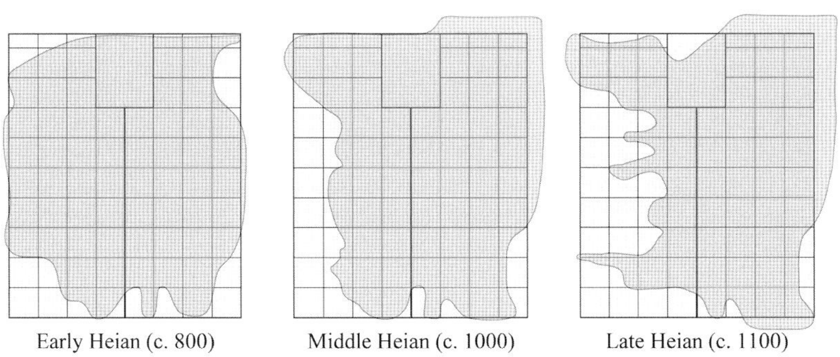

2.1. Heian-kyō's urbanization over time. Shaded areas indicate where excavations have unearthed evidence of urbanization associated with each period. After Kyōto-shi, ed., *Yomigaeru Heian-kyō*, 18–19

The Unrealistic Grid

Not only was Heian-kyō's urban grid not finished, the way its blocks were defined and used in practice appear to have departed significantly from the original, ultimately unrealistic, top-down planning scheme. The private activities of both high and low contributed to several trends that from the beginning subverted imperial codes yet ultimately made the city more user-friendly.

Heian-kyō inherited the Heijō-kyō system of status-based land allocation. Despite documents that call the scheme "law," all indicators suggest that it never functioned quite as planned.[7] One strong indicator of dysfunction is the simple fact that there was not enough land within the city to distribute residential plots faithfully according to the entitlement scheme. The higher members of the aristocracy, those of fifth rank and above, probably received their full allotments, not only due to their superior status but also because of their small numbers. At the time of Heian-kyō's establishment, there were only five men of the first three ranks entitled to a full city block. Those of the fourth and fifth ranks, entitled to half a block, probably numbered around seventy-five. Below this, the number of officials entitled to land, albeit a fraction of that given to their superiors, swelled dramatically. If the Nara-period prescriptions were followed, the five to seven thousand members of the imperial hierarchy would have been entitled to a total land area equal to more than 1,250 blocks.[8] As we have seen, however, even decades after the capital was founded, not half this amount had been created. Even if the entire grid had been completed, there would have only been about a thousand blocks available, hardly enough to suffice. Archeological evidence suggesting there was little or no demand for residential development in the south and southwestern areas leads to the conclusion that lower-ranking officials were likely choosing to reside in the city's east and northeast, on plots even smaller than those to which they were entitled. Why this might have been the case is discussed in chapter 3.

A further deviation from the status-based land scheme became apparent in the tenth century. Under the statutory system, midlevel aristocrats were appointed as provincial governors, called *zuryō*, and tasked with the primary duty of ensuring that grain taxes flowed steadily from the provinces to the capital. Over time, state affairs became increasingly privatized, and *zuryō* enjoyed greater degrees of private wealth and personal influence. Eventually, many migrated to the capital, where they could enjoy better lifestyles and potentially engage in high politics. The metropolitan palaces of the *zuryō* that appear in documents from this period are striking for their sprawling size and ostentation, both of which were inconsistent with the formal statuses of their owners. As midlevel officials, *zuryō* would have been entitled to no more than one-fourth of a block. Many, however, constructed palaces that covered whole blocks, a few even more.[9] An entry in *Nihon kiryaku* from 1030 highlights the specific problem while also shedding light on the broader breakdown in rules related to status-based building practices:

> The governors of various provinces should not build homes larger than one-fourth of a block. Lately, however, many are building whole-block residences. . . . Furthermore, people of the sixth rank or lower should be stopped from building walls [around their homes] and covering their roofs in cypress bark.[10]

Cypress-bark roofing (*hiwada-buki*) was reserved for noblemen of the third rank or higher. The same year the document above was issued, the capital residence of a provincial governor named Minamoto no Sōkō was punitively dismantled by the imperial police reportedly for the offense of "building a large home with cypress bark."[11]

Inside these palatial residences, *zuryō* sometimes built large, fire-resistant storehouses (*kura*), which, filled with precious objects and being clearly visible from surrounding streets, stood as unabashed monuments to their owners' material wealth.[12] The *zuryō* building boom of the eleventh century highlights how wealth could make possible the subversion of at least one of the guiding principles of Heian-kyō's planning scheme. It also shows, however, that it was seldom carried out without reproach, both formal and informal.

Provincial governors were not the only people who came to Heian-kyō in search of better lives yet whose presence was not part of the original urban plan. Countless craftsmen, traders, laborers, and peasants likewise flocked to the city, drawn by the prospect of lucrative work in a society with salaried public servants. Records documenting such commoners are inherently flawed due to that social stratum's mobility, but impressionistic evidence puts the number between twenty and thirty thousand by the end of the first millennium. Added to the estimated seventy thousand official residents, this number pushes Heian-kyō's total population to about one hundred thousand, making it one of the largest cities in the world. Indeed, it was rivaled only by its Chinese counterparts.[13]

From the outset, commoners showed little respect for the lofty ideals of central planning. Their living patterns impacted how space was used and defined, and they eventually adapted the urban landscape to their own needs. The first major change took place within the residential *machi*. As explained in chapter 1, the original urban plan called for each of the city's blocks to be divided into thirty-two separate administrative units, called *henushi*, arranged into four rows divided by two interior laneways. Perhaps due to the narrowness of the interior lanes or, conversely, the superiority of the wider surrounding roads, within a short time urbanites began to repartition land within *machi* so that all residential lots provided access to the surrounding roads. The material effects of this change include individual residential lots becoming narrower and longer, *machi* coming to possess an interior courtyard, and finally, and in contrast to the original plan, homes began facing roads to the north and south of blocks rather than just those to the east and west (see Figure 2.2). The driving force behind these changes was the importance of the road, not only as a medium of transportation but

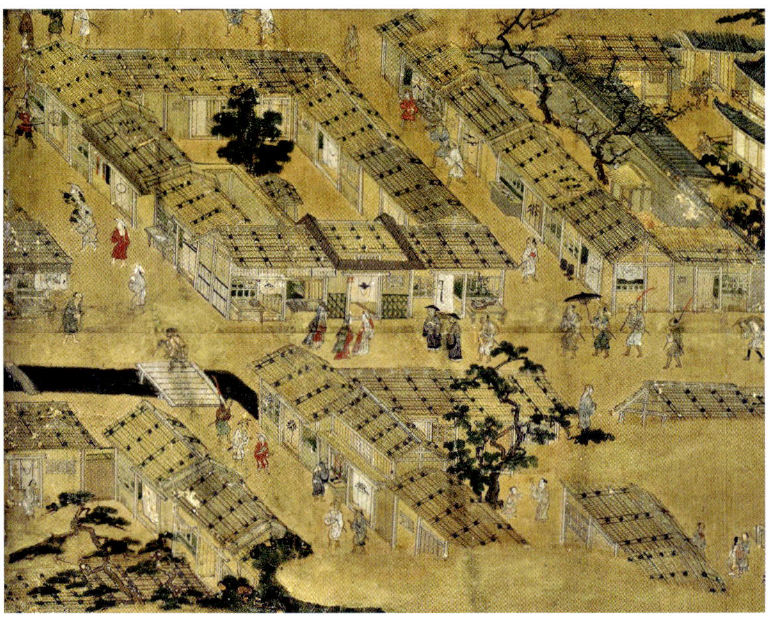

2.2. Residential blocks and "market houses" (*machiya*) in late medieval Kyoto, in Rekihaku kōbon version of *Rakuchū-rakugai-zu byōbu*. Courtesy of the National Museum of Japanese History

also the center of daily life. The public space provided by Heian-kyō's wide thoroughfares came to facilitate a thriving commercial culture and economy that, in terms of its size and complexity, was entirely unforeseen by city planners. As commoners oriented their lives increasingly toward the street (a term used in this book to signify a social phenomenon distinct from the "road"), their most important social, economic, and eventually political bonds came to be held with those people with whom they shared a street rather than those with whom they shared a block.[14] As illustrated in Figure 2.3, an evolution occurred in both the meaning and reading of the ideograph used to indicate the block: 町. Read as "*machi*," it originally signified the physical area of a single, square, urban block, the basic spatial unit of the master-planned city. With the street as the center of daily life, however, residents who occupied each of the four block faces thought of themselves as belonging to discrete social units, with the members of each sharing personal and professional bonds more important than those engendered by the administrative blocks. To describe themselves, these nascent social units appropriated the same ideograph used for *machi*, yet read it as "*chō*."[15] The difference in reading indicated a shift in meaning from a predominantly top-down spatial designation into a self-defined social unit. Later, during the early medieval era, the meaning of the word "*chō*" changed yet again. As streets took on an even more central role in the lives of commoners, roads became the adhesive that bound together the lives of people whose homes faced each other. In other words, they became a medium of community rather than division. The result was a mutation in the meaning of the word "*chō*," which from about the twelfth century signified a cohesive social unit composed of two opposing block faces. Incidentally, this practice, which emerged from the grass roots during the medieval era, is now a defining feature of Kyoto's official political geography.

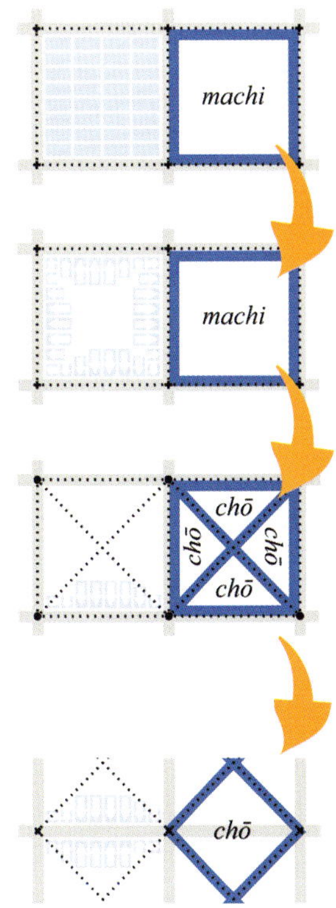

2.3. Evolution of blocks: from *machi* to *chō*. Illustration by Osamu Umatani and the author

Square city blocks were rational from a planning perspective and useful in terms of centralized administration. For urban residents, however, it was the street that mattered most. One place where the street's social significance was readily apparent was in the emergence of a new method for indicating locations: an address system devised entirely from the grass roots that privileged local identity over central planning. The new system was made initially possible through the important step of assigning names to all the capital's roads, big and small. Whereas all the "major roads," or *ōji*, seem to have been given names from the outset, many of the smaller "minor roads," or *kōji*, remained unnamed until as late as the tenth century. Many of the names that began appearing in documents, those such as "lamp-oil road," "brocade road," and "salt road," suggest they were related to a certain dominant commercial activity undertaken by the people who lived and worked on each.[16] These names became the basis for a new addressing system that used intersections as primary points of reference. Whereas Heian-kyō's original system identified and envisioned every unit of space as an elemental fraction of the whole, the new system referred only to a site's relationship vis-à-vis its nearest intersection. The latter, being a far more localized approach, resulted in addresses that looked like the following, which appeared on a deed of sale for a property located near the intersection of Rokkaku and Aburanokōji in Sakyō:

> ORIGINAL: 六角油小路下東面南北二丈八尺九寸東西五丈七尺五寸
>
> TRANSLITERATION: Rokkaku-Aburanokōji sagaru; higashinotsura; nanboku: 2 jō, 8 shaku, 9 sun; tōzai: 5 jō, 7 shaku, 5 sun
>
> TRANSLATION (ABBREVIATED): South of the Rokkaku-Aburanokōji intersection, the block's eastern face. Dimensions: over 6 meters, north-to-south; over 15 meters, east-to-west.[17]

Whereas the new address system lacked the clinical accuracy and rationality of the original (see chapter 1), it was far more user-friendly because it reinforced commoners' sense of belonging to a local community, something that was always more important than their belonging to a centrally planned administrative unit.

Vanishing Venues of State

The grid was a potent and immediate expression of top-down urban planning, but the several sites of state authority that punctuated the cityscape were the most powerful reminders that Heian-kyō was first and foremost the base of a centralized imperial government. Whereas the state may not have had the money or the political will to complete an urban grid it did not need, all evidence suggests that the critical venues of statecraft, practical and performative, were initially finished.

Many, however, were short-lived. The reasons behind their respective disappearances are various, but all relate in some way to a growing gulf separating the idealized capital model from the real-world needs of the state. Frankly, from the time of Heian-kyō's establishment, the Japanese state itself had already become a profoundly privatized operation. While emperors, ministers, and other officials derived their authority from their positions within the system, the individual organs of that system were increasingly controlled by these same people in ways indicative of private enterprises. The details of this breakdown, discussed at length in previous scholarship, need not detain us here.[18] Nevertheless, it is critical to point out that it was because of this trend toward the private control of state institutions that so many of Heian-kyō's most important monuments to state authority began to dissolve almost as soon as they were created.

As mentioned, the Eastern and Western Markets were among the first facilities transferred from Nagaoka-kyō to Heian-kyō. They were also among the first to disappear. The Western Market declined particularly fast. Business was so bad there that in 835 the imperial court took steps to revive the market by designating several commodities over which its traders could enjoy a monopoly.[19] Protests from the vendors of the thriving Eastern Market, however, led to the cancellation of the policy a mere five years later. By 842, the Western Market was clearly on the verge of irrelevance. A document from that year describes: "[p]easants moving east to trade their goods. The stalls [in the Western Market] are already empty and the official gates are not being kept up."[20]

Official state-to-state relations with continental countries were already in decline by the time of Heian-kyō's establishment. The once powerful Tang dynasty had become a mere shadow of its former self and was leaning inexorably toward eventual collapse in 907. Only two official Japanese embassies visited the Tang court during the Heian period. None traveled in the other direction. The last envoy from the Korean kingdom of Silla arrived in 779. Vigorous trade relations with the Kingdom of Parhae (Bohai), located in what is now northeastern China, resulted in dozens of missions to Heian-kyō until 926, just prior to that kingdom's fall.[21] Besides the several factors that inhibited more robust diplomatic activity, the official movement of people between Japan and the continent was always lopsided: far more Japanese traveled abroad than Chinese or Koreans visited Japan. As a result, the several urban facilities built to either impress foreign dignitaries or accommodate them might have seemed lavish and inordinately expensive to maintain. Perhaps for this reason, they were among the first of Heian-kyō's early infrastructure to disappear. Among them was the great Rajō Gate, Suzaku Road, and the twin Kōrokan compounds. While the first two were ostensibly just as useful to the emperor and high aristocracy as to foreign visitors, there is little evidence to suggest either was used with any regularity.

The Rajō Gate was destroyed by high winds in 816 but was quickly rebuilt at state expense. Following a similar calamity in 980, the state was more reluctant to make outlays, instead leaving reconstruction to a provincial governor seeking court favors in return. When that plan fell through, the gate was never rebuilt. Its foundation stones were eventually dragged away for use by Fujiwara no Michinaga (966–1027) in the construction of his private temple of Hōjōji.[22]

Perhaps because it was a space rather than a material object, Suzaku Road's disintegration is less well documented. The few textual records that mention change suggest the impractically wide road was made more narrow through the introduction of crop cultivation and cattle grazing along its shoulders. A document from 862 orders the dispatch of soldiers to guard a series of gates built along the adjacent eastern blocks in response to a claim that nighttime Suzaku had become "an abyss of thieves."[23] Under such circumstances, the Kōrokan compounds, which faced Suzaku, were clearly unsustainable. Not only was urban infrastructure dissolving around them, so too were the diplomatic activities for which they were built. Ambassadors from Parhae were reliable boarders, but their visits were infrequent. A decade or more could pass between missions, during which both complexes might stand completely vacant. Except for passing mention in a document from 1168, we have no other evidence the Kōrokan structures were maintained after the final Parhae mission departed in 920.[24]

Saiji, the state-sponsored Buddhist temple to the west of Suzaku, suffered the same fate as its urban surroundings: it all but disappeared from the documentary record by the close of the first millennium. Besides being on the wrong side of town, Saiji declined partly because of its exclusive function as a venue of state-sponsored Buddhism. While it continued to depend entirely on the state for financial backing, its counterpart to the east, Tōji, diversified and eventually changed its institutional identity entirely. In 823, Emperor Saga (786–842) permitted the monk Kūkai (774–835) to take over administration of the temple, thereby transforming it from a wholly state-sponsored institution into a headquarter temple of the emerging Shingon sect.[25] As Shingon grew in popularity, Tōji thrived. Saiji, on the other hand, declined as the state weakened and its noble patrons became increasingly interested in sectarian Buddhism. A fire in 990 destroyed all of Saiji's structures except for its five-storied pagoda. Several imperial funerals and memorial services followed, but the documentary accounts of each suggests none were particularly grand or of any special public significance. The pagoda might have survived beyond 1233, but the rest of the temple probably did not. Today, there is no trace of Saiji save for a few archeological remains.[26]

Of all the early state structures, compounds, and urban monuments discussed so far, there was no more poignant a symbol of Heian-kyō's failure than the disappearance of the Daidairi imperial enclosure. The most immediate factor that contributed to the Daidairi's eventual decline was fire. Fires were so common in premodern Kyoto that hardly a decade went by without a major conflagration claiming large portions of the wood-built city. Separated from the rest of the urban landscape by a high earthen wall, the structures of the Daidairi were protected but hardly immune. The Chōdō-in burned down in 876. Although it was rebuilt immediately on this first occasion, it took fourteen years for construction to be completed after a similar calamity in 1058. It burned down again and for the last time in 1177 when a great fire devastated a third of Sakyō. The Buraku-in was destroyed earlier in 1063.[27]

Besides the enormous costs and logistical complications involved in rebuilding such large venues of state, a critical factor stymieing their reconstruction was a decisive shift in the conduct of the statutory government. During the Heian period, high government posts and their corresponding offices became increasingly hereditary and thus monopolized by aristocratic families. As privatization progressed, government offices gradually migrated from their original facilities, located within the Daidairi, to the private homes of the aristocracy. As a result, much of the Daidairi was rendered vacant, becoming little more than home to the emperor and the symbolic seat of imperial government.[28]

The work of emperors likewise became more intimate and personal. Increasingly, sovereigns used the Imperial Palace, the Dairi, to hold court amidst a correspondingly small segment of the ruling elite. But this compound too suffered frequent fire damage. It burned down fourteen times between 960 and 1082, and again during the great fire of 1177. On each occasion, the emperor took up temporary residence in compounds located outside the imperial enclosure. At first, the period of residence at these provisional palaces, called *sato-dairi*, was limited to the time needed to complete repairs on the Dairi.[29] The atomization of government, however, which had been progressing from early in the Heian period, had made statecraft portable, and the emperor's duties were no exception. Gradually, the imperial presence at *sato-dairi* grew longer and the functionality of the several palaces expanded accordingly.[30] Eventually, with the emperor's almost constant absence, justification for maintaining the original Dairi declined before disappearing completely. A fire that swept through the largely vacant grounds of the greater palace enclosure in 1227 laid waste to the last few structures that remained and erased any residual pretext that the site continued to be the formal seat of imperial government. Although never entirely forgotten, Heian-kyō's most imposing monument to imperial authority, the Daidairi, was gone. The land on which it stood was eventually transformed into an inextricable part of the expanding urban landscape.

The *Shinden* Style in Practice

The previous chapter described how *shinden*-style palaces proliferated from the eighth century as members of the aristocracy began engaging in various ceremonial activities as a means of demonstrating their membership in the Ritsuryō hierarchy. Serving as the prescribed venue of a highly scripted form of performative statecraft was, after all, *shinden* style's first and foremost function. From the outset, however, there was a yawning gulf separating the style's idealized role and the way it was used in practice. To be sure, elite palaces, including the Imperial Palace itself, were much more than sterile venues of ritual and ceremony. They were also fully functioning personal and family residences. Circumstances necessitated their accommodation of entertainment, household businesses, and private worship, as well as the more mundane acts of everyday life such as sleeping, eating, washing, and procreating. Modification of the original and largely impractical model was as inevitable as it was immediate.

The practice of temporarily partitioning interior *shinden* space through the use of folding screens, curtains, and bamboo shades began concurrently with the adoption of the style.[31] The rooms created in this way were customarily outfitted (*shitsurai*) to accommodate specific non-Ritsuryō functions. Early on, the practice of temporarily accoutering interior space was limited to secondary structures such as corridors (*rō*) or fountain pavilions (*izumi-dono*). Before long, however, the impulse to better accommodate non-Ritsuryō activities, as well the desire to expand dedicated living space, contributed to the creation of permanent interior rooms. When in about the twelfth century the importance placed on Ritsuryō customs began to wane, even central *shinden* (plural) began to be partitioned with stationary walls and sliding doors. Creating these rooms—which appeared in documents as *tsune-gosho*, or "living quarters"—on the northern faces of their *shinden* enabled the elite to hold, for example, poetry contests, drinking parties, and any number of other private functions in ways that minimized the impacts of those activities upon the south-facing parts of their compound, parts that remained reserved for traditional rituals.[32]

Yet another departure from the *shinden* ideal that appeared soon after adoption was the construction of small religious facilities on the grounds of elite palaces. Used to accommodate private religious observances, these oratories, called *jibutsudō* or *bodaiji*, were usually quite modest. They generally possessed no sectarian affiliation, housed no permanent clergy, and were always sequestered behind private palace walls. Their existence, nevertheless, was an early modification of the *shinden* grounds plan as well as a subversion, though a restrained one, of the taboo against temples within the city.[33] As we shall see in later chapters, while architectural prescriptions and proscription remained broadly valid, adaptations to elite palaces continued to challenge capital norms.

Conclusion

Heian-kyō was meant to be a mononuclear capital: the imperial institution was its political, economic, and social center of gravity, and every constituent element of the cityscape was ostensibly oriented around a single, unified, public core. As we have seen, however, private interests and the activities of the high and low alike undermined this ideal from early on. Not only did the city fail to materialize as planned, alternative development patterns soon emerged that revealed a society no longer organized around a single political or economic nucleus. These medieval development patterns are the subject of the next chapter.

3

Making Kyoto Medieval

A Fractured, Privatized, and Pluralistic City

THE EMPEROR AND the state never ceased being the ultimate sources of legitimacy. Moving toward the medieval era, however, power—real power—shifted from the Imperial Palace to the homes of court aristocrats, religious institutions, and, in time, the palace-headquarters of retired emperors and warriors. Appearing in documents as *kenmon*, a word literally meaning "great gate," each of these entities of private influence drew to itself substantial human and material resources. Many of them became the nuclei of dense nodes of development located in and around the capital. The formation of these *kenmon*-centered nodes constituted a profound spatial transformation whereby the master-planned capital became a composite of urban islands, each with a unique identity and distinct set of occupants enjoying a high degree of political and economic autonomy.[1] Most significant about the phenomenon of nodal urban development is how it so vividly reflected a divergence from the classical ideal of a mononuclear political, economic, and social universe. Indeed, the fragmentation of urban space was a stark indicator that, by about the eleventh century, the capital had departed its classical era to become a medieval city. It had made the transition from "Heian-kyō," the "capital of peace and tranquility," to "Kyoto," a fractured, privatized, and pluralistic metropolis.[2]

This chapter focuses on the phenomenon of nodal urban development as it occurred in three separate areas in and around early medieval Kyoto. The first is the city's northeast, a district that came to be called Kamigyō, meaning the "upper capital." There, the palaces of the aristocracy, emperors, and retired emperors clustered with greater density than anywhere else. Earlier research has treated Kamigyō as a single unit, focusing on its character as an aristocratic enclave. Here, greater attention is given to individual complexes, their owners, and the people who condensed around them. The history of elite palaces in medieval Kyoto is important not merely because their sizes and opulent styles symbolized vast wealth and influence. The physical compounds themselves—as government offices, the headquarters of rich family enterprises, and the birthplaces of future emperors—played material roles in the process by which power became privatized and state institutions were weakened.

Kamigyō's geographic and social antipode was the dynamic commercial area that grew up in the shadow of Heian-kyō's Eastern Market: the southern district of Shimogyō, or the "lower capital." As regulatory state institutions waned and expendable wealth increased, commercial activity in Kyoto expanded. As the official markets disintegrated, their functions were replaced by countless stalls and workshops that lined the roads. The nodal development that took place in Shimogyō was different from that of Kamigyō in that it was based mainly around commoners rather than *kenmon* (plural). Nevertheless, there was a fundamental similarity: the clustering of people and institutions was related to the pooling of wealth and influence almost entirely outside the purview of the statutory state.

The next section of this chapter explores the fields and hills surrounding the capital, a place where countless religious institutions built large bases of worship, wealth, and political influence. The most prominent of these exurban temples and shrines exhibited the same kind of basic nodal development patterns seen in Kamigyō: a central *kenmon* surrounded by affiliated administrators, craftsmen, merchants, and others, all drawn together by their sponsor's wealth and ability to shelter them legally and economically.

The final section examines several large temple-palace complexes built on Kyoto's outskirts by retired emperors during the century after about 1075. These complexes empowered members of the imperial family to freely accumulate massive private wealth and political influence rivaling that of even the most powerful aristocratic families and religious institutions. Retired from office, these ex-sovereigns operated outside the frameworks of traditional state apparatuses and, not coincidentally, did so from bases located outside the boundaries of the capital.

Readers familiar with medieval Japanese history will notice a glaring omission from this chapter. There is only passing mention of the rise of warriors and the tremendous impact fighting men began having on the capital from about the twelfth century. They receive much greater attention in the next chapter. While warrior interaction with Kyoto coincided with the trend toward nodal urban development highlighted here, their long-term impact was much more complicated and deserves the sustained examination given later in this book.

Suburbs: Kamigyō and Shimogyō

By the mid-tenth century, Ukyō, the "right" or western half of the old capital, was well on its way to extinction. Writing in about 982, Yoshishige Yasutane describes the area as a deserted wasteland where "homes are rare" and "people leave but nobody new comes."[3] In *The Tale of Genji*, written at about the same time, Prince Genji is asked to intervene to prevent the "pitiful" prospect of a princess coming of age in the capital's west.[4] Yasutane explains that people of wealth, such as the princess, "wouldn't be able to stand living there even a day."[5] A map produced several decades earlier for inclusion in *Engishiki*, an official court record, shows in striking visual detail that Ukyō was almost devoid of official facilities, elite residences, and pretty much anything else (Figure 3.1). Except for inscriptions indicating the Imperial Palace and the Council of State (Dajōkan), the Daidairi appears empty. The two great halls of court ritual, the Chōdō-in and Buraku-in, might still have existed at the time of the map's production, but their omission, like that of the many government offices, suggests they had ceased to function as originally intended.

In marked contrast, Sakyō, the capital's "left" or eastern half, was booming. Yasutane reports intense urban development stimulated by the activities of elites and commoners alike. The *Engishiki* map is embedded with clues suggesting that the east had taken over several formal functions originally shared with Ukyō. One example relates to the two official markets. Built on either side of the city, the Western and Eastern Markets were supposed to operate on an alternating basis. The map suggests, however, that by the tenth century the Western Market had disappeared altogether and that the Eastern Market had expanded dramatically to encompass eight surrounding "outer markets" (see Figure 3.2).[6]

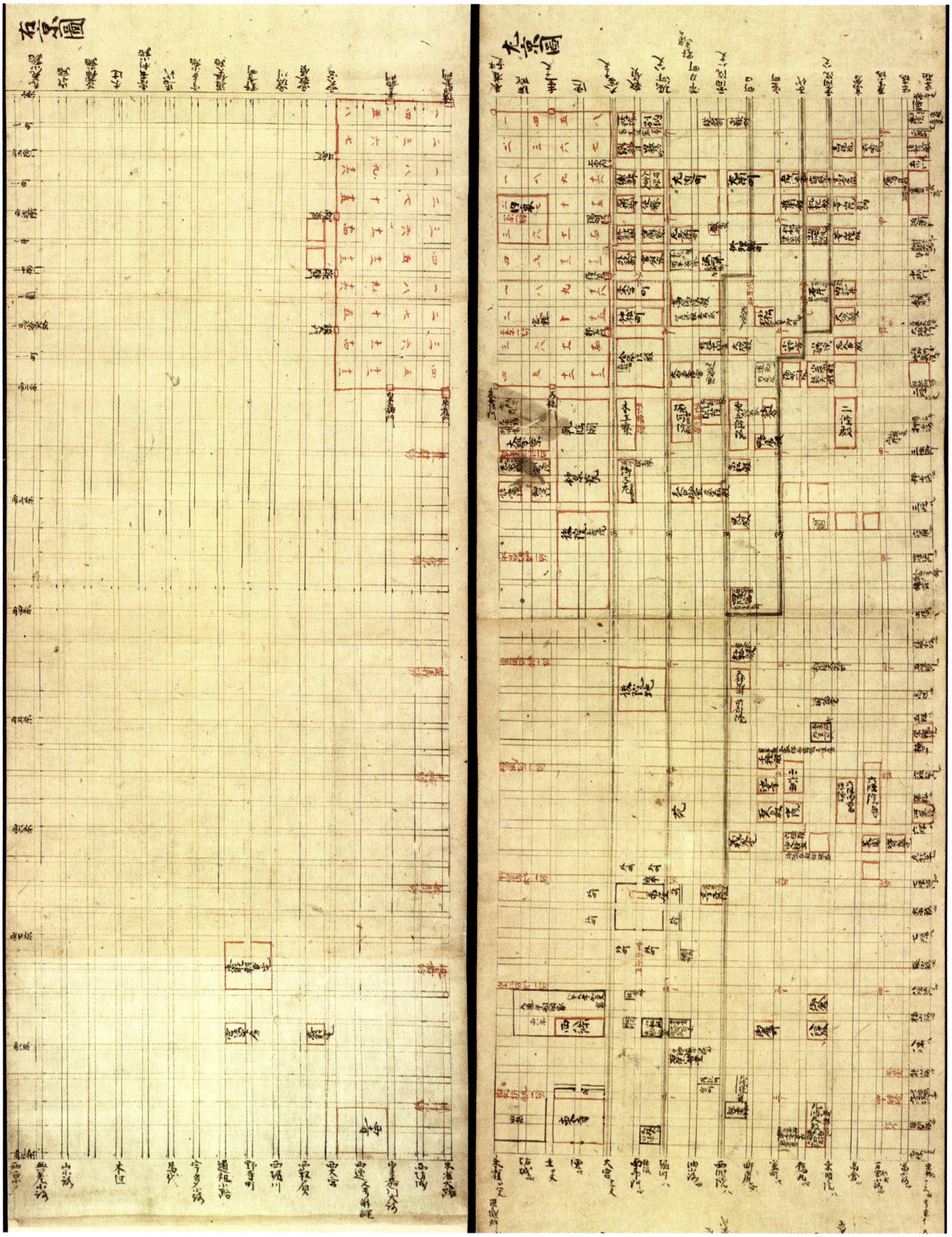
右京圖
左京圖

An additional example of Sakyō's broadened official capacity is apparent in the area's exclusive use for imperial processions. Such processions traditionally took place primarily along the great Suzaku Road. Dark lines on the *Engishiki* map, however, reveal that the emperor and his retinues had come to prefer traveling up and down the urban grid mainly along the Sakyō roads of Ōmiya, Horikawa, and Nishinotōin (see Figures 3.1 and 3.4).[7] With Ukyō having become mostly farmland, the Daidairi being hollowed out, and urbanization exploding in Sakyō, the capital's geographic and ritual center of gravity had shifted decisively toward the east.

3.1. Maps of Ukyō and Sakyō, in *Engishiki*. Courtesy of Tokyo National Museum

Before long, the names Ukyō and Sakyō virtually disappeared from the historical record. As the former was absorbed into the hinterland and the latter took on much greater significance, the Heian-era distinction between a "left" and "right" capital ceased to be meaningful. In *Chiteiki*, Yasutane suggests that a new essential geographic distinction had emerged, one that instead differentiated between the city's "upper" and "lower" parts. According to the narrative, urban development was most concentrated in the north, where high prices had made land ownership prohibitive for the likes of the author himself, a low-ranking government official. In contrast, the land in the south was

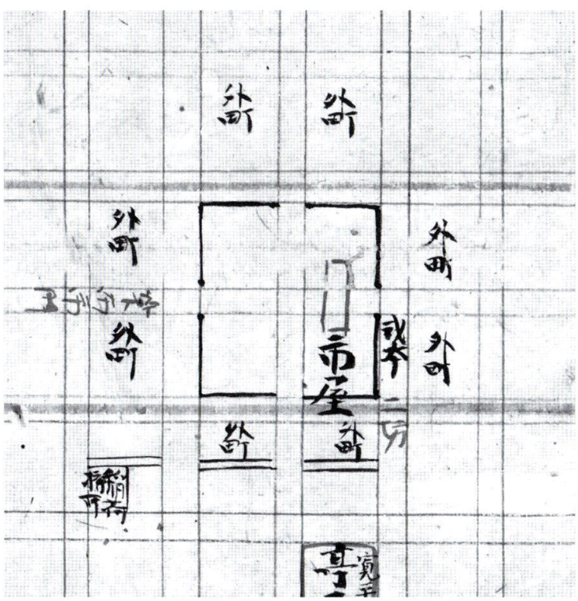

3.2. Eastern Market surrounded by "outer markets," in *Engishiki*. Top of image is west. Courtesy of Tokyo National Museum

reportedly "desolate," a place where "wheat alone bears fruit."[8] It was there, near Rokujō, where Yasutane finally bought property and built a home. The *Engishiki* map is less dismissive of the south. It indicates the existence of several elite palaces, the temple of Tōji, and, as mentioned, an expanded commercial area around the Eastern Market.[9] This final point is important because it was the south's identity as a commercial district, populated mainly by commoners, that would eventually distinguish it from its more elite counterpart to the north.

The earliest textual evidence of a discursive distinction between the city's north and south appears in *Konjaku monogatari*, a literary text from the early twelfth century. It refers to "upper" and "lower" parts of the capital with the words "*kami-watari*" and "*shimo-watari*" respectively.[10] A document from 1275 reports that the "gravely ill" were stalking about the capital's "upper and lower towns," begging for food.[11] By about the fourteenth century, the distinction had become quasi-official, with court documents referring to the toponyms of "Kamigyō" (上京) and "Shimogyō" (下京), meaning "upper capital" and "lower capital" respectively. The ideographs used in these names are significant because they demonstrate that the urban landscape indeed possessed two distinct districts, yet confirm that each was an elemental components of a single whole, one "capital" (*kyō*). This close relationship between Kamigyō and Shimogyō would eventually take on profound significance when, as we shall see, the rise of temple and warrior influence led to an impulse to resuscitate classical-era notions about the capital's status as an exclusive geographic space where state control reigned supreme.

Kamigyō

Explanations for why Kamigyō became the elite district tend to focus on several factors. Its higher, drier, and cooler topography is cited frequently, as is the proximity to the Daidairi imperial enclosure. The former topography argument is tied to a broader assumption that the failure of the capital's western half was due to its boggy, more humid conditions. The standard narrative suggests that Heian-kyō's population generally gravitated toward more favorable land in the east, with the elite preferring the north for its proximity to the Daidairi. But bogs were hardly rare in the east and the northeast in particular was by no means safe. Seasonal floods from the nearby Kamo River regularly wreaked widespread damage.[12] If, therefore, the significance of topography can be de-emphasized and the relevance of proximity instead privileged, we are left with the question of why elites tended to settle with such high concentration on the Daidairi's eastern face rather than the west or south. What made it so special?

There were several factors that influenced settlement trends, but one was much more important than the rest.[13] Quite simply, that was convenience. During the early Heian period, government officials worked within the Daidairi yet lived outside it. When commuting to and from their offices, they accessed the grounds of the palace enclosure through the Yōmei Gate, the Daidairi's most important egress on the eastern side (see Figures 1.3 and 3.3). The central southern gate of Suzaku was reserved for only the most formal occasions, and even then, it was used by only the highest-ranking members of the court. It was this proximity to and orientation toward the Yōmei Gate that stands as the single strongest explanation for why Kyoto's northeast, from early on, became the residential location of choice for the capital elite. In the lingo of urban geography, the Yōmei Gate was the nucleating factor that led to the formation of an elite district. In time, as the offices of imperial government gradually moved from the Daidairi into the homes of the high aristocracy, and after the Daidairi itself had finally disappeared, the city's northeast took on more importance as a center of power and wealth in its own right.

Chiteiki's narrative conveys a sense of dismay about development taking place in the northeast, outside the boundaries of Heian-kyō. Indeed, numerous other sources confirm that urbanization was particularly pronounced north of Ichijō, the northern edge of the classical city. Development in that area has traditionally been interpreted as urban sprawl, understood to mean that urbanization must have reached a saturation point within the city and begun overflowing into the surrounding areas.[14] Some sprawl is undeniable, but the impulse to build outside the city, which had begun almost as soon as the capital was established, was also inspired by certain political and symbolic factors. As discussed in chapter 1, a panoply of laws and customs defined what could and could not be built within the city's formal boundaries, by whom, and for what purposes. It was these codes that proscribed temple construction and burial, and tied the sizes of residential plots and the styles of palace architecture to formal statuses. Some rules,

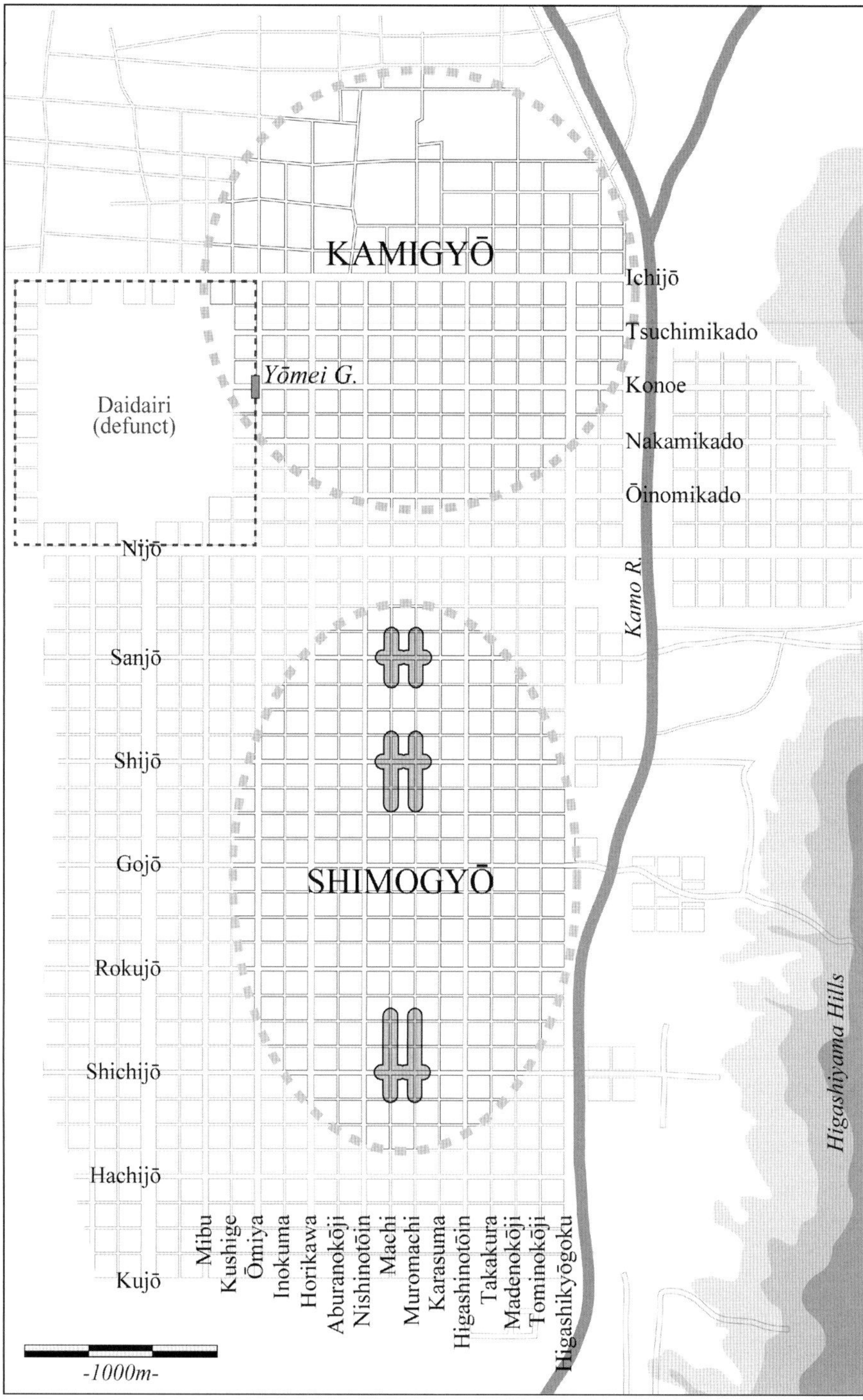
KAMIGYŌ
Ichijō
Tsuchimikado
Konoe
Nakamikado
Ōinomikado
Yōmei G.
Daidairi
(defunct)
Nijō
Kamo R.
Sanjō
Shijō
Gojō
SHIMOGYŌ
Rokujō
Shichijō
Hachijō
Kujō
Higashiyama Hills
Mibu
Kushige
Ōmiya
Inokuma
Horikawa
Aburanokōji
Nishinotōin
Machi
Muromachi
Karasuma
Higashinotōin
Takakura
Madenokōji
Tominokōji
Higashikyōgoku
-1000m-

such as property size, proved flexible as the city and its political structure changed. Others, however, were remarkably resilient. Only outside the capital, for example, could the elite build freely and according to their whims, including both opulent palaces of brazen audacity and simple hermitages considered unbecoming of their august ranks. Almost all exhibited strong religious traits and many were fully fledged temple-palace complexes.

From about the twelfth century, the existence of palaces north of Ichijō stimulated nearby development, which in turn led to the extension of the capital's roads in the same direction.[15] Urbanization was so intense north of Ichijō that the area eventually became indistinguishable from the landscape of the capital proper. While Kamigyō's geographic boundaries seem never to have been explicitly defined, by the time the word came into common usage, it signified a broad zone of dense urbanization north of Nijō, including a substantial area beyond Ichijō (see Figure 3.3). This point about Kamigyō's area is important because, as we shall see, despite profound material transformation and the superimposition of new geographic divisions, the capital's original, formal boundaries continued to be relevant both in Kamigyō and elsewhere.

Scholarship has traditionally treated Kamigyō as a monolithic geosocial phenomenon. The impulse to do so is justifiable, in part, by the district's overwhelming concentration of elites who self-identified as members of a unified interest group. They were "*kuge*," a word translated here and elsewhere as "aristocrat," "courtier," or "nobleman," but one whose ideographs unambiguously signify the role of public servant. Thinking of Kamigyō as a single, homogeneous unit, however, is problematic for several reasons. First, the district was hardly devoid of merchants, craftsmen, traders, and many others of common stock. Their historical profile is simply overshadowed by their elite counterparts. Second and more important, it is wrong to think of the *kuge* as a single interest group, despite what they themselves may have claimed when doing so was somehow advantageous. The progressive neutering of the statutory state's practical power was carried out mainly by *kuge* who operated in their own self-interests, not those of their class or social stratum, and most certainly not for the sake of the state. The individuals and families that were ultimately the most successful became powerful political and economic institutions in their own right, exercising broad control over members of the imperial family, imperial offices, and vast private wealth.

3.3. Map of early medieval Kyoto, showing urban development north and east of the classical grid and the approximate boundaries of Kamigyō and Shimogyō. Areas shaded by double cruciforms correspond to "markets" (*machi*). By about the tenth century, the entire western half of the original grid (Ukyō) had disappeared.

The plurality of aristocratic power was readily visible in Kamigyō's urban landscape. The palaces of the elite were not merely the settings or backdrops of high politics, they played a material role in the advancement of private influence. First, and in the most basic sense, they provided the infrastructure to accommodate increasingly complex and lucrative household enterprises. These enterprises grew as a result of the privatization of government offices and direct familial control over wealth-producing provincial estates. Even from the dawn of the Heian period, when aristocrats were generally expected to attend court six days a week and tend their offices located within the Daidairi, afternoons were reserved for individual household business. The households of the most powerful aristocrats, those of third rank and higher, were particularly large and they consequently required considerable personnel to handle their economic, bureaucratic, and social affairs. Recognizing these needs early on, the Law of Household Administrative Appointment (Karei shokuin-ryō), promulgated in 719, allocated administrative staffers, called *karei,* in numbers corresponding to the ranks of their respective aristocratic masters.[16] Initially employed in such tasks as drafting documents, keeping records, and tutoring younger family members, *karei* were different from other government officials because their appointments were considered more private than public. They were personally attached clients of the households they served.

During the Heian period, the number of *karei* positions grew substantially as a result of the expansion of the *shōen* system, which, among other things, converted tracts of provincial land into designated tax bases to fund specific government offices. As the posts controlling those offices became hereditary, *shōen* and the wealth they produced became the de facto private property of certain aristocratic families. Greater income and more responsibility led to the expansion of palace-headquarters and the employment of more *karei*—also called *keryō* or *keishi*—for accounting, policing, protocol, and the administration of storehouses and granaries. Even the maintenance of the physical plant itself could require enormous human resources. Engineers and builders were retained to construct and maintain walls, stables, granaries, private oratories, and sumptuous residential and administrative buildings. Gardeners, craftsmen, cooks, wet nurses, animal minders, and an army of cleaners could swell the ranks of a household's staff to as high as several hundred. The many people involved in these enterprises were generally not accommodated within the grounds of the palaces they served. Instead, they occupied dormitories, workshops, and offices in nearby neighborhoods. Appearing in documents as "storehouse blocks" (*mikura-machi*), the largest of these were created near the great Fujiwara palaces of Higashisanjō and Tsuchimikado (see Figure 3.4).[17] There, weavers, hatters, metalworkers, *tatami* makers, painters, traders, and other skilled craftsmen lived and worked amidst the large, fire-resistant storehouses from which the blocks took their names.[18] While not all these workers were necessarily *keryō*, they enjoyed a similar status. That is, their relationship with the Fujiwara was based on private, patron-client bonds, a circumstance that afforded them legal protections such as exemption from state taxation and corvée labor. The commoner communities that clustered around Fujiwara palaces were remarkable for their size, but they were not unique. Similar nodes of development existed elsewhere in Kamigyō, constituting highly autonomous social and geographic units oriented around aristocratic *kenmon*.[19]

The palaces of the most successful aristocrats were powerful tools for engaging in sexual politics. They could be used to manipulate the imperial institution because they functioned as incubators of future

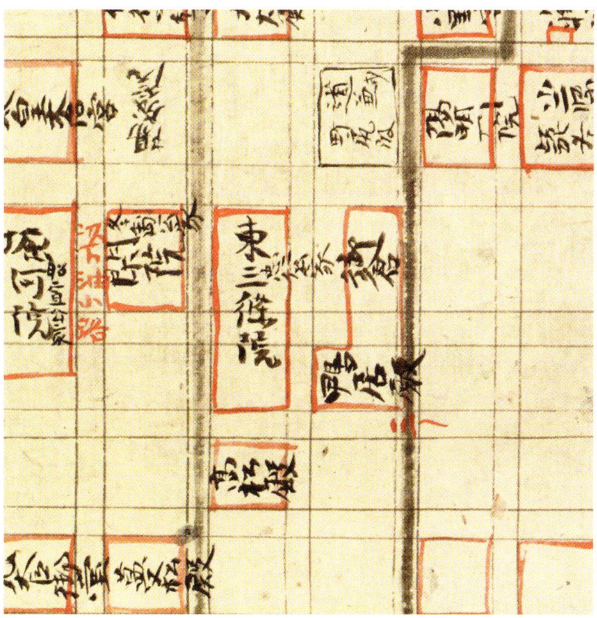

3.4. "Storehouse block" (*mikura-machi*), in *Engishiki*. The storehouse block illustrated here—located adjacent to the Higashisanjō Palace and indicated with the inscription "Kamoi-dono"—covered an area of about 5.3 acres. Top of image is north. Courtesy of Tokyo National Museum

emperors. Imperial regent Fujiwara no Michinaga and his successor, Yorimichi (992–1074), were particularly skilled at exploiting a custom in which aristocratic children were raised at the homes of their maternal grandparents.[20] Fujiwara scions arranged for their daughters to become wives and consorts of reigning emperors. The princes born of these unions were raised at Fujiwara palaces where they came to have strong personal ties of trust and affection with their maternal grandfathers and uncles. Should one of those princes someday become emperor, Fujiwara men would inevitably be appointed to high court positions. If an emperor took the throne as a child, as increasingly became the case, a Fujiwara head (again, the young sovereign's grandfather or uncle), would frequently be made imperial regent (*sesshō* or *kanpaku*), a position that afforded him de facto rule.[21] Fujiwara domination of this uniquely potent form of imperial regency during the ninth and tenth centuries has led some historians to refer to a "Fujiwara era" (*Fujiwara jidai*) or, more commonly, the "regency era" (*sekkan-ki*).

When a prince became emperor, standard protocol dictated that he move to take up residence in the Imperial Palace. His childhood home, however, could remain useful, functioning as a retreat villa on occasions when fire, repairs, or even extreme boredom forced him out of his official residence. In the task of providing retreat villas, again the Fujiwara took the lead. Early on, emperors in need of temporary lodging could simply be welcomed "home" to the places where they were born and raised. Such an arrangement helps explain why these complexes were called "*sato-dairi*," a word that can be translated, albeit clumsily, as "natal home imperial palace." Recognizing the significance of providing for the livelihood of a reigning emperor, Fujiwara scions began preparing palaces specifically for the purpose.[22] By the time the official Imperial Palace, the Dairi, was destroyed for the last time in 1227, most *sato-dairi* possessed all the architectural and stylistic traits necessary to facilitate the full repertoire of imperial rites and duties, and could do so on a permanent basis. One of the earliest and most important among these was Fujiwara no Kanemichi's Horikawain. First used by Emperor En'yū (959–999) after a fire consumed the Dairi in 976, Horikawain is referred to in *Eiga monogatari* as "the current imperial palace" (*ima dairi*) and is described as being "built just like the Dairi."[23] A similar description was applied to Fujiwara no Michinaga's Biwa Palace when it was used by Emperor Ichijō from 1009. In that case, Michinaga went so far as to ascribe names to the buildings that corresponded to analogous structures within the Dairi.[24] Such architectural mimicry should not be interpreted as imitation for the sake of flattery or, as some have asserted, meant to ensure that a visiting sovereign felt comfortable.[25] The relationship between form and function was such within the context of *shinden*-style complexes that building to resemble the Imperial Palace was required in order to ensure a reigning emperor had at his disposal the physical infrastructure necessary to conduct imperial business and rituals despite his relocation. Creating *sato-dairi* in such a way is what made longer stays possible. It might have also led to the eventual determination that the original Dairi was no longer necessary.

Fujiwara palaces dominated Kamigyō's urban landscape during the Fujiwara heyday, but the palaces of other aristocratic families served similar functions and exhibited similar traits. Although on a smaller scale, they too were centers of substantial household enterprises and personalized clientage, and hotbeds of sexual politics. Even after Fujiwara power waned, Kamigyō continued to be a very special place. It was an elite district, without doubt, but one perhaps best characterized as a conglomeration of heterogeneous nodes of power, each with its own independent political, economic, and social foci.

Shimogyō and the Appearance of "*Machiya*"

Widespread commerce and production—and the people engaged in both—were not integral to the original capital plan. They were not forbidden per se, simply not planned for. As we have seen, commoners who serviced the elite were not unusual. They fulfilled important functions and ultimately contributed to the transformation of Heian-kyō from an inert realm of imperial statecraft—a "capital" in an austere sense—into an infinitely more diverse and undoubtedly more interesting social milieu, a medieval "city." Nowhere was the dynamism of commoners more pronounced than in the capital's south, in the district that came to be called Shimogyō, the "lower capital" (see Figure 3.3). Shimogyō was distinct from Kamigyō in two basic ways. First, it possessed a far greater concentration of commoners and their shops, trading stalls, workshops, street markets, storehouses, and the like. Second and more important, Shimogyō's commoners were more detached from the aristocracy. They were freer agents, engaging in market-based commercial activity and, in many cases, making a good living doing so. What gave Shimogyō its distinct commercial flavor and made it so different from its elite counterpart to the north was not merely the magnitude of its commercial activity. Rather, it was that its commercial activity took place largely without state or aristocratic intervention. The formation of an urban district that was almost exclusively common, demographically and occupationally, was an important part of Kyoto's medievalization because it was indicative of the emergence of new, characteristically "medieval" economic institutions and the general waning of state power.[26]

Heian-kyō's two official markets were the nucleating forces that initially drew commercial activity to the capital in general and the southern half in particular. There, countless traders, skilled craftsmen, and laborers were provided a window through which they could access the urban marketplace, fueled by robust demand from a large population of salaried officials. After the Western Market disappeared along with its half of the city, the Eastern Market expanded to take over many of its formal and informal functions. Official oversight of the Eastern Market, however, receded early. Court officials charged with management were clearly ineffectual by as early as the late ninth century.[27] The weakening of state institutions in general was one factor, but even more important was increased demand for commercial activity. Elites who commanded greater private wealth needed skilled commoners to help them dispose of it. Precisely when the physical market finally disappeared is unknown, but its absence in documents describing a fire that swept through the area in 1178 suggests it was gone by at least the mid-twelfth century.[28]

Insipient commercial activity had begun to take place on roads and in blocks long before the Eastern Market disappeared. Heian-kyō's excessively wide roads were identified early on as ideal places to set up stores and workshops.[29] They afforded squatters wide-open land that was flat, well drained, and ideally placed for the conduct of business. Just as important, because roads were considered public or "unaffiliated space" (*kugai*), they were not initially subject to taxation.[30] State officials tried to enforce laws banning the use of roads for anything other than transportation. Their efforts, however, proved ineffectual for the same reasons market oversight failed: the state was too weak and commercial demand too great. Other commoners acquired residential land by more orthodox means, gaining the right to occupy small plots within the capital's formal blocks, the *machi*. As discussed in chapter 2, land within blocks was quickly reorganized to give more properties direct access to the surrounding roads.[31] Commoners built long, narrow row houses and converted the fronts into shops, workshops, and other commercial facilities. Midsections were used as homes while the backs, which often opened onto a shared courtyard at the center of the block, were generally used for storage (see Figures 3.5 and 3.6). Called "*machiya*," these multipurpose buildings eventually became hallmark architectural elements of Kyoto's historical landscape and monuments to the city's robust commercial culture.

Exploring the origins of the word "*machiya*" provides the context for describing several conventions and phenomena that are fundamental

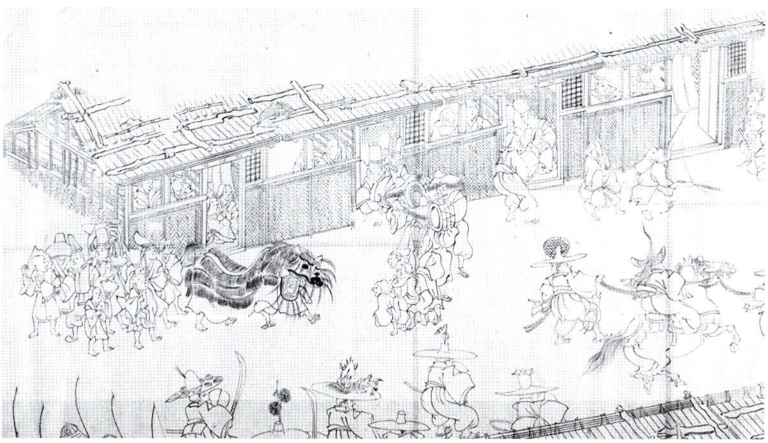

3.5. "Market houses" (*machiya*). This illustration, from *Nenjūgyōji emaki*, is the earliest known pictorial representation of commoner houses in Kyoto. Courtesy of Kyoto University Faculty of Letters

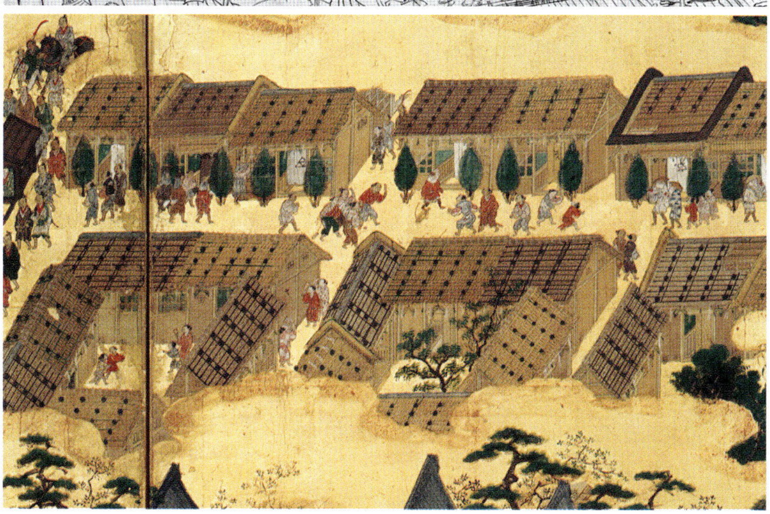

3.6 "Market houses" (*machiya*), in Uesugi version of *Rakuchū-rakugai-zu byōbu*. Defining traits of early *machiya* include direct access to the road, a shared rear courtyard, and timber-plank roofing secured by logs or stones. Courtesy of Uesugi Museum, Yonezawa

to understanding Kyoto's urban landscape, past and present. The types of structures first called *machiya* were most densely clustered along the north-south roads of Machi and Muromachi, particularly at the intersections of Sanjō, Shijō, and Shichijō (see Figure 3.3). Land was several meters higher there, probably making it less prone to flooding.[32] These intersections became major hubs of commercial activity, full-fledged markets born organically of demand and necessity rather than state planning. As sites of social and economic importance, they began appearing in documents with ever-greater frequency. Following convention—which, incidentally, remains the same today—the authors of contemporary documents indicated each intersection by combining the names of its two intersecting roads, with the east-west road usually written first. The intersection of Sanjō and Machi Roads, therefore, appears in historical records as "Sanjō-Machi." The Shijō and Machi intersection appears as "Shijō-Machi," and so on. Commercial activity was so highly concentrated along Machi and Muromachi that the word "*machi*" itself, used as a de facto suffix, came to be synonymous with "market." A document, for example, that might refer to "Shichijō-Machi" in the tenth century was, therefore, not merely specifying an intersection. It was using a proper noun to signify what is perhaps best rendered in English as the "Shichijō Market," a site that would have been universally understood to be located at the intersection of Shichijō and Machi Roads. As *machi* came to be synonymous with "market," the types of homes typical of the most important of those markets, those along Machi and Muromachi Roads, came to be called "*machiya*," which, according to the usage of the day, signified "market houses."[33] Recent excavations in Shimogyō along Machi (which is now called Shinmachi) have unearthed swords and their accoutrements, metal casts and melting pots. The findings support a rich body of textual evidence documenting the clustering of swordsmiths, founders, filigree workers, and artisans who fashioned, among other things, gold and silver leaf. It was an enclave of skilled craftsmen, *shokunin*, who were heavily patronized and made wealthy by the Kamigyō elite.[34] When a fire swept through Shimogyō in 1234, this is what Fujiwara no Teika (1162–1241), writing in *Meigetsuki*, had to say about the area and its people:

> The number of storehouses (*dosō*) is innumerable; the place is flooded with people engaged in commerce. It's said to be the center of wealth for the entire country. . . . Reconstruction

> began the next day. [Other] wealthy commoners came to offer their commiserations, piling up [gifts] like mountains. Erecting large curtains around their properties, they stay inside with no shortage of rice, *sake*, and fish.[35]

Teika's reference to *dosō* is significant because it shows that commercial activity in Shimogyō was not limited to the buying, selling, and producing of goods. To be sure, the owners of such "storehouses," along with *sake* brewers (*sakaya*), served as financiers for the Kamigyō elite and the most powerful religious institutions, Enryakuji preeminent among them.[36] They provided, among other things, a channel for the conversion of *shōen* income into more liquid assets such as gold, copper, silk, and all sorts of fineries. In return, they received various legal benefits such as tax exemptions.[37] Sometimes appearing in documents less euphemistically as *kashiage*, a word meaning "lender," these commoners were Shimogyō's most wealthy by far. An encyclopedia of ailments from the late twelfth century includes an illustration of just such a lender. Supported by two attendants on either side of her bloated body, the accompanying text explains that her wealth and access to rich foods has inflicted her with "extreme obesity" to the point where she is "unable to walk without grave difficulty."[38] Shimogyō's complexion as a district of commerce and commoners only sharpened over time. Tax rolls from the early fifteenth century make it possible to plot the locations of more than three hundred *sake* brewers, oil retailers, and pawnbrokers, which together constituted the backbone of the urban economy (see Figure 3.7). While they maintained a prominent profile throughout the city and surrounding hinterland, their concentration was greatest south of Nijō and north of Shichijō, between Ōmiya in the west and Higashikyōgoku in the east.[39] This area corresponds closely to what contemporary writers meant when referring to Shimogyō. Except for a few exceptions, it was virtually devoid of notable aristocratic palaces by about the twelfth century. Perhaps as a result, Shimogyō boasted a cultural tradition distinct from its elite counterpart, elements of which linger today. For example, from about the ninth century, more than a dozen of the neighborhoods of Shimogyō began constructing massive portable shrines (*yama* and *hoko*) to be put on display and paraded through the streets of the capital during the annual Gion Festival (*Gion-sai*). While the whole city took part in the festivities, only the commoners of Shimogyō deployed portable shrines. It was the

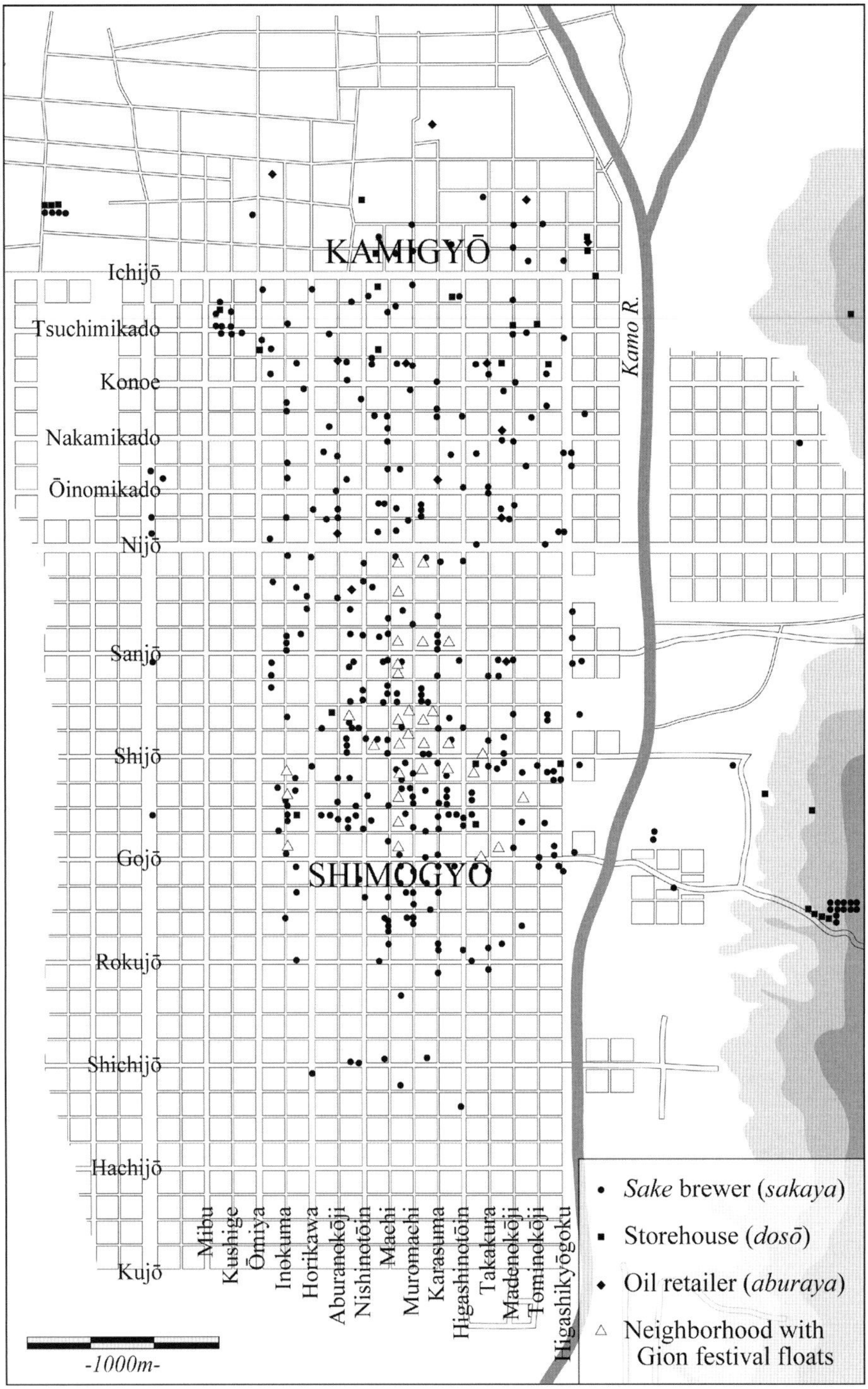

KAMIGYŌ
SHIMOGYŌ
Kamo R.
Ichijō
Tsuchimikado
Konoe
Nakamikado
Ōinomikado
Nijō
Sanjō
Shijō
Gojō
Rokujō
Shichijō
Hachijō
Kujō
Mibu
Kushige
Ōmiya
Inokuma
Horikawa
Aburanokōji
Nishinotōin
Machi
Muromachi
Karasuma
Higashinotōin
Takakura
Madenokōji
Tominokōji
Higashikyōgoku
Sake brewer (sakaya)
Storehouse (dosō)
Oil retailer (aburaya)
Neighborhood with Gion festival floats
-1000m-

associated spectacle that became the festival's highlight as well as its signature event.[40]

The formation of Shimogyō meant the tacit acceptance of commoners as a large and increasingly integral segment of the capital's population. Without doubt, the activities of those commoners created and sustained an economy far more complex and dynamic than anything envisioned by early state planners. Despite their profound demographic, occupational, and cultural differences, Kamigyō and Shimogyō maintained some key economic, legal, and political bonds. First, Kamigyō was the single largest and most lucrative market for Shimogyō's commoners. Their smelters, potters, leather workers, painters, silk weavers, architects, entertainers, gardeners, *sake* brewers, moneylenders, and people of countless other professions kept the elite fed, clothed, financed, and serviced in the styles to which they were accustomed.[41] In return, they made a good living doing so and some—especially moneylenders—received legal protections from taxation and corvée labor. Finally, the land in Shimogyō that commoners occupied was usually owned (or wholly controlled) by members of the aristocracy or certain religious institutions.[42] In the final analysis, the commoners of Shimogyō were freer agents than their counterparts in Kamigyō, who were often attached, physically and professionally, to aristocratic palaces. Nevertheless, Shimogyō continued to be an integral part of the capital. The Kamigyō elite and Shimogyō commoners were engaged in a symbiotic and increasingly interdependent relationship. As we shall see in the next chapter, when Kyoto was threatened by those considered outsiders, one of the first steps the aristocracy took to insulate the city was to rearticulate the geographic boundaries of the capital. In doing so, at least one of their objectives was to ensure that they remained masters over the area of Shimogyō. To them, it was the "lower" capital, perhaps, but an integral part of the capital nonetheless.

3.7. Map of Kyoto's medieval economy. After Takahashi et al., eds., *Zushū Nihon toshi-shi*, 86

Exurbs: Temple Towns and Temple Palaces

The focus now shifts to the capital's immediate surroundings. There, during the medieval era, influential sectarian temples and shrines became the nuclei of large, diverse, and staunchly autonomous quasi-urban communities. In similar fashion, temple-palace complexes built by retired emperors catalyzed the formation of exurban microcities. These *kenmon*-centered communities are archetypes of the kind of nodal urban development indicative of the rise of private power. At the core of each was a nucleating *kenmon* that, while deriving its underlying legitimacy from its ties to the statutory state, exercised its most substantial influence through the control of vast private wealth, strong ties of personal clientage, and, in some cases, the ability to project military force. People and resources clustered around each, forming communities with discrete identities and corporate benefits.

It is of profound significance that the development nodes discussed in this section were universally located outside the capital's formal boundaries. The original taboo that excluded religious institutions from Heian-kyō was only part of the equation. Throughout the premodern age, there remained a clear and consistent distinction between the capital's "inside" and "outside" that impacted a broad range of building and behavior patterns. For its complexity and interrelationship to so many other phenomena, a full explanation of this particular topic must wait until the next chapter.

Temple Towns on the Outskirts

The decision to abandon the capital at Heijō was partly motivated by Emperor Kanmu's desire to separate the state from the influence of the early Buddhist sects. The polity had become infused by sectarian intervention, and the city itself was saturated with temples large and small. In contrast, Heian-kyō had no temples except for Tōji and Saiji, the two official state institutions, both of which originally had no sectarian affiliation. The precise nature of the temple/shrine taboo is not known; we have no primary sources that explain it in any detail. Circumstantial evidence suggests, however, that it applied only to the area within the capital's formal boundaries and not the surrounding fields and hills. The founding of Heian-kyō exerted a strong gravitational pull on religious institutions seeking to be close, geographically and politically, to the center of national power. As we explore these institutions, it should be made clear from the outset that in the Kyoto basin, temples were generally much larger, richer, and in many cases the institutional superiors of their shrine counterparts.[43] As a result, they receive more attention in the narrative that follows. Throughout Kyoto's history, there was a steady stream of temple and shrine construction in the areas surrounding the city. In retrospect, however, the establishment of substantial religious institutions prior to about 1400 took place in three great waves. The first began during Kanmu's reign and occurred very much with the emperor's blessing and support. He sponsored the travels and studies of Saichō and Kūkai, two monks who, respectively, founded the esoteric sects of Tendai and Shingon, perhaps two of the most influential schools of the Heian period. In 788, Saichō (767–822) established the temple of Enryakuji on Mount Hiei, the highest peak surrounding the Uta basin, where Heian-kyō would be built six years later (see Figure 3.8). Enryakuji's fortuitous northeastern location, the direction in which malevolent deities reside, and Saichō's close relationship with Kanmu might have affected the decision about where Heian-kyō was located. Kūkai (774–835) built his headquarters on Mount Kōya, closer to the former capital of Heijō, but later created a foothold in Heian-kyō by converting the official state temple of Tōji to Shingon in 823. Tōji and Enryakuji were of matchless importance to the premodern history of the capital. Both institutions had a profound and long-lasting impact on politics, economic matters, and eventually, as armed and fortified compounds, conflict.

In the long run, Shingon was to enjoy stronger ties to the court and its members, but it was Enryakuji whose presence was most palpable in the capital region. Dozens of Enryakuji-affiliated subtemples and shrines surrounded the city, standing with particular density along the eastern hills of Higashiyama. Many, called *shukubō*, served as sectarian outposts and bases for charismatic monks who received patronage from the capital elite.[44] Others, called *monzeki*, functioned as destinations for members of the imperial family or other high aristocracy seeking to escape capital politics while remaining politically relevant and financially well endowed. The great Gion Shrine, home of the annual Gion Festival, was also under Enryakuji's institutional control.[45] All played a role in extending the influence of the Enryakuji establishment, which deftly blended its official status, vast wealth, private ties to the elite, and its command of a substantial militia into a virtually irresistible lobbying force.

A second wave of temple construction began in the late ninth century with the meteoric rise of the Amida movement of Pure Land Buddhism. Concerned with individual salvation at a time when many considered the world in a state of irrevocable spiritual decline (*mappō*), Pure Land thought generated broad interest among the capital elite just as many began constructing private retreat palaces outside the city.[46] While these same individuals often maintained discrete, nonsectarian

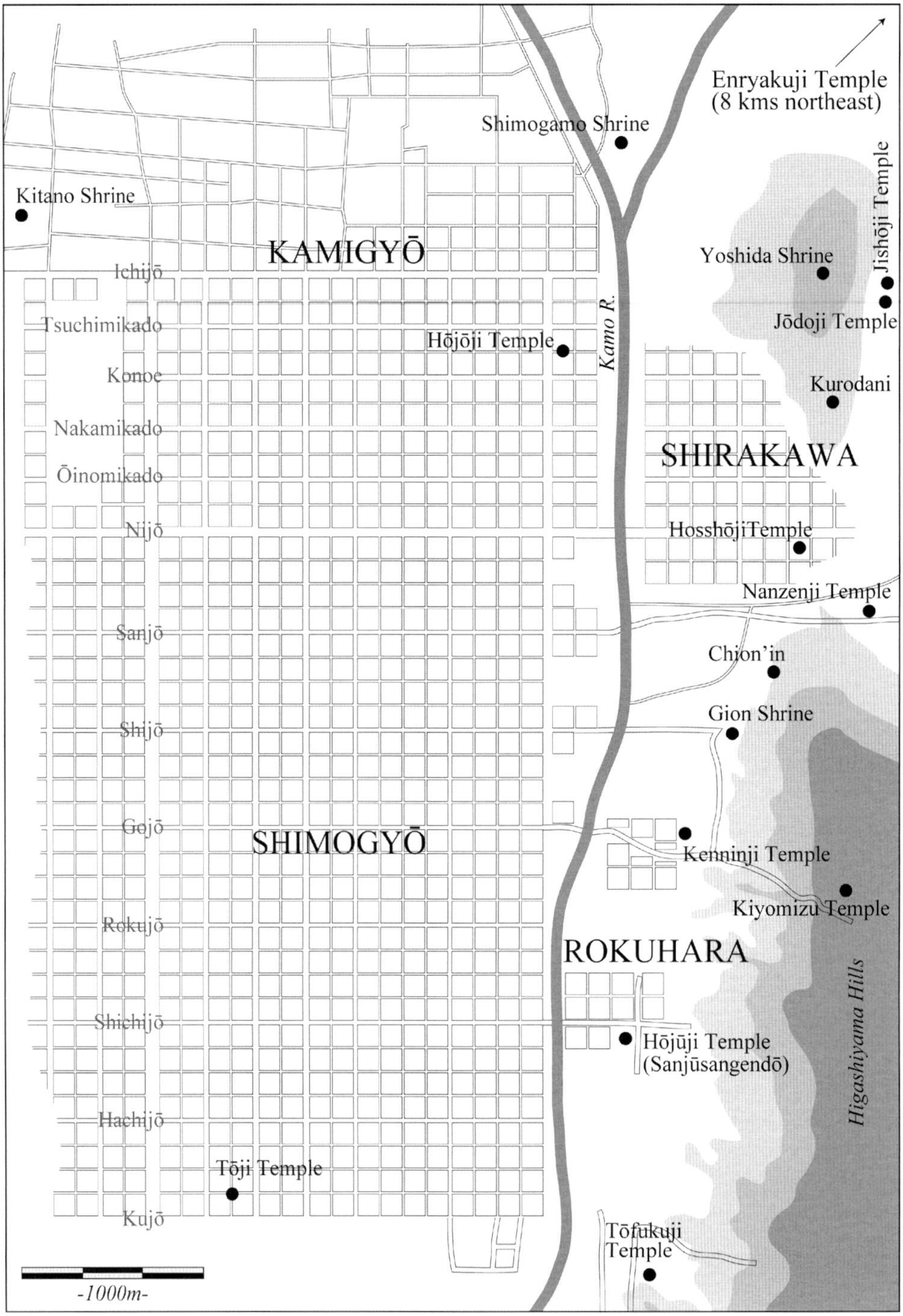
Enryakuji Temple
(8 kms northeast)
Shimogamo Shrine
Kitano Shrine
KAMIGYŌ
Ichijō
Tsuchimikado
Konoe
Nakamikado
Ōinomikado
Nijō
Sanjō
Shijō
Gojō
Rokujō
Shichijō
Hachijō
Kujō
Yoshida Shrine
Jishōji Temple
Jōdoji Temple
Kurodani
Hōjōji Temple
Kamo R.
SHIRAKAWA
HosshōjiTemple
Nanzenji Temple
Chion'in
Gion Shrine
SHIMOGYŌ
Kenninji Temple
Kiyomizu Temple
ROKUHARA
Higashiyama Hills
Hōjūji Temple
(Sanjūsangendō)
Tōji Temple
Tōfukuji
Temple
-1000m-

oratories on the grounds of their urban residences, many saw the creation of exurban retreats as an opportunity to construct more substantial religious facilities. And true to the zeitgeist, most of these were inspired by Amida thought and would eventually become part of the emerging Pure Land establishment. The result of this trend was the creation of many of Kyoto's largest and most opulent temples, including Byōdōin, Jōdoji, Kurodani, Kiyomizu, and Chion'in. Many still exist today, and their concentration in the Higashiyama Hills east of Kyoto makes that area one of the densest conglomerations of Buddhist temples in the world.

From about the thirteenth century, Pure Land temples began receiving smaller yet vastly more numerous financial contributions from commoners who flocked to temples as pilgrims. Besides religious fervor, many were drawn by pure spectacle. Visiting a temple or shrine to worship amidst grand halls and towering pagodas, sonorous bells and chanting monks, gilded icons, and the scent of incense enabled commoners to see and, to a limited extent, take part in a world of grace and refinement unlike anything available to them in the city.

The third religious wave that resulted in a spate of temple construction took place in the mid-thirteenth century with the patronage of Zen Buddhism, primarily by warrior elites. The flourishing of Zen inspired the construction of dozens of temples, mostly located in the metropolitan centers of Kyoto and Kamakura. The most famous of these built near Kyoto include Kenninji, Nanzenji, and later Tenryūji.

3.8. Map of temples, temple-towns, and exurban districts outside Kyoto. For the location of Tenryūji, see Figure 3.11.

From its adoption in the sixth century, Buddhism in Japan was tied on a fundamental level to sacerdotal imperial rule, elite pageantry, and the functioning of the statutory state.[47] Despite dramatic institutional changes, both to the Buddhist establishment and to the state itself, this cardinal connection between church and state persisted throughout Heian and beyond. The building of temples, their formal recognition, and the number of priests ordained annually were all matters of close court oversight. Monks and priests were expected to perform rites and rituals at the Imperial Palace and other public venues that served to protect the state and the body of the emperor as well as legitimize the enlightened rule of the imperial government. Competition among doctrinal persuasions—what can be called "sects" only in hindsight—for monopolies over certain state rituals was fierce, sometimes violent. Economic incentives were one motivation; for their service to the state, religious institutions were granted *shōen* estates from which they could draw taxes. Prestige, however, was just as valuable. Institutions and eminent priests with the highest public profiles—meaning formal ranks and titles—were the first to receive private patronage, which could far outweigh ties to the state in terms of long-term rewards. Members of the imperial family, the aristocracy, and later elite warriors lavished upon them gifts of cash, precious heirlooms, animals, and even greater tracts of land. They might sponsor the construction of temples and subtemples, the overseas study of promising novices, and the commissioning or purchase of sutras and icons. Vast sums were given to institutions for their performance of certain annual observances, while special occasions such as funerals, exorcisms, and prayers for the sick commanded even greater recompense.

Temples and shrines were, in principle, extraterritorial, meaning they enjoyed exemption from taxation and their grounds were (usually) off limits to imperial police. Midlevel aristocrats sought to exploit the special legal status of religious institutions and in so doing boost their own incomes. Those serving as provincial governors (*zuryō*), for example, might commend newly developed provincial lands under their supervision to a powerful religious institution. In so doing, they removed that land from state tax rolls, thus channeling its wealth instead to the temple or shrine. And of course, for engaging in an act of such piety, the governor would receive a portion of the income generated annually.[48] Extraterritoriality was nowhere more apparent than in some institutions' maintenance of militias or, in some cases, full-scale armies. The armed monks of Enryakuji are the most famous. They used the threat of force not only to protect their financial interests but also to launch raids on the capital aimed at asserting their rights to monopolize certain religious posts and public rituals.[49]

In sum, despite their foundational association with the state and unflagging enthusiasm for public rewards, religious institutions—not dissimilar from the aristocracy—came to enjoy a high degree of financial, legal, and territorial autonomy. They commanded vast private wealth and flourished due to the benefits of private patronage. Any one of the countless temples that stood along Kyoto's eastern hills during the medieval era, for example, might have accommodated as many as several hundred novice and ordained monks who lived, worked, and practiced within a walled and gated compound encompassing dozens of large and small structures typically spread over a hectare or more. The proliferation of attached subtemples (*tacchū* or *shiin*), which was particularly pronounced around Zen temples, increased these figures exponentially.[50] To sustain such substantial populations and large physical plants, temples, like Kamigyō palaces, retained the services of countless skilled and unskilled laborers. Teams of administrators, clerks, and even private police were employed to look after landed and other economic interests. Hundreds more were needed to maintain buildings and gardens, procure food, paper, and other daily necessities, weave robes, produce devotional art, manufacture *tatami*, brew *sake*, and much more. As de facto retainers but not formal members of the ecclesiastic community, these people generally took up residence just outside the gates of the institutions they served, usually along the road leading to the capital. There, they built homes, shops, and workshops, maintained roads, and formed neighborhood associations that were, despite their otherwise rural settings, unmistakably urban in character.[51]

These clusters of development evolved into lively and diverse urban communities that appear frequently in documents as *monzen-machi*.[52] The word literally means "town in front of the gate," but it signified much more than a geographic juxtaposition. *Monzen-machi* became important economic bases and resource pools to their respective religious *kenmon*. They provided critical goods and services, and due to their usefulness, temples and shrines sought to protect their residents legally from the intervention of outsiders, including the court, aristocrats, warriors, and rival religious institutions. In practice, this meant claiming *monzen-machi* as exclusive territory, making them and their occupants off-limits from outside policing or criminal investigation, taxation, and corvée labor. The most successful religious institutions could exercise legal prerogatives over adjacent lands even beyond their *monzen-machi*, including cultivated fields and forests. Medieval documents refer to a temple or shrine's expanded territory as *keidai*.[53] The word itself means "within the boundary" but the articulation of a "boundary" of any kind beyond temple or shrine walls signified an expansion of territorial jurisdiction. Examples of institutions that claimed formidable *keidai* include the temples of Nanzenji, Tōfukuji, Tōji, Kenninji, Tenryūji, and the shrines of Kamo (Shimogamo), Kitano, and Gion (Yasaka) (see Figure 3.8).

After the Ashikaga shogunate was established in Kyoto in 1336, warrior leaders sought to exert greater legal, economic, and, particularly in the case of Enryakuji, martial control over religious institutions in the capital region. Their success in the long run is undeniable, but it is important to note that military officials frequently showed deference to the principle of temple and shrine extraterritoriality. When problems arose, for example, rather than simply issuing dictatorial commands, shogunal officials tended instead to admonish religious leaders to enforce "temple law" (*jihō*) over the people and territories of their *keidai*. The very existence of "temple law" itself suggests an outstanding degree of autonomy.[54] This is not to say that religious institutions were entirely exempt from forceful shogunal intervention on occasion. It does appear, however, that force alone trumped the otherwise complete control that powerful temples or shrines exercised over their affiliated *keidai*.

During the tumultuous Age of Warring States (1467–1580s), many temple- and shrine-based communities surrounding Kyoto, like Kamigyō and Shimogyō themselves, built walls and dug moats around their *keidai* in self-defense (discussed in chapter 6). Fortifications stood as stark indicators of the era's extreme danger and lawlessness. In a sense, however, they merely made more materially obvious circumstances that had existed for centuries: religious institutions were the nuclei of discrete territories that encompassed both sacred and profane space, a diverse population, and robust commercial and agricultural activity. Over all this, they exercised a high degree of political, legal, and economic autonomy. Temples and shrines generated nodes of development whose very existence signified the fractured state of medieval politics and society.

Temple-Palaces of Retired Emperors

For a period of just over a century starting in about 1086, a series of former emperors effectively challenged the influence of the Fujiwara to seize sweeping control over political affairs. As the embodiment of state and public authority, reigning emperors were meant to possess no private power or wealth, no individual control over land, and no personal or familial ambitions. Thus, in an environment where private wealth and political ties were becoming increasingly critical to the exercise of real-world power, the imperial family was at a stark disadvantage. During the heyday of Fujiwara domination, however, a few independently minded princes and emperors who were not tied by blood to that aristocratic family began seeking ways to remedy their situation. The solution was found by Shirakawa (1053–1129), who, at the age of thirty-three, formally retired from the position of emperor and took the tonsure. Having left public office—and, as a cloistered oblate, "the world"—Shirakawa was suddenly free to engage in politics in ways similar to the Fujiwara. That is, he could begin amassing unrestricted wealth, engaging in sexual politics, and establishing strong personal ties with temples, aristocrats, and warriors. Succeeding in all these respects with the support of provincial governors and the great warrior houses of Minamoto and Taira, Shirakawa and his several successors—including retired emperors Toba, Goshirakawa, and Gotoba—exercised almost unmitigated influence over the court and state institutions from the comfort of massive temple-palace complexes built on Kyoto's outskirts. Like the Kamigyō palaces and exurban temples discussed so far, these sites too drew to themselves substantial and diverse populations, eventually growing to become satellite cities in their own right.

In 1075, while still in office, Emperor Shirakawa commissioned the construction of the temple of Hosshōji along an extension of Nijō Road east of the city (for location, see Figures 3.8 and 3.11). Boasting an eight-sided, nine-story pagoda that was a staggering eighty-one meters tall, Hosshōji was merely the first and largest of six major temples built at the site, in addition to two administrative palaces, and several smaller oratories (Figures 3.9 and 3.10).[55] Shirakawa's retirement in 1086 and subsequent relocation to the nascent district—which itself came to

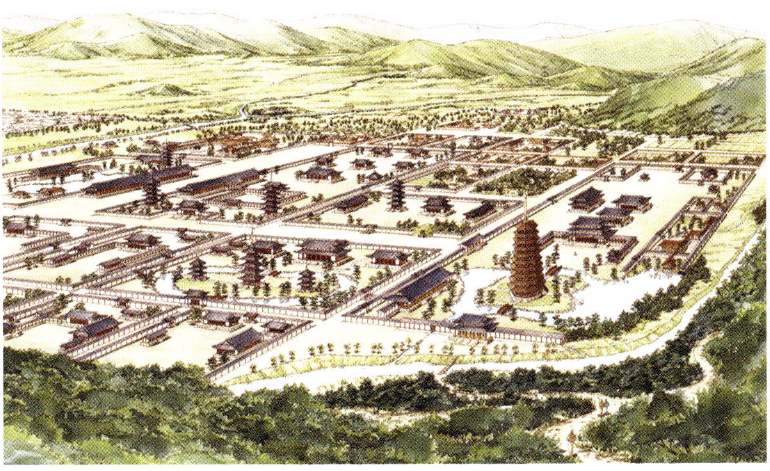

3.9. Shirakawa temple-palace complex, featuring Hosshōji Temple in foreground (with pagoda). Bird's-eye representation from the south-southeast. For Shirakawa's location, see Figures 3.8 and 3.11. Courtesy of Kyoto City Library of Historical Documents

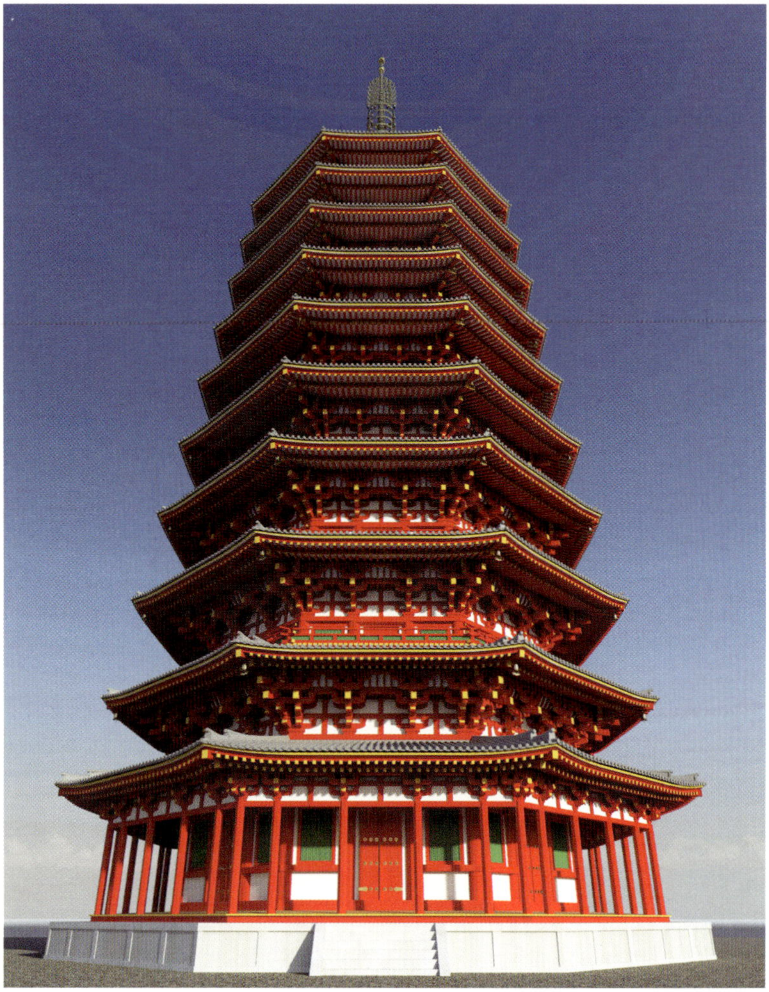

3.10. Hosshōji Temple's eight-sided, nine-story pagoda (81 m). Computer-generated image created by Tomishima Yoshiyuki and Takegawa Kōhei

be called "Shirakawa"—stimulated even greater urban development. Scores of minor officials and their families flocked to the new center of political and economic concentration, where they, along with countless craftsmen, artisans, traders, and laborers, built homes, offices, and workshops.[56] Fighting men who served in the retired emperor's de facto private army further augmented the population. During Shirakawa's tenure, warriors associated with the Seiwa Genji under the command of Minamoto no Yoshiie (1039–1106) occupied large, purpose-built barracks near the exurb's northern edge. That location earned them the toponym "Warriors of the North Face" (Hokumen no bushi).[57] Recent archeological excavations have shown that Shirakawa, now completely gone, covered a staggeringly broad area of more than two hundred acres and that its numerous structures and compounds were linked by a grid-road system similar to that of the capital.[58] While *Heike monogatari*'s mention of "forty or fifty thousand homes" is most certainly an exaggeration, it is undisputable that Shirakawa indeed grew to be an urbanized community of substantial size and demographic diversity.[59] With the retired emperor's palaces at its core, it was a hub of highly autonomous political power, religious practice, and economic activity, located just outside Kyoto.

A similar description can be applied to two other complexes built and used by retired emperors during the so-called "Era of Rule by Retired Emperors" (Insei-ki, roughly 1086 to 1192). The first, the temple-palace complex of Toba, was located where a southern extension of the great Suzaku Road intersected with the lower Kamo and Katsura Rivers (see Figures 3.11 and 3.12).[60] Construction began in 1086 with the building of a residential headquarters, followed in close succession by the creation of Jōnanji Temple, several oratories, and yet another palace. Shirakawa's patrons, those who both bankrolled his administration and provided him and his successors with the political clout to dominate the court, flocked to the area. The scale of the resulting boom is evident in this account from *Fusōryakki:*

> On a broad area of over a hundred blocks in size, each of the vassals, ministers, attendants, and various officials were given residential plots upon which they all built houses. It was as if another movement of the capital had taken place![61]

Goshirakawa (1127–1192), the third emperor to rule from retirement, based his "cloistered administration" (*insei*) at the temple-palace of Hōjūji, located just east of the Kamo River, parallel to Shichijō (see Figures 3.8 and 3.11).[62] While the greater Hōjūji complex was similar to Shirakawa and Toba in terms of its opulence and functional diversity, the size of its military component was incomparable. Taira no Kiyomori (1118–1181), the head of the Taira house and a strong initial ally of Goshirakawa, had established at the site the large warrior enclave

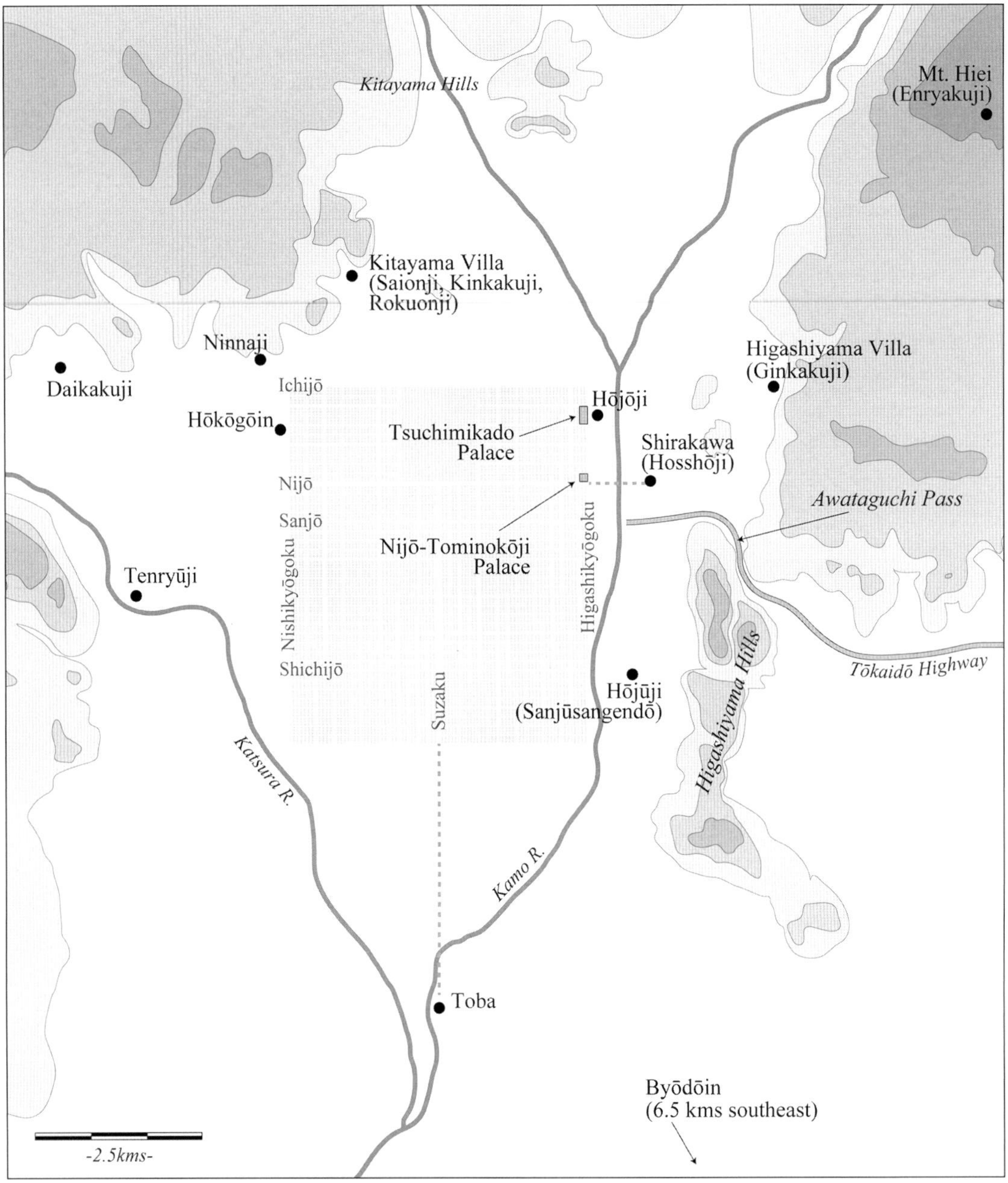

3.11. Map of greater Kyoto basin, showing the temple-palace complexes of retired emperors and major *betsugyō* vis-à-vis the Heian-kyō grid.

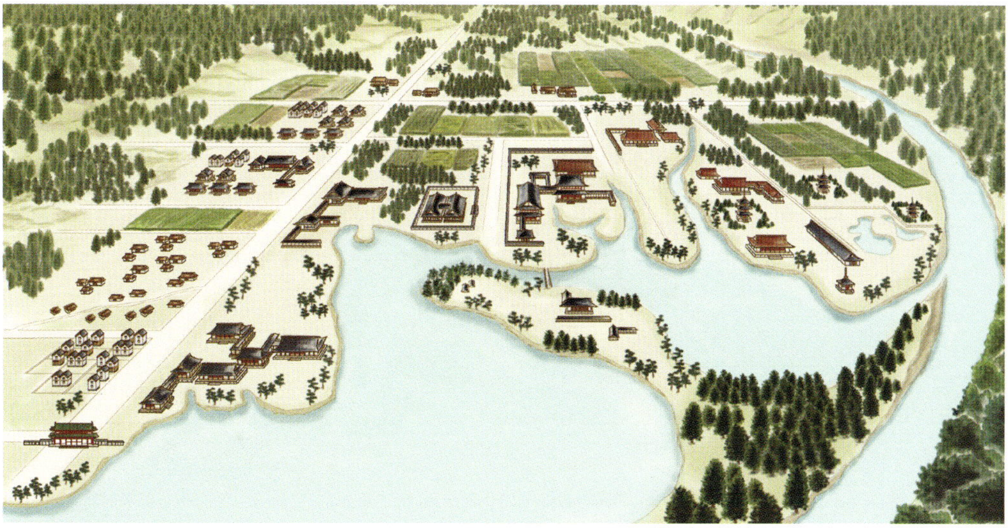

3.12. Toba temple-palace complex. Bird's-eye view from the south. For Toba's location, see Figure 3.11. Illustrated by Yoriko Igari

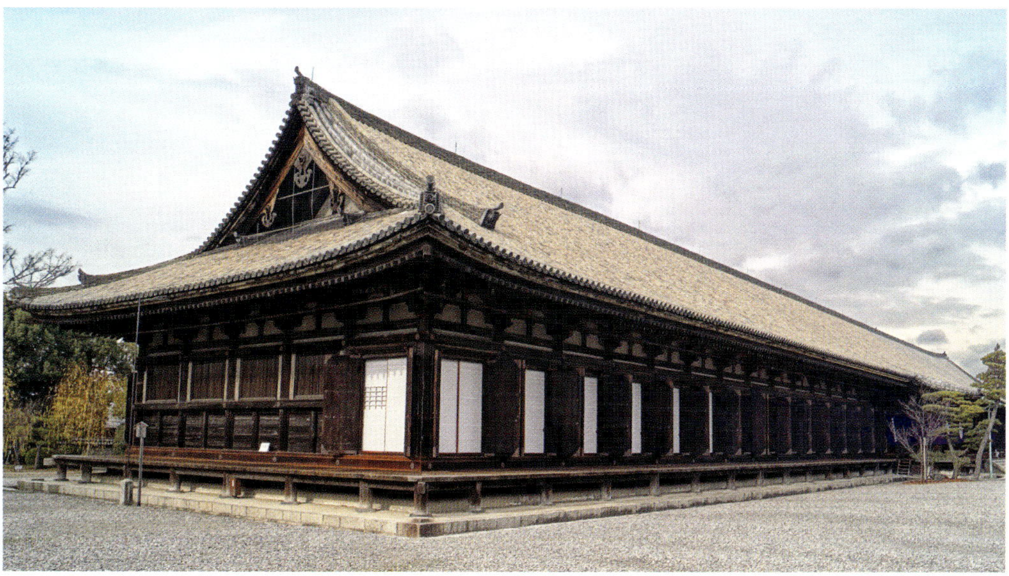

3.13. Sanjūsangendō Hall, originally part of the Hōjūji temple-palace complex of retired Emperor Goshirakawa at Rokuhara.

of Rokuhara (see Figure 3.8). Rokuhara's very creation and location immediately adjacent to Kyoto likely played a key role in Kiyomori's meteoric rise to the position of grand chancellor of state in 1167. It served as a base of operations from which the warrior-aristocrat could protect Goshirakawa while at the same time intimidate his political rivals in the capital. Before losing favor a decade later, Kiyomori paid for the substantial expansion of Hōjūji through the addition of Rengeōin. That temple's central structure, the thirty-three-bay Sanjūsangendō Hall, remains standing today and is the only architectural remnant of a glorious age of exurban temple-palace construction by and for retired emperors (Figure 3.13).

Conclusion

Kyoto's transformation into a composite of *kenmon*-centric urban islands represented the advancement of private wealth and the fragmentation of political power. This characteristically medieval trend notwithstanding, the tendency for *kenmon* of similar ilk to gravitate to or otherwise avoid certain areas in and around the city should not be ignored. It was, for example, no coincidence that the Fujiwara built each and every one of their *sato-dairi* within the city while the temples and temple-palace complexes of the great retired emperors were universally located on the outside. The pattern stands as evidence that several key classical-era ideas about space, place, and identity continued to influence decisions about what and where people built in the medieval city. In the next chapter we shall see that despite the unrelenting rise of private influence and the corresponding emergence of multiple, often competing power centers, the capital continued to be a tangible symbol of the real and conceptual efficacy of public institutions and state authority.

4

Rakuchū-Rakugai

Inside/Outside, Public/Private

The Hōgen and Heiji disturbances of the mid-twelfth century, followed by the Genpei Wars (1180–1185) a few decades later, were only the most violent and well documented of numerous upheavals that wreaked havoc on Kyoto's urban landscape at the dawn of the medieval era. Together, they accelerated the urban disintegration described in the previous chapter and aggravated a general sense of crisis among capital dwellers. The underlying cause of upheaval was the progressive weakening of the state and the inversely proportional rise of private power.

Despite profound political and physical changes, the capital elite throughout the medieval era continued to reinforce the notion that Kyoto was an exclusive domain where public authority reigned supreme. The impulse for such an anachronistic and ultimately unrealistic view was the same as that which motivated the almost universal coveting of imperial ranks and posts: Reinforcing and respecting the classical state in both its abstract and material forms remained elemental to claims of legitimacy. The state's traditional hierarchy continued to be the universal benchmark of elite status, and the capital city continued to be the formal venue of imperial ritual and statecraft. Working to maintain the integrity of both, however imperfect (or at times disingenuous), was an indicator of membership in the traditional order, a membership that medieval power holders of all stripes sought to attain and maintain with no less enthusiasm than their classical counterparts.

A discourse about the capital being an exclusive realm was as old as the city itself. After all,

Heian-kyō was envisioned as an inert venue of imperial government and ritual, a place meant to accommodate the emperor, state institutions, the lives of its officials, and little else. As discussed in the first chapter, notions about functional purity informed taboos proscribing religious institutions, violence, killing, and burial. Rarefied and wholly impractical ideas such as these remained part of elite discourse despite the dramatic changes the city underwent in terms of its form, functions, and demographic composition. The turmoil that characterized the dawn of the medieval era, however, seems to have catalyzed a renewed, more energetic discourse about exclusivity. The impulse was, perhaps, a reaction to what Amino Yoshihiko called a "crisis of kingship," a sense that the efficacy of classical institutions was being dangerously eroded or even swept away by the rising tide of *kenmon* influence.[1] Attempting to physically insulate the capital from the intrusions of temples, warriors, and others whom the traditional elite deemed to be outsiders and threats to their primacy sent an unambiguous message that the capital and the institutions it housed were still relevant and viable.

This chapter explores the medieval discourse on capital space, which conveys an unmistakable impulse to insulate Kyoto, quite physically, from the growing influence of certain *kenmon*. From the late eleventh century, court documents and noble diaries began referring, with increasing frequency and vehemence, to the capital's formal boundaries, usually within the context of a violation perpetrated by temples or warriors. Using language that frequently suggests an appeal to "propriety" and a respect for "age-old customs," the capital elite appear to have begun caring a great deal more about what should and should not take place within the city, who should be allowed to enter, and what they should and should not bring with them. As we shall see, a general spirit of compliance on the part of would-be perpetrators suggests that they remained beholden to the state for their own legitimacy. This circumstance is on particularly stunning display in the context of the Kamakura shogunate's activities in Kyoto. Even at the height of its power, the military regime frequently deferred to the emperor, the imperial police, or the court on matters of capital administration. They even went so far as to limit the activities of their own vassals within the capital's formal boundaries.

Within this context, precisely where Kyoto's formal boundaries were drawn became an important question, and a difficult one to answer due to the erosion of Heian-kyō's urban grid and the advancement of urban sprawl. The need for a clear geographic border, one that unambiguously defined capital space and separated it from its surroundings, became acute after 1221, when a failed attempt to overthrow the Kamakura shogunate led to a substantial increase in the presence of warriors in and around the city. Such circumstances help explain why, from about the second quarter of the thirteenth century, the authors of documents began using an alternative name to signify the physical space of the capital: "Rakuchū." The eventual mainstreaming of "Rakuchū" during this period, along with its binary opposite, "Rakugai" (meaning "surroundings" or "environs"), was indicative of an impulse to redefine Kyoto's medieval geopolitical area and, in so doing, reinforce notions of an inviolable realm, however small, where traditional state authority remained valid. As we shall see, the choice of this particular word to achieve this objective entailed a compromise. Replacing more traditional names for Kyoto with a word that signified a much smaller area suggests an admission that the classical city was well and truly gone.

"Rakuchū-Rakugai," an ideographic compound that was later to become the most common term used to refer to Kyoto, gave linguistic form to an idea that the capital basin was composed of two discrete and concentric spatial components, an "inside" and an "outside." In the last section of this chapter, it is argued that this articulation was new in the thirteenth century but that the underlying idea was not. For centuries, the Kyoto basin had exhibited a two-tiered spatial structure that split the city into a well-defined core—the capital proper—and a surrounding buffer zone. The elite engaged in a concentric building pattern that mapped neatly onto this layered structure, dividing their lives along the distinction with striking consistency. Simply noticing and then examining this pattern sheds light on the dichotomy of elite power in premodern Japan. Influential aristocrats, clergymen, and, in their time, elite warriors all enjoyed a sort of dual identity: one as officers of the state, endowed with public ranks and posts, and another as private individuals, commanding landed wealth and influence through their control of family enterprises and institutions. The land within the capital's formal boundaries continued, well into the medieval era, to be imagined as a rarefied realm of sustained public authority. The people who sought to claim legitimacy through their formal membership in the imperial hierarchy maintained official residences there that generally adhered to status-based codes of comportment. At the same time, however, they sought out areas, usually on the city's outskirts, where they could escape the performative mandates of public status to enjoy lifestyles more in line with their identities as private power holders. As we shall see, the geographic dichotomy of Rakuchū and Rakugai was a material manifestation of the dichotomy of public authority and private power.

Temples and the Capital Ideal

An early catalyst for a more explicit definition of capital space appeared in the eleventh century with the increased political and military assertiveness of religious institutions. Temples and shrines had long challenged the absolute authority of the state, using spiritual suasion, landed wealth, and private, sometimes kinship-based ties with court families to secure various imperial titles, privileges, and even greater wealth. In the late eleventh century, however, the impact of sectarian influence became physical. Demanding that the court act in their favor, the monks of Enryakuji, Onjōji, and Kōfukuji—to name just the most aggressive—began engaging in mass, sometimes violent protests that included dramatic ritualized marches on the capital.[2] Noble diaries convey a profound sense of foreboding as they describe long, menacing processions of rowdy monks and acolytes approaching the city bearing weapons of both secular and sacred efficacy. Religious institutions threatened the capital collaterally as well, engaging in warfare against their sectarian rivals over such issues as land rights, official appointments, and matters of doctrinal validity. There were more than three hundred demonstrations (*gōso*) during the medieval era and no less than thirty-three cases of intersectarian warfare in and around Kyoto during the twelfth century alone.[3] In response to such a high level of disruption, it appears the court began attempting to systematically exclude religious actors from the capital through both legal and military means. The diary of Fujiwara no Munetada (1062–1141) describes in great detail the events surrounding several large demonstrations that took place around the turn of the eleventh century. His narrative captures both the general sense of crisis as well as critical details about how the author, an aristocrat and member of the imperial court, envisioned the capital and defined its exclusivity (here and below, locations and space-related terms are indicated in Japanese for their relevance to the discussion ahead):

> [T]he sectarians of Kōfukuji entered the capital (*nyūraku*) at about 6 p.m. Even though there is a proscription (*seishi*) [on entry], they disregarded it. Their route took them past the intersection of [Higashi] Kyōgoku and Sanjō, before arriving at [their destination,] the Kangakuin university. . . . Among the more than two thousand, there were some on horseback. Warriors surrounded each formation. The capital (*kyōchū*) is in an uproar.[4]

In legal terms, the word used here to indicate a proscription on capital entry, *seishi*, is not particularly strong. It suggests an admonition to respect the customary taboo barring temples from Heian-kyō rather than an absolute prohibition. As we shall see, however, it was not long before the court began deploying stronger language and laws.

Reference to the intersection of Higashikyōgoku and Sanjō is significant for what it reveals about the author's sensitivity to the capital's formal boundaries. Considering Kōfukuji's location in Nara, a two-day walk to the east, it is probable that the sectarians traveled to Kyoto, at least in the final stage, along the Tōkaidō Highway. Therefore the head of the long procession would have appeared to city dwellers the moment it emerged from the high pass at Awataguchi along the Higashiyama Hills, about 1.5 kilometers east of the city proper (see Figure 3.11). From there, the sectarians would have proceeded westward down the basin's gentle eastern slope, passing along the way countless suburban homes, shops, temples, and monuments before crossing the Kamo River at a location approximately parallel to Sanjō Road or, more likely, a bridge near Shijō to the south. Despite the high drama of such an occasion, the author provides no information on the procession's advance toward the city until it reached the intersection of Higashikyōgoku and Sanjō. The paucity of geographic detail can be explained, however, by recalling the special significance of Higashikyōgoku as the boundary defining Heian-kyō's eastern edge. The mob's crossing of Higashikyōgoku at Sanjō was the singular act that most disturbed the diarist. Indeed, the greatest threat posed on this occasion came not from the prospect of physical violence, but rather from the sectarians' possession of a portable shrine (*mikoshi*). An object of such religious power, placed before the gates of a government institution such as the Kangakuin, could bring official business to a screeching halt indefinitely.[5] Outside the city's formal boundaries, a *mikoshi* would have had far less impact on the court and its institutions, if any at all. Undoubtedly, preventing such disruptions was a key motivation behind the classical proscription against temples in the first place.

The following two entries narrate temple demonstrations that took place in 1095 and 1108 respectively:

> 1095.10.26: I have heard that the chief abbot [who returned to Enryakuji yesterday] has sided with the "mountain sectarians" [who are now threatening the capital]. An [imperial] decree has banned them from entering the capital (*kyōto*). They have come as far as the [Kamo] riverbed. [Minamoto no] Yoshitsuna has been ordered to the riverbed with his troops to defend against entry. . . . Warriors are filling up Kyoto.[6]

> 1108.3.30: This evening, the "mountain masses" [of Enryakuji] came to the capital (*gekyō*). Like a line of stars, they carried torches, wending their way down the mountain. Because imperial police and warriors defended along the [Kamo] riverbed, the sectarians did not enter the city (*nyūraku*). Nevertheless, Kyoto (*kyōchū*) is in an uproar. [The balance] between Kingly Law and Buddhist Law is destroyed. . . . Troops of the Minamoto and Taira families have been stationed east of Hōjōji Temple, near the riverbed.[7]

The issuance of a direct imperial decree in 1095 suggests that the court no longer relied upon customs or taboos to insulate the city. When that legal deterrent failed, however, warriors were deployed along the Kamo River, a position immediately east of Higashikyōgoku. The second passage's reference to the temple of Hōjōji, located on the narrow sliver of land between Higashikyōgoku and the riverbed, further underscores the author's acute consciousness of Heian-kyō's original boundaries (see Figure 3.11). By the same token, the absence of any mention that the court might have sought to use the considerable military capacity at its disposal to extend the front line of defense, perhaps even to block the several mountain passes leading into the capital basin, shows a marked indifference to insulating anything other than formal capital space.

The discourse of exclusion in these and other accounts from the period seem to reveal a sense of golden-ageism with regard to the capital's physical space. At the time of Munetada's writing, the western half of the old city had long ago been converted into cultivated land and was no longer a viable part of the urban landscape. At the same time, rapid growth in the east had led to massive residential and commercial expansion well beyond Heian-kyō's northern and eastern boundaries. Under the circumstances, the attention paid to Higashikyōgoku appears either anachronistic or perhaps just out of touch. It can be explained, however, as part of an attempt to translate the capital's idealized status as the exclusive realm of imperial statecraft into a symbol of sustained state, imperial, and aristocratic potency. To be sure, when it came to asserting the authority of traditional institutions, the capital itself, as both a thing and an idea, would have proven a useful functionary. Invoking the notion that capital space was inviolable would have elicited a host of traditional ideals, rules, taboos, and customs that underscored the supremacy of the imperial state, its institutions, rituals, and officials. The discourse reveals a regressive impulse, a desire to turn back the clock and restore the capital to its "original" state of functional purity, free from the corrupting influences of temples and other *kenmon.* But of course there was no such thing as a golden age for Kyoto. It, like the institutions it was created to house, was imperfect from the start. Physically mutated and institutionally degenerate, the city was a monument to the constant struggle between public and private interests. In a word, there was a yawning gulf separating the ideal from the real.

This gulf is on clear display in the following imperial decree, issued in 1087, that attempts to interdict an elite practice that was both widespread and long-held. It also, at the same time, blindly ignores the city's contemporaneous geography:

> The Ministers of the Left and the Right hereby convey this imperial decree. Numerous oratories have, in violation of court law, recently been built in the two capitals [Sakyō and Ukyō]. This must not be. In accordance with the earlier decree, the executive officers of Sakyō and Ukyō, along with the imperial police, are ordered to enforce, from now on, the ban on oratories within the capital (*kyōchū*).[8]

As touched upon in chapter 3, by the time this decree was issued, members of the civil aristocracy had been subverting the customary proscription on temples by building small oratories (*jibutsudō*) on the grounds of their private residences for at least a century.[9] Much more modest than their "temple" (*-ji* or *-tera*) counterparts, which remained exurban, these private devotional facilities had correspondingly narrow functions. They were used predominantly to accommodate low-key, personal religious observances or family memorial rituals.[10] In light of their proliferation and the high status of their owners, attempting to ban oratories in 1087 seems unrealistic. After all, this particular decree was issued by the imperial court to enforce a law being broken with the highest frequency by none other than members of the court itself. Such circumstances, of course, do not necessarily mean the law would be dismissed out of hand. Nevertheless, that is precisely what happened when, a few years later, former grand chancellor of state and imperial regent, Fujiwara no Morozane (1042–1101), built an oratory at his residence in honor of his deceased first wife. Either he was in flagrant violation of the decree—which he suggests in his diary was little more than an entreaty to exercise "self restraint"—or, more likely, the decree itself was more symbolic than effectual, meant to reinforce a sense of capital exclusion at a time when incursions were becoming rampant.[11]

The decree's reference to "two capitals" is likewise out of touch with real-world circumstances. The impulse to apply laws equally to the entire space of Heian-kyō at a time when more than half the original area had essentially been converted into farmland appears either romantically idealistic or flatly delusional. Again, however, the dissonance can be explained by interpreting the decree as part of a conservative campaign to stanch the growing influence of *kenmon* and reassert the authority of the statutory state. Attempting to physically exclude outside political actors, to reinstate foundational customs and rules, and to use language that suggests physical integrity rather than breakdown, all point to a desire on the part of the traditional elite to return, against overwhelming odds, to a former glory. For its emblematic representation of the classical past, the capital city was a tool useful for achieving this objective.

It should be added that customs related to capital space were not just about exclusion. Certain things were also considered requisite. These included the presence of the emperor, his imperial palace, and the three sacred imperial regalia.[12] When the child emperor Antoku (1178–1185), for example, visited retired emperor Goshirakawa at Hōjūji in 1180, Fujiwara no Tsunefusa (1143–1200) expressed dismay that the sovereign would make the journey east of the [Kamo] river "in possession of the sacred mirror."[13] Three years later, Antoku would again leave the capital in possession of one of the three sacred regalia, that time as part of the Taira army's full retreat during the Genpei Wars. Writing in *Gukanshō*, the monk Jien (1155–1225) lamented the emperor's absence, yet his choice of words suggests the object of his concern was propriety rather than person: "It is understood that a sovereign must be present in the capital."[14]

The final example dates to 1371, when preparations were underway for the enthronement of Emperor Goen'yū (1358–1393). Even during this much later period, when we might expect changes to the city and its politics to have rendered classical customs obsolete, Sanjō Kintada (1324–1384) had this to say about the location of the ceremony (see Figure 5.2):

> There is to be an imperial succession ceremony today, held at the Yanagihara Palace, the residence of Hino Tadamitsu. Is there no precedent for the holding of a succession ceremony outside capital boundaries (*jōgai*)? We have been concerned about this for several days, but because there is no appropriate palace within the capital [the ceremony is to go forth at the Yanagihara Palace].[15]

Well into the medieval era, there remained a strong sense of what should and should not take place within Kyoto.

Warriors and the Capital Ideal

Warriors were an essential part of the early campaign to insulate Kyoto. In time, they became part of the problem. The epic twelfth-century struggle between the Fujiwara and several retired emperors over control of court politics led to the proxy wars of Hōgen (1156) and Heiji (1159). As war became a more critical element of imperial politics, so too did the individuals who fought them. The leaders of the warrior families of Minamoto and Taira were, each in their turn, rewarded for services rendered to their aristocratic masters by being granted high imperial ranks and posts, statuses that gave them sweeping—and entirely legal—political prerogatives. After becoming grand chancellor of state in 1167, for example, Taira no Kiyomori was able to dominate the court and retired emperors with perfect legitimacy.[16] His establishment of a warrior enclave and familial headquarters at Rokuhara further augmented his influence by bringing to Kyoto a large contingent of his own army (see Figure 3.8). In 1180, as part of a fraught drama involving his manipulation of imperial succession, Kiyomori attempted to engineer a relocation of the capital from Kyoto to Fukuhara (modern-day Kobe). Although initiated, the move was soon abandoned when war broke out against the Minamoto. Besides subjecting Kyoto to another round of destruction, this protracted series of conflicts, known collectively as the Genpei Wars, occasioned the fall of the Taira and the establishment of the Kamakura shogunate under the imperially sanctioned leadership of Minamoto no Yoritomo (1147–1199). Although ostensibly an arm of the statutory state, charged with the duty of protecting public interests, the Kamakura regime was to become the greatest threat to Kyoto's political primacy over the next two centuries.

The threat posed by warriors was obvious to traditional members of the Kyoto aristocracy long before the rise of Kiyomori and Yoritomo. A growing apprehension about the physical and political incursions of fighting men helps explain the appearance of court documents that, not unlike those directed at temples, attempt to exclude them from the capital. An early example dates to 1091 when Minamoto no Yoshiie revolted and set out from his provincial base to march on Kyoto. Upon hearing of the advance, an imperial decree was issued explicitly forbidding the renegade's army from "entering the capital" (*nyūkyō*).[17] The language of the text is interesting for its almost singular concern with the matter of capital entry. It never, for example, challenges Yoshiie's prerogative to rebel, nor the means by which he might do so.

Similar—and similarly futile—attempts to insulate the capital are apparent in documents dating to the time of the Hōgen Disturbance. In the seventh month of 1156, the emperor handed down a decree empowering the imperial police to "interdict warriors."[18] Four months later, "military weapons" were banned.[19] In both cases, the decrees refer specifically and exclusively to the space "within the capital" (*kyōchū*). Violence was undoubtedly a concern, yet insulating Kyoto was paramount.

Other documents that refer to weapons underscore the relevance of capital boundaries vis-à-vis matters of jurisdiction. In 1028, for example, the emperor issued a decree that prohibited people who were not "of the proper employ" from stalking about the capital with bows and arrows.[20] Since it was the imperial police (*kebiishi*) who enjoyed an official monopoly on capital law enforcement, contemporaries would have understood the decree to be aimed specifically at reining in the martial capacity of provincial warriors (*bushi*) who had come to Kyoto. Discrimination based on location was on even more stark display following the Battle of Dannoura in 1185. Upon the conclusion of hostilities, the emperor's sacred mirror was returned to Kyoto under the armed escort of provincial soldiers. When entering the city, members of the retinue were compelled to dismount their horses and walk, an action that, if not completely stripping them of military potential, greatly diminished their offensive profile.[21] Incidentally, once inside the city, it is likely these soldiers were met and escorted by a special detachment of imperial police called Yamashiro kokanshi, whose sole duty was to patrol the capital's outer border. An entry in a court diary from 1311 explains that these same officers were permitted to carry arrows only when accompanying the emperor north of Ichijō, the northernmost boundary of Heian-kyō.[22] It appears that at least certain weapons, regardless of who possessed them, were meant to be banned from Kyoto well into the medieval era. When it came to keeping the peace and the means to do so, the capital's formal boundaries continued to be relevant, and within them the imperial state was meant to be supreme.

The impulse to exclude warriors from Kyoto most probably stemmed from two interrelated sentiments, one cultural, the other a matter of status. First, they were provincials and as such were considered boorish, violent, and generally uncivilized. Second and more important, although they were able to exert tremendous influence, the vast majority did not possess formal statuses within the state hierarchy. They were outsiders, not merely because of their occupations or origins, but because they were ill-equipped, status-wise, to legitimately engage in capital affairs. Stressing the idea of an inert imperial capital helped assert the validity of the traditional order, an order to which most warriors were not meant to belong.

But it is precisely within the realm of status distinctions where things get murky and interesting. The leaders of the Kamakura shogunate, just like Kiyomori and a few others before him, did in fact possess formal court ranks and posts. As chancellors, shoguns, regents, and high-ranking generals, they were servants of the state. As such, they became—indeed they were obliged to be—fierce advocates of court customs and capital norms, including exclusion. As we shall see, numerous cases can be found where Kamakura officials deferred to the court on matters of capital policing and taxation while enforcing codes that physically excluded even their own vassals from the city. Demonstrating familiarity with spatial dictates and a willingness to adhere to traditional conventions might have helped warrior leaders periodically authenticate their status as loyal servants of the state and, as such, possessors of orthodox authority. In fact, it should become apparent that the most elite among them—and incidentally the most successful—consistently sought more to infiltrate traditional institutions than to change them.

The Kamakura Shogunate and Capital Space

The conclusion of the Genpei Wars and successive establishment of the Kamakura shogunate in 1192 made possible the restoration of a level of peace and stability Kyoto had not seen in decades. Initially, the Kamakura regime (a toponym deriving from the name of the town where the shogunate made its headquarters, 350 kilometers east of Kyoto) remained largely aloof of the capital, both physically and politically. Circumstances changed in 1221, however, when retired emperor Gotoba (1180–1239) staged a deeply flawed and ultimately disastrous armed campaign aimed at toppling the warrior polity.[23] His proxy army of twenty thousand was easily overmatched by the superior numbers and martial capacity of the shogunate's forces. Only thirty days after Gotoba issued an imperial decree ordering Kamakura's chastisement, shogunal deputies marched on Kyoto to arrest the former sovereign on the grounds that he represented a threat to the state and the legitimate rule of the reigning emperor. Endowed with imperial ranks and posts, these deputies could play the role of loyal servants of the state, restoring order and balance to what in their assessment was a broken system. Thus concluded the Jōkyū Disturbance, an attempt by the Kyoto establishment to reassert political primacy that resulted in the strengthening of shogunal power and a substantially increased warrior presence in and around Kyoto.

The material aftermath of Jōkyū, both within the capital and beyond, was dramatic. The shogunate confiscated more than three thousand provincial estates controlled by capital elites, transferring their administration (and their tax wealth) to loyal retainers. The Kamigyō properties of aristocratic conspirators were likewise confiscated, the palaces that stood on them destroyed in overt public displays of the regime's newly justified assertiveness.[24] Finally and perhaps of the most long-term impact, the shogunate established a satellite headquarters in the district of Rokuhara, the same exurban site formerly used in the same way by the Taira. Staffed at any given time by two senior constable officers (Rokuhara tandai), a pool of skilled bureaucrats, and a substantial contingent of foot soldiers, Rokuhara was charged with administering shogunal affairs in the western provinces. After 1238, its soldiers took on the added responsibility of policing the capital from small guard boxes called *kagariya*, built at most major intersections.[25] These, however, were their formal, sanctioned duties. In practice, Rokuhara's most important function was to sniff out and quash antishogunal sentiment among the Kyoto elite.[26]

The establishment of Rokuhara meant the introduction of fighting men to the capital on a more permanent basis than ever before. Kyoto had previously endured its fair share of war. In the past, however, the end of fighting had in general meant the withdrawal of troops. A few elite warriors had, during their respective heydays, occupied residences in and around the capital.[27] In each case, however, they were able to justify their presence through their possession of court posts and ranks. Everything was different after Jōkyū. While Rokuhara constables indeed possessed imperial titles, as did a few of their highest generals, the foot soldiers who swelled their ranks and policed the city did not. These "light foots," as rank-and-file soldiers were called, were beholden to their military masters through feudal bonds of vassalage, yet they possessed no formal (or informal) connection to the imperial state. Their presence in the capital was particularly aggravating to the city's traditional leaders, some of whom were apparently not shy about expressing discontent. Graffiti scrawled on the walls of the retired emperor's palace in 1260 enumerated at length the infelicitous incidents and circumstances of the day. Among the more than twenty items, "warriors in the capital" (*kyōchū bushi*) was listed third, ahead of "immoral governance," "famine in the provinces," and an abundance of "bleached skeletons by the riverbed."[28]

Had soldiers remained largely sequestered within their exurban base at Rokuhara, circumstances might have been different. But they did not, and the court reacted vehemently, on each occasion asserting that capital spatial norms must be respected. To this, Kamakura officials responded with remarkable deference, uncharacteristic of their otherwise assertive post-Jōkyū posture. In about 1227, for example, word reached Hōjō Yasutoki (1183–1242), a senior shogunal leader, that soldiers were using the site of the then-defunct Daidairi imperial enclosure as riding grounds. He responded with the following letter, addressed to his son Tokiuji (1203–1230), who at the time was the chief Rokuhara constable:

> It has come to my attention that in recent years soldiers stationed in the capital are shooting arrows at things and that they have made Uchino a riding grounds. There has been a secret appeal [from the court], saying that it is dreadful for horses' hooves to trammel the former site of the Imperial Palace. . . . Above all, soldiers should not leave Rokuhara to travel to Uchino. You should establish an appropriate site out in the countryside for when young soldiers need a place to test themselves by running their horses and firing off arrows.[29]

Besides limiting warrior access, Kamakura also took steps to moderate warrior behavior, particularly with respect to comportment. In 1240, the shogunate drew up a code explicitly banning vassals from riding ox carts when traveling through Kyoto.[30] Since the ox cart (*gissha*) was the prescribed mode of transportation for a civil aristocrat of high status, such an ordinance served to prevent the blurring of status lines while also sharpening the definition of capital space.

There is clear evidence showing that Kamakura's recognition of a discrete jurisdictional division between itself and the court was tied to geography. One example relates to the shogunate's standard practice of confiscating and demolishing the homes of criminals. Outside Kyoto, such punishment was meted out regularly and with impunity. In cases where a perpetrator's home was located "within the capital," however, the regime explicitly forbade its officers from taking direct action, instead requiring them to send an appeal to the imperial police requesting that commensurate punishment be meted out by them.[31] In 1215, the shogunate issued a decree prohibiting warriors stationed at Kyoto from patrolling "within the city," and decreed that punishments (and commendations) would be issued according to soldiers' adherence to this new law.[32] Examples such as these suggest that Kamakura officials recognized and respected the court's sustained efficacy and, more important, that the imperial institution continued to represent ultimate authority within the physical space of the capital. The very fact that the shogunate, even at the apex of its power following the Jōkyū Disturbance, built its local headquarters at Rokuhara, rather than at a site within the city, is itself a powerful example of warrior deference.

Kamakura's motivation for respecting the capital's boundaries and spatial customs might not have been entirely unselfish. There was probably a keen desire to keep up appearances by fulfilling the performative dictates of their imperially sanctioned offices, particularly in ways that did not substantially limit their influence. Indeed, by doing such high-profile yet largely inconsequential things as expelling foot soldiers from Kyoto and leaving public safety to the imperial police, the leaders of the regime could play the role of good servants of the state and emperor. Besides the individual statuses of warrior leaders, it should not be forgotten that the shogunate was itself a legally sanctioned branch of the imperial government. The regime's founder, Minamoto no Yoritomo, had himself decided in 1192 to fold his fledgling yet potentially autonomous government into the classical state order.[33] Institutionalized warrior legitimacy, as it came to be, was predicated upon the existence of an imperial state with the capacity to fulfill its institutional and, perhaps more important, ritual functions. Key to the latter was the existence of an emperor as supreme and sacerdotal sovereign, an imperial hierarchy as the universal benchmark of public status, and a capital city with the material infrastructure necessary to accommodate the trappings of ritualized statecraft. Warrior elites who rose to power during the medieval era bowed to the first, infiltrated the second, and showed respect for the third. As we shall see in the following chapter, the leaders of the succeeding warrior regime were no less enthusiastic about respecting Kyoto space.

Defining Rakuchū, Redefining "The Capital"

The authors of historical documents going back to Kyoto's establishment in the eighth century used a variety of common nouns to identify the physical area of the capital. Among them, the most common were *kyō-chū* (京中), *kyō no uchi* (京内), and *kyō no chi* (京地).[34] While each is a subtle variation on the idea of "within" or "throughout the capital," the precise geographic meaning of the word "capital" ("*kyō*") is itself almost never explicitly indicated. Originally, no explanation would have been necessary. "The capital" inevitably referred to the area encompassed by the urban grid of the master-planned, classical city. As we have seen, however, Heian-kyō had never been completed as planned and almost the entire western half of the city, Ukyō, was given over to agriculture by at least the eleventh century. We are left, therefore, with the question of how contemporaries living, for example, in the twelfth, thirteenth, and later centuries—many of whom cared deeply about Kyoto's physical and political integrity—conceptualized "*kyō*," or "the capital."[35] One of the earliest unambiguous indications that the word did not signify the whole of the classical grid appeared, perhaps predictably, in a literary text. Describing the aftermath of a famine that devastated the region in about 1181, Kamo no Chōmei (1155–1216) wrote the following in his *Hōjōki*, an extended reflection on the impermanence of the world:

> Within the capital (*kyō no uchi*)—[which includes the area] south of Ichijō, north of Kujō, west of [Higashi] Kyōgoku, and east of Suzaku—the number of dead along the roadside numbered more than 42,300. . . . If we include those in the adjacent areas (*henchi*) such as Shirakawa, the banks of the Kamo River, and the Western Capital (Nishi no kyō), there would be no limit to the number.[36]

Chōmei's specific reference to the roads of Ichijō, Kujō, Higashi-kyōgoku, and Suzaku confirms that he equated the land "within the capital" with the area of Sakyō, the eastern half of Heian-kyō. At the same time, he reduced Ukyō—what he calls the "Western Capital"—to the status of peripheral "adjacent area." It was *near* the capital but no longer *of* the capital (see Figure 4.1).

It is curious that Chōmei used the term "*kyō no uchi*" ("within the capital") to signify the land bounded by the roads he mentions instead of the more specific and geographically accurate "Sakyō." An explanation can be proposed by pointing out that at the time of his writing, the word Sakyō was rapidly becoming obsolete. The notion of a "left capital," after all, ceased to be meaningful in a context where a "right" counterpart no longer existed. Critically, Chōmei's evolved definition of the capital was not merely a function of urban shrinkage or geographic drift. We know this because he reinforces three of Heian-kyō's original four boundaries and explicitly excludes the densely populated exurb of Shirakawa and the built-up banks of the Kamo River, both of

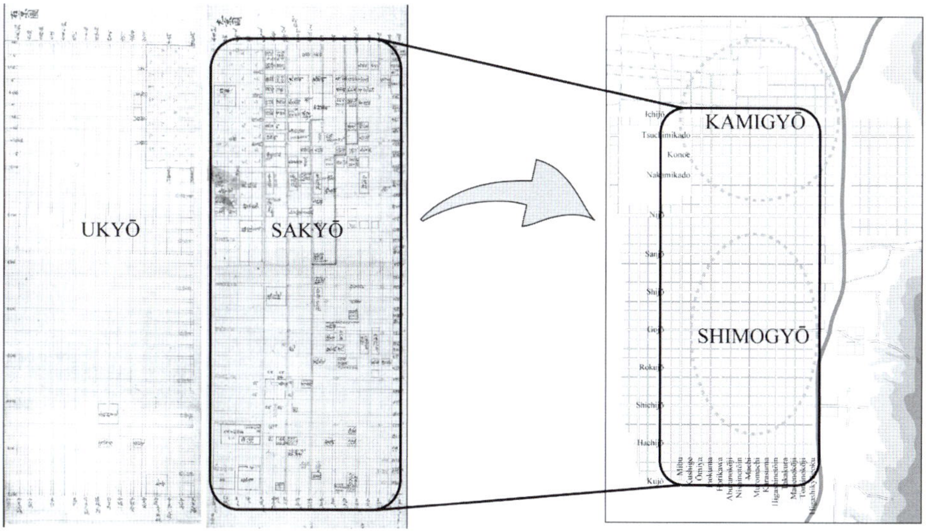

4.1. Evolving capital boundaries.

which were appended to the old city contiguously by roads and thick bands of urban development. Rokuhara fit this same description, yet it is not even mentioned. Incidentally, when that warrior enclave appears a century later in *Taiheiki*, it is described much like Ukyō is in *Hōjōki*: it is a place "very *close* to the capital" (author's emphasis).[37]

In the minds of early medieval authors, exurbs such as Shirakawa and Rokuhara existed within the "*henchi*," a term for the liminal space immediately surrounding and contiguous with the capital, yet not formally part of it. It was from about the twelfth century that people began to conceptualize the greater Kyoto basin as being divided into two concentric or "nested" parts that were, like the public and private identities of the elite who divided their time between them, distinct yet inseparable.

As discussed, following the Jōkyū Disturbance of 1221 and the subsequent establishment of a shogunal outpost at Rokuhara, there emerged a heightened sense of crisis among members of the capital elite, many of whom saw the rise of warriors as a threat to political orthodoxy and the status quo. In addition to shogunal confiscation of aristocratic lands and the exiling of the retired emperor, there was the disturbing introduction of a large and persistent population of fighting men who possessed no formal status within the imperial state hierarchy. Their presence in Kyoto and habitual flouting of capital norms undermined the efficacy of the state, which, significantly, continued to be the ultimate arbiter of much-coveted formal statuses. For those who sought to sustain the traditional order and the fundamental source of their authority, there needed to be an effective means of limiting the impact of warriors upon imperial politics. At least one solution was found in a revised definition of capital space, one in particular that helped reinforce notions about exclusivity.

Evidence of this change was manifested in the proliferation and eventual mainstreaming of the word "Rakuchū." The word itself was not new. Emperor Saga, a devout Sinophile, used "Rakuyō" and "Chōan" to describe Sakyō and Ukyō respectively. Such terms perhaps reflected the sovereign's aspiration that Kyoto should be like the great Chinese capitals from which those names derived. The word "Rakuchū" was a simplification of "Rakuyō," where the second character is replaced with "*chū*," which, as in the case of *kyō-chū*, means "within." Rakuchū, therefore, literally meant "within the area of Rakuyō," or, more accurately, "Sakyō." Whereas variations on the word "*raku*" appear in documents from as early as the eleventh century, there was a threefold increase in usage from the second quarter of the thirteenth century, roughly following the Jōkyū Disturbance.[38] In addition to "Rakuchū" and "Rakunai" (洛内) (or "Raku no uchi"), related neologisms included "*jō-raku*" (上洛) (to go to the capital), "*nyūraku*" (入洛) (to enter the capital), and later Rakugai (洛外), a proper noun signifying the area immediately surrounding Rakuchū yet distinct from the encompassing province of Yamashiro.

There were profound political and jurisdictional implications to this discursive shift. In geographic terms, "Rakuchū" (or any one of its several variations) unambiguously signified the limited geographic area of Sakyō. Politically, however, and this is key, the word signified a *whole* capital city. Taxation and policing documents confirm that "Rakuchū" was the area over which state bureaucratic bodies continued to exercise direct and unmitigated authority.[39] Elsewhere, including parts of the basin such as Ukyō that had originally been part of Heian-kyō's urban grid, the state's influence was attenuated by the legal and customary claims of temples, warriors, and other *kenmon*.[40]

This change was an acknowledgment that the capital had transformed profoundly and irrevocably from its classical prototype. The traditional elite who sought to better and more explicitly insulate Kyoto as a material and political realm might have felt compelled to stop using a term such as "*kyō*," which, due to its intrinsic association with the grand yet defunct Heian grid, had become not merely antiquated but ultimately unrealistic. The proliferation of a more geographically accurate term for "the capital" was a function of the impulse to better define imperial space and, in so doing, reinforce notions of exclusion, exclusivity, and state efficacy. The choice of the word "Rakuchū" to achieve this objective, however, reveals something of a compromise. Substituting "*kyō*" with a word that signified a much smaller land area shows an admission that the classical capital and its institutions had become diminished versions of their former selves. That said, the very act of refashioning the discourse itself shows that neither the state nor the capital, however shrunken, ceased being relevant and worth preserving.

Inside/Outside, Public/Private: *Honjo* and *Betsugyō*

Yanagita Kunio (1875–1962), a modern scholar of folklore, referred often in his work to a tendency in traditional Japanese society for people and institutions to make a clear, binary distinction between the realms of public and private life.[41] Drawing on historical sources, Yanagita used the term "*hare*"—literally meaning "sunny" or "clear"—to specify occasions and activities that were public or formal, such as rituals, festivals, annual observances, and rites of passage. In contrast to *hare*, he referred to the notion of *ke*, signifying the private or mundane, the profane, or even the defiled. According to Yanagita and those who subscribed to the idea of a *hare*/*ke* binary, the distinction between public and private life was particularly sharp before the dawn of the modern era. Premodern Japanese people, they suggest, saw themselves as having two interrelated, yet sharply distinct, social profiles: one as a private individual and another as a member of a social unit such as a family, temple, or other institution, endowed with certain duties and a public persona.

In the late 1960s, Kawakami Mitsugu applied the *hare*/*ke* binary to an examination of residential architecture in medieval Kyoto.[42] With striking clarity, he showed that the distinction between public and private life took on physical form within the homes of the capital elite. As touched upon earlier, palaces built in the *shinden* style were ostensibly meant to be the prescribed venues of ritualized imperial statecraft.

Possessing a central *shinden* and its associated structures endowed members of the civil aristocracy with the physical infrastructure to conduct public rituals that—in their adherence to strict, status-specific protocols—reinforced and authenticated their membership in the imperial hierarchy.[43] From the outset, however, there was a gulf separating the idealized public functions of elite palaces and the day-to-day needs of those who occupied them. To be sure, palaces were much more than sterile venues of ritual or public ceremony. They were also fully functional private residences, homes to large, multigenerational aristocratic families, and the headquarters of dynamic household enterprises. It was therefore necessary for them to accommodate the everyday lives of their occupants as well as those unofficial (or quasi-official) social, economic, and political activities through which members of the aristocracy accumulated and maintained their influence. Kawakami's findings showed that from as early as the eighth century, the elite began partitioning the interiors of their palace structures so as to create private spaces along the north, or "back-facing," sides.[44] Appearing in documents as *tsune-gosho* ("living quarters") or even *ke-gosho* ("mundane palace"), the names of these spaces clearly capture their informal functions (see Figure 4.2). They also distinguish them sharply from their south-facing and, perhaps not coincidentally, sunnier counterparts, which continued to be reserved for public rituals, events, and official court business. Incidentally, it was the impulse to create more and better private spaces—while not too much compromising ritual spaces—that led to the emergence in about the fourteenth century of an entirely new, free-standing type of structure called *kaisho* ("meeting place"). Structurally and stylistically distinct from their *shinden* counterparts, early *kaisho* became the prototypes of *shoin*-style architecture, which, as the preferred venue of non-Ritsuryō business and cultural pursuits, proliferated from the early fifteenth century.[45]

The basic principle that informed a division of public and private space within elite palaces can be transposed onto Kyoto's entire premodern urban landscape. As we have seen, despite how much the city had evolved over time, there continued to be a strong sense that capital space was public space and that it should be free from the mitigating forces of outside influence. While there was tacit acceptance of household enterprises and even private religious facilities, evidence suggests that social pressures forced a high degree of compliance regarding the principles of architectural comportment. Elaboration and expansion

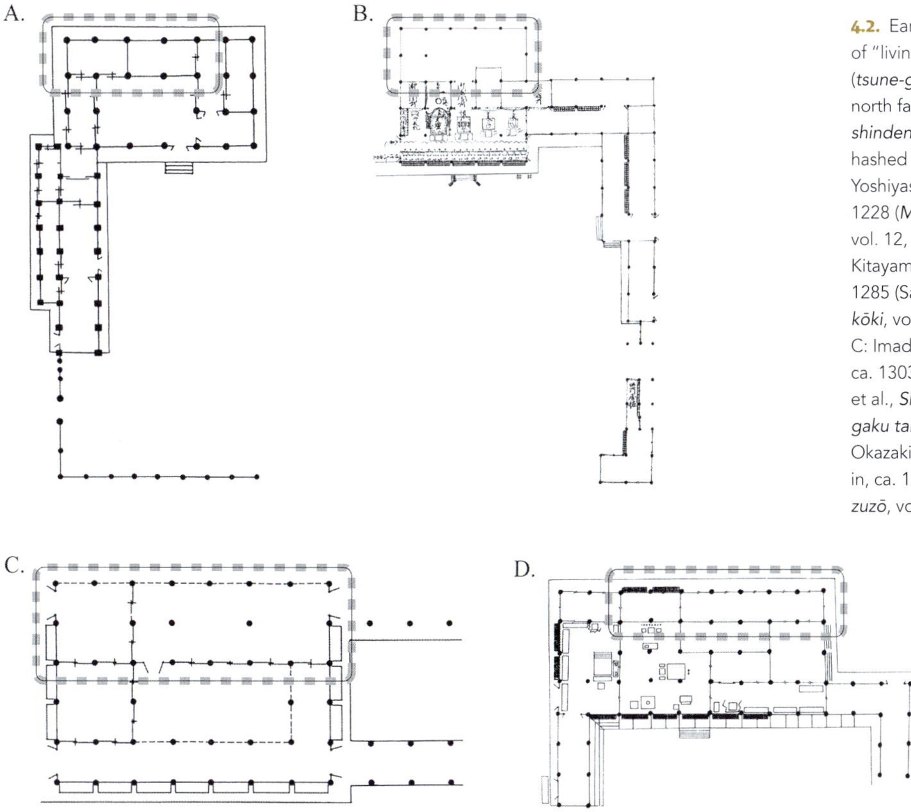

4.2. Early examples of "living quarters" (*tsune-gosho*) on the north faces of central *shinden* (indicated with hashed lines). A: Sōjō Yoshiyasu palace, ca. 1228 (*Mon'yōki, zuzō*, vol. 12, 71); B: Saionji Kitayama Palace, ca. 1285 (Saionji, *Kinhira kōki*, vol. 1, 149–150); C: Imadegawa Palace, ca. 1303 (Sawamura et al., *Shin kenchiku-gaku taikei*, 278); D: Okazaki-bō Sanenori-in, ca. 1319 (*Mon'yōki, zuzō*, vol. 12, 199).

had to take place in ways that did not violate—at least not flagrantly so—certain taboos or the basic tenet that a Kyoto residence was an official domicile, a *honjo*, built to a size and style consistent with its owner's formal status. *Tsune-gosho* and *kaisho*, consequently, were always created on the northern or "back" sides of official palaces, separated by walls and distance from the south-facing formal and public venues. Private oratories, though numerous, remained relatively small, unremarkable fixtures and, perhaps because they generally possessed no sectarian affiliation, were never called "temples." Those who broke the rules, for example by building palaces that were inordinately opulent or unjustifiably large, were frequently censured and sometimes even punished.[46] By maintaining multiple capital residences of enormous size and architectural ostentation, the heads of the Fujiwara family during the ninth and tenth centuries were the worst offenders. They alone, however, could justify their extravagance on the grounds that they were creating *sato-dairi*, temporary imperial palaces, outfitted with the structures and spaces necessary for the emperor to conduct imperial rituals and government.[47] In sum, it is difficult to find cases where members of the Kyoto elite flagrantly and without either justification or reproach gave material form to their often substantial private wealth or influence within the context of their official capital residences. To give form to their wealth, they turned to a place free of public pretentions and sumptuary restrictions: the capital's immediate surroundings.

Throughout the Heian period and the first half of the medieval era, the most successful of the Kyoto elite—including imperial princes, civil aristocrats, and, later, warrior leaders—engaged in a layered building practice that can be read as a homology of their dual identities, first as civil servants and members of the imperial hierarchy, and second as men of great private power.[48] Within the capital, they maintained official family residences that, in terms of their adherence—albeit imperfectly—to status-specific codes dictating sizes and styles, were emblems of their formal public profiles. Outside, they built residential compounds that, in their architectural and artistic lavishness, large sizes, and frequent incorporation of religious apparatuses, were monuments to their extra-public lives, private influence, and spiritual inclinations. Close examination of elite building patterns over time—including attention to who built what, when, where, and for which types of functions—reveals a public/private binary that maps neatly onto the geographic distinction between the capital and its surroundings. There emerges what can be read as an equation of Rakuchū with *hare*, the realm of public authority, officialdom, and the state; and Rakugai with *ke*, the world of the individual, a place where the rich and powerful could play, worship, and sometimes exercise sweeping influence in ways unencumbered by the strictures of formal public institutions.

The tendency for the elite to build exurban retreats—most often appearing in documents as *betsugyō* or *bessō*—has traditionally been attributed to a desire to engage in private leisure activities amidst sites of extraordinary natural beauty (for the locations of major *betsugyō*, see Figure 3.11). This interpretation, however intuitive and probably not entirely incorrect, overlooks the fact that because *betsugyō* tended to incorporate substantial, sometimes monumental, religious facilities (indeed some encompassed full-fledged monasteries), their construction within the capital was probably considered taboo. More important, the greatest among them ended up being much more than mere retreats or temples, however grand. Upon their owner's retirement from public office, they became full-time retirement palaces of substantial size, religious potency, and, most significantly, institutional consequence.

The pattern by which some of Japan's most influential politicians retired from public office only to exercise greater power from behind the scenes is a well-rehearsed narrative. While retired emperors Shirakawa, Toba, and Goshirakawa are the most emblematic examples of the phenomenon, such was also the case with Fujiwara no Michinaga and his son Yorimichi, as well Saionji Sanekane (1249–1322) and the Ashikaga shoguns Yoshimitsu (1358–1408) and Yoshimasa (1436–1490). What often goes unnoticed about the late careers of these political giants is that in each case, the departure from public life corresponded with a departure from the capital. Formal retirement coincided with the quitting of an official capital residence and the promotion of a pre-established exurban *betsugyō* to the status of full-time palace, temple, and administrative headquarters. In sum, an individual's transition from public authority to private power often meant a move from Rakuchū to Rakugai, from the capital to its surroundings.

Not all men of consequence retired to the capital's outskirts. In fact, most did not. Those whose influence increased after leaving public office, however, almost always did. Again, the best examples are the several retired emperors who ruled in retirement from the massive temple-palace complexes of Shirakawa, Toba, and Hōjūji. As we have seen in the previous chapter, in addition to lavish private living quarters, each of these sites included monastic structures as well as considerable spaces dedicated for use by teams of administrators, retainers, and military personnel. With only minor adjustments, a similar description can be applied to the retirement villas of the several figures mentioned above. Fujiwara no Michinaga's Hōjōji, for example, was more than merely a temple or even a luxurious retirement palace. It included a variety of nonmonastic structures that enabled the former regent to maintain a high level of political engagement, particularly with respect to marriage politics and the management of land wealth.[49] Although his son, Yorimichi, was not as successful, the latter's retirement complex at Uji, which encompassed the temple of Byōdōin,

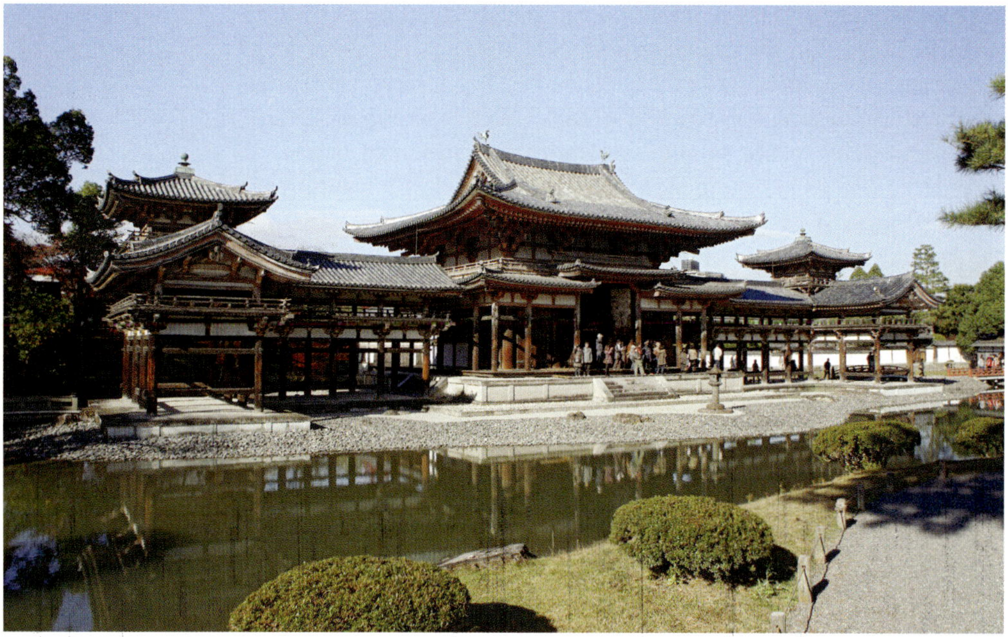

4.3. Phoenix Hall (Hōōdō) of Byōdōin Temple, originally part of the temple-palace complex of Fujiwara Yorimichi in Uji, south of Kyoto.

was likewise designed to facilitate substantial political and economic engagement (see Figure 4.3). About a century later, Saionji Sanekane retired from the lofty imperial post of grand chancellor of state and withdrew to his family's memorial temple located in the Kitayama Hills northwest of the capital.[50] Not only did the eponymously named Saionji Temple serve as a potent political base for Sanekane over the following twenty-nine years, it was later used in much the same way by Ashikaga Yoshimitsu. It was at this Kitayama Villa (Kitayama-dono) that Yoshimitsu—having retired from precisely the same imperial post as Sanekane—built a three-storied reliquary covered in gold leaf and famously received an embassy from the Ming court addressing him as "King of Japan" (Figure 4.4). Not only had the former shogun stepped outside the capital, he had assumed a title entirely outside the framework of Japanese politics. Finally, his grandson, Yoshimasa, built the Higashiyama Villa (Higashiyama-dono) east of the city very much in the mold of his predecessors. The site included elaborate facilities both for administrators and vassals, as well as a Kannon Hall dubbed the "Silver Pavilion" that resembled the "Golden Pavilion" at Kitayama (Figure 4.5).[51]

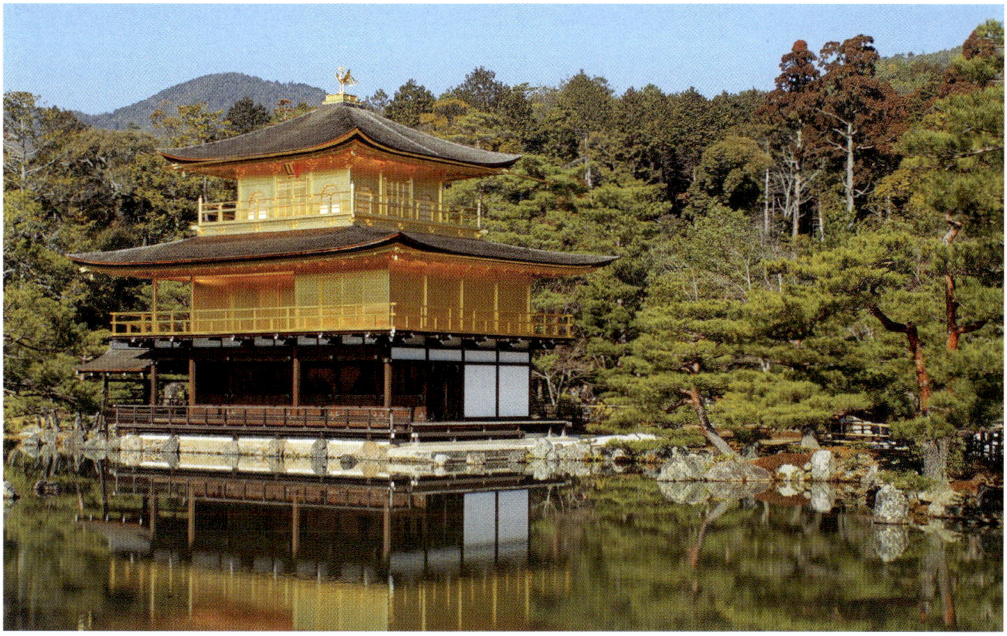

4.4. Golden Pavilion reliquary (Kinkaku shari-den) of Rokuonji Temple, originally part of the Kitayama Villa of Ashikaga Yoshimitsu.

The pattern is clear.[52] Capital elites who retired from formal imperial posts to exercise greater power from behind the scenes consistently did so from sites outside Kyoto. Incidentally, it is intriguing that the word used most frequently to describe these sites, *betsugyō*, can signify a "side business" or at least an alternative occupational profile.[53] In this respect, these "retreats" might be though of as the linguistic and functional opposites of official *honjo.* Whereas *honjo* were the stately yet conventional capital residences of public servants, *betsugyō* were the luxuriant exurban homes of hereditary landholders who enjoyed expansive influence by right of their land wealth and close personal ties to both the court and religious establishments. Of critical importance is the fact that in this equation both the public servant and the landholder were the same person, each with a distinct power profile and each possessing a discrete base of operations. One was *in* the capital and *of* the state. The other was neither.

The impulse to leave the capital to establish an alternate center of political power should not be interpreted as a rejection of the imperial system, the state, or the emperor. On the contrary, it was a validation.

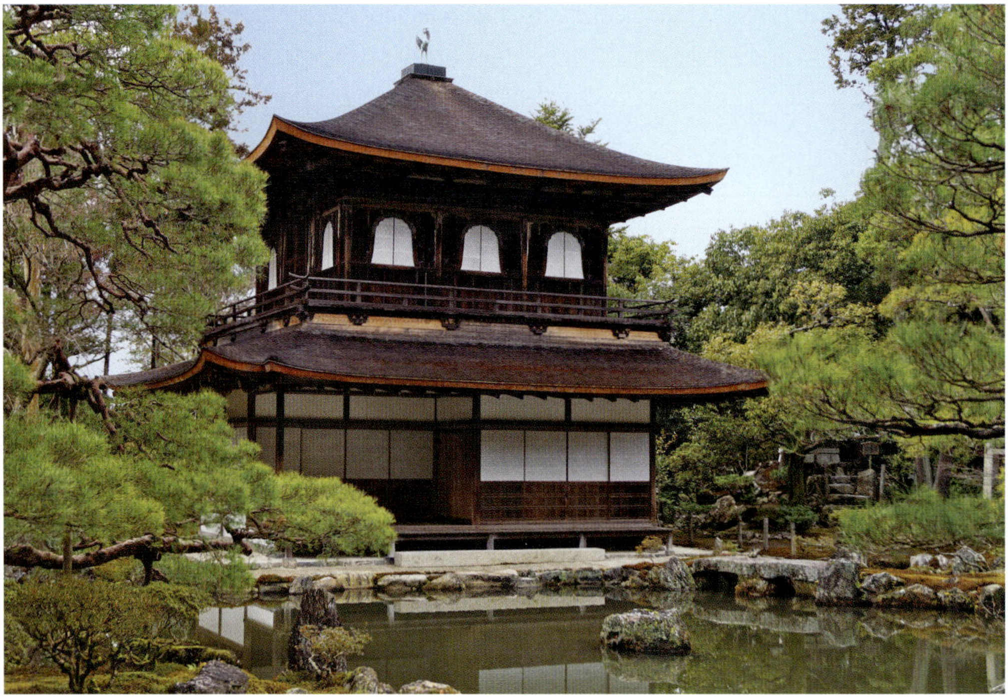

4.5. Silver Pavilion Kannon Hall (Ginkaku Kannon-den) of Jishōji Temple, originally part of the Higashiyama Villa of Ashikaga Yoshimasa.

That no *betsugyō* were built within the boundaries of the old city throughout most of the premodern age suggests a sustained respect for the principle of capital exclusivity and, by extension, imperial relevance. Indeed, the acuteness with which the elite remained conscious of Heian-kyō's borders—again, despite how irrelevant they had become from a development perspective—is perhaps illustrated best in the location of Michinaga's Hōjōji. The former imperial regent built his retirement complex immediately adjacent to his official residence at Tsuchimikado. Nevertheless, it stood, critically, on the eastern side of Higashikyōgoku Road, just outside the old city (see Figure 3.11). This is to say that it was as close to the formal zone of imperial power as physically possible, yet still technically outside it.

An additional example comes from 1130. That year, Fujiwara no Shōshi (1101–1145), the first wife of retired emperor Toba, built the temple-palace complex of Hōkōgōin near the intersection of Konoe and Nishikyōgoku Roads, just outside Heian-kyō's original western boundary.[54] Construction occasioned a complete rebuilding of Nishikyōgoku, which indicates at least two things. First, the need to reconstruct the road in the first place shows the degree to which that part of the city had declined by the twelfth century. More important, the impulse to reconstruct the road at all—merely to locate a temple-palace complex on the other side—suggests a sustained sensitivity to the classical urban ideal and, by association, a desire to underscore its continued relevance.

Inclusion was just as important as exclusion. Indeed, equal attention was paid to ensuring that certain structures—imperial palaces in particular—were not only located within the city but that their regular use did not require venturing outside. In 1317, for example, a decision was made to reorient the imperial residence built near the intersection of Nijō–Tominokōji. The reason given for such a decision, which required substantial human and financial resources, was that the property's original main gate opened onto Higashikyōgoku, an orientation that forced the emperor into the infelicitous position of having to venture out into "Rakugai" when departing his palace (see Figure 3.11).[55]

These and other examples suggest that reinforcing classical ideas about capital boundaries and exclusivity bolstered the efficacy of the institutions the city was built to accommodate. Maintaining the trappings of a relevant and viable state was key to maintaining the imperial hierarchy. And critically, it was the exploitation of that hierarchy that continued to be—well into the medieval era and beyond—the surest way of accumulating and eventually wielding private wealth and power.

Conclusion

Medieval Kyoto was a homology of medieval power. The center, "Rakuchū," was the public and formal core, the venue of state rituals, court ceremony, and the seat of the emperor. To insulate the city from the influence of private political actors, public servants of various occupational origins deployed classical taboos, imperial decrees, soldiers, and even an entirely new discourse about capital space. Many even went so far as to exclude themselves when their private personas overshadowed their public profiles. They did not go far, however. Kyoto's immediate surroundings, "Rakugai," provided elites with a space where they could build and behave in ways inconsistent with—and usually well beyond—their roles as public servants. The medieval capital basin became divided into layered public and private parts, just like the identities of its most prominent political figures.

5

Warriors in the Capital

The Ashikaga and the Classical Ideal

THE KAMAKURA SHOGUNATE, which had been economically and politically weakened by the Mongol invasions of the late thirteenth century, was toppled in 1333 by a coalition of warriors fighting at the behest of Emperor Godaigo. Flushed with victory and determined to rule in the manner of a classical, Chinese-style sovereign, Godaigo sought to become the sole arbiter of formal rewards and commendations.[1] Provincial warriors seeking recognition and recompense for services rendered in the recent conflict were compelled to make the journey to Kyoto personally. Large-scale migration forced the greater capital basin to accommodate a sudden and dramatic influx of fighting men, and by no means were the newcomers kept outside the capital's traditional boundaries. On land adjacent to his own palace, Godaigo granted prime real estate to prominent generals such as Kusunoki Masashige (d. 1336) and Nawa Nagatoshi (d. 1336).[2] Former proscriptions on warriors in the capital appear to have had no meaning in the new order. Indeed, had Godaigo's regime prevailed, such circumstances might not have constituted a threat to imperial authority. In fact, it should have signified the advent of an even stronger centralized state, one able to accommodate and dominate political interests irrespective of their locations, inside or outside the capital. But alas, within three years of its proclamation, the restoration came crashing down. By the summer of 1335, Godaigo had been hounded out of Kyoto by the Ashikaga and their supporters, who quickly moved to replace him through the enthronement of Kōmyō (1321–1380), a prince from a rival branch of the imperial family. Meanwhile, the exiled Godaigo established a "Southern court" in the mountains of Yoshino from which he and his successors challenged the primacy of Kyoto's "Northern Court" for more than half a century.[3] The war of attrition that ensued helped justify the establishment of a robust warrior regime in Kyoto. The general state of unrest that characterized the 1330s in fact transformed Kyoto into a cityscape infused with warriors and other "outsiders," a circumstance that substantially eroded notions of capital exclusivity. Surprisingly, it was the Ashikaga who attempted to restore them.

This chapter begins by exploring the ways warriors interacted with Kyoto's urban landscape following the establishment of the Ashikaga shogunate in 1336.[4] Some of the regime's earliest policies reveal a remarkable level of deference toward traditional spatial paradigms. Whereas the trend toward a greater level of inclusion had become inexorable by this period, warrior residence remained largely limited to the city's margins. This tendency remained true even during the transformative reign of Ashikaga Yoshimitsu, the third and most powerful Ashikaga shogun. Yoshimitsu's several large-scale building projects had a dramatic impact on Kyoto's medieval urban landscape. Notably, however, not one was located within the classical city's original boundaries. The shogun, it seems, remained reticent about violating the foundational taboo barring warriors and temples from the city. He even went so far as to defer to the court on questions of capital land distribution. The findings of this first section force a re-evaluation of the extent of Ashikaga assertiveness in medieval Kyoto, even at the zenith of the regime's power. The standard narrative depicts the shogunate as a growing and eventually ineluctable force of political, economic, and physical change, one that ruled by fiat and according to supposedly unique "warrior" sensibilities. We discover here, however, evidence of a marked reluctance to violate age-old customs and a powerfully conservative impulse vis-à-vis capital spatial norms. This stance, it is argued, helped the Ashikaga gain legitimacy by enabling them to play the part of dutiful servants of the state.

The impulse to become fully endowed members of the state bureaucracy helps explain the findings of the second section, which show that successive Ashikaga leaders consistently built residential headquarters in the *shinden* style. Doing so endowed them with the architectural infrastructure necessary to conduct rituals of state that helped authenticate their membership in the imperial hierarchy. The findings reinforce the suggestion that the Ashikaga sought to influence traditional spheres of influence through infiltration rather than coercion. This section also calls into question a widely accepted impression that the Ashikaga shoguns were pioneers of *shoin*-style architecture, the precursor of traditional Japanese residential architecture. As we shall see, to the extent that the Ashikaga shoguns built structures in that emerging style at all, they were more likely responding to pre-existing trends instead of forging new ones.

The same section concludes with a brief reflection on yet another way warriors used architecture to "build" legitimacy in medieval Kyoto. Following the establishment of the shogunate, the Ashikaga sought to transform the Tsuchimikado Palace in Kamigyō from a luxurious yet temporary imperial abode—a *sato-dairi*—into the official and permanent Imperial Palace, the *kōkyo*. The campaign was significant because it signaled the Ashikaga's public acceptance of responsibility for the reigning emperor's material well-being, a duty indicative of political primacy carried out with equal relish by the Fujiwara, Taira, and Minamoto before them. Just as important, any plan that contributed to a sense of imperial stability underscored the legitimacy of the Kyoto court (and its military protectors) vis-à-vis its "Southern" rivals.

The third section of this chapter looks more closely at the urban legacy of Ashikaga Yoshimitsu, this time to consider the possibility that the shogun had a master plan for medieval Kyoto that entailed a fundamental reorganization of capital space. A synthesis of textual and archeological evidence reveals that all the major building projects commissioned by Yoshimitsu—including several major temples, the Imperial Palace, and his own shogunal headquarters—lined up along a series of axes that together constituted a complex and highly contrived urban matrix. The evidence suggests the shogun was constructing a cityscape in which each of the powerful bodies of interest had a clearly defined place within the greater order, an order that he himself was defining and constructing in the process. While the calculated incorporation of *kenmon* into the capital's urban landscape was novel, there was something deeply conservative about Yoshimitsu's vision. By reorganizing Kyoto into a more unified political and material entity, he was restoring the classical ideal of monocentrism and turning back the clock on the nodal development that had for centuries made the city a fractured and pluralistic medieval landscape.

In the conclusion, we consider how the success of Ashikaga rule affected the discourse of capital exclusion. As the shogunate expanded its power to eventually control all key matters of policy and the economy, the differentiation between Rakuchū and Rakugai became less emphatic, and from about the fourteenth century, those two words began appearing with the greatest frequency as part of a single, compound term signifying the entire capital basin: "Rakuchū-Rakugai." No longer, it appears, was it necessary to sharply define spheres of autonomy and jurisdiction in an environment where there existed a strong centralized governing authority.

Restoring the Spatial Status Quo

The establishment of the Ashikaga shogunate in Kyoto can be interpreted as an extreme measure justified by the state of civil war that ensued following Godaigo's 1335 exile. Early shogunal authority was predicated upon the regime's role as protector of the Kyoto-based "Northern Court," a duty that carried with it the obligation of safeguarding the traditional capital order. Accordingly, several of the shogunate's earliest policies impart a determination to redress matters related to court and aristocratic entitlement. Among these, one of the most urgent was the issue of land rights, which had been disrupted not only by Godaigo's failed experiment with direct imperial rule, but also by the preceding Kamakura shogunate.

Article 5 of the regime's founding legal document, the Kenmu Formulary (*Kenmu shikimoku*), addressed the issue of land in Kamigyō that had been confiscated from members of the aristocracy implicated in the 1221 plot to overthrow the Kamakura shogunate, the Jōkyū Disturbance.[5] Acknowledging the "need to return vacant lots within the capital to their former owners," the article can be interpreted as a gesture of conciliation to those elite families who had been disenfranchised by the former warrior polity. It sent a clear message to the emperor that the current regime was different from its predecessor because it was sympathetic to the interests of traditional capital elites.

The influx of warriors that occurred in the wake of Godaigo's restoration caused the displacement of thousands of commoners. The scale of the problem is captured in the following account of mass migration recorded in *Taiheiki*:

> Once the eastern and western provinces were calm, the [warrior] houses of Shōni, Ōtomo, Kikuchi, and Matsuura came

> to the capital aboard more than seven hundred large boats. Nitta Sama'nosuke and his younger brother, Hyōgo'nosuke, arrived [leading] more than 7,000 cavalry. From all the other provinces too, it was as if not one [soldier] had been left behind. Kyoto and Shirakawa had become utterly inundated by warriors.[6]

Most of the newcomers found accommodations in Shimogyō through a sanctioned quartering system called *shitaku tenjō*, which permitted the temporary commandeering of commoner homes. Despite codes meant to ensure the right of return for the displaced, the practice resulted in the sudden and indefinite eviction of thousands.[7] *Shitaku tenjō* is often cited as one of many ill-conceived policies of the Godaigo regime that led to widespread dissatisfaction. As a first step toward addressing the problem, Article 4 of the Kenmu Formulary specifically prohibited the commandeering of private homes by warriors. The article's concern for the former residents of houses "built by the diligent application of slender means" was as much a gesture of good will to Shimogyō's commoners as it was a sign of passivity toward the Kamigyō elite, many of whom continued to have vested economic interests in the area.[8]

For the shogunate, restoring and protecting capital land privileges meant, at times, giving precedence to the interests of traditional landowners even at the expense of the regime's own vassals. A dispute that unfolded between a shogunal deputy named Kogushi and the aristocratic house of Nakahara in 1367 indicates the kinds of problems the Ashikaga faced. In the autumn of that year, Kogushi began building a house in Shimogyō, claiming he had been ordered to do so by the shogun, Yoshiakira (1330–1367). The project, however, was put on hold and eventually canceled when Nakahara Moroshige (1312–1378), the head of the Nakahara family, lodged a complaint with Yoshiakira's office stating that the block in question had been under the proprietorship of the Nakahara for generations. "So vital is this particular plot to our family," Moroshige explained in a letter to the shogun, "the Nakahara are sometimes referred to as the 'Record Keepers of Sanjō,'" a toponym derived from the site's location along Sanjō Road. "We are talking about land with a name attached to it," Moroshige pleaded.[9] The contest ended in victory for the Nakahara, whose traditional proprietary rites apparently trumped warrior priorities.[10]

Scholars who have considered warrior movement into the capital after 1336 are quick to point out how the first functioning headquarters of the shogunate, the Sanjō-bōmon Palace, and most vassal residences were located in the district of Shimogyō. Not until Yoshimitsu moved to Kamigyō in 1378 do we find any significant or sustained warrior presence in that elite district. The prevailing argument holds that land in Shimogyō was relatively easy for warriors to acquire because it was populated predominantly by commoners.[11] There is an assumption that Kamigyō, with its high concentration of aristocrats, would have been much more difficult to break into. It should be remembered, however, that urban commoners in the fourteenth century did not generally own the land they occupied. Rather, in most cases they were tenants who leased plots from aristocratic or temple proprietors, the former of which usually lived in Kamigyō.[12] As we can see in the above case of Kogushi versus Nakahara, these aristocratic landowners were not only intent upon preserving their hold over Shimogyō real estate, in many cases they were exceedingly good at it. With this in mind, it becomes necessary to reconsider early Ashikaga gravitation toward Shimogyō. After all, having just noticed that one of the earliest policy objectives of the new regime was to roll back previous warrior advances in Kyoto, how then do we explain large-scale Ashikaga settlement there?

Answering this question requires careful consideration of precisely where warriors settled.[13] Figure 5.1 shows the locations of known residences built by top Ashikaga generals during the 1350s.[14] While it is clear that they—in addition to the regime's headquarters at Sanjō-bōmon—were predominantly clustered south of Nijō in Shimogyō, it is notable that none stood within the most developed part of that district along Muromachi Road between Sanjō in the north and Gojō in the south (see Figure 3.7).[15]

5.1. Map of Kyoto in the 1350s, showing the residences of Ashikaga leadership. Shaded areas correspond to urbanized portions of the city during the Age of Warring States (1467–1580s).

The extent of early warrior peripherality comes into even sharper focus through an examination of Shimogyō's size during the succeeding Age of Warring States (1467–1580s). During this long phase of protracted violence, the urbanized portions of Kyoto shrank and retreated into fortified islands surrounded by walls and moats. Within these makeshift urban fortresses, townspeople organized into grassroots self-governing bodies called "neighborhood federations" (*chō-gumi*), which provided for a degree of self-government amidst a largely ungoverned urban landscape. If we make the safe assumption that the shrunken sections of wartime Shimogyō corresponded with the most highly developed core of the prewar district, we discover just how

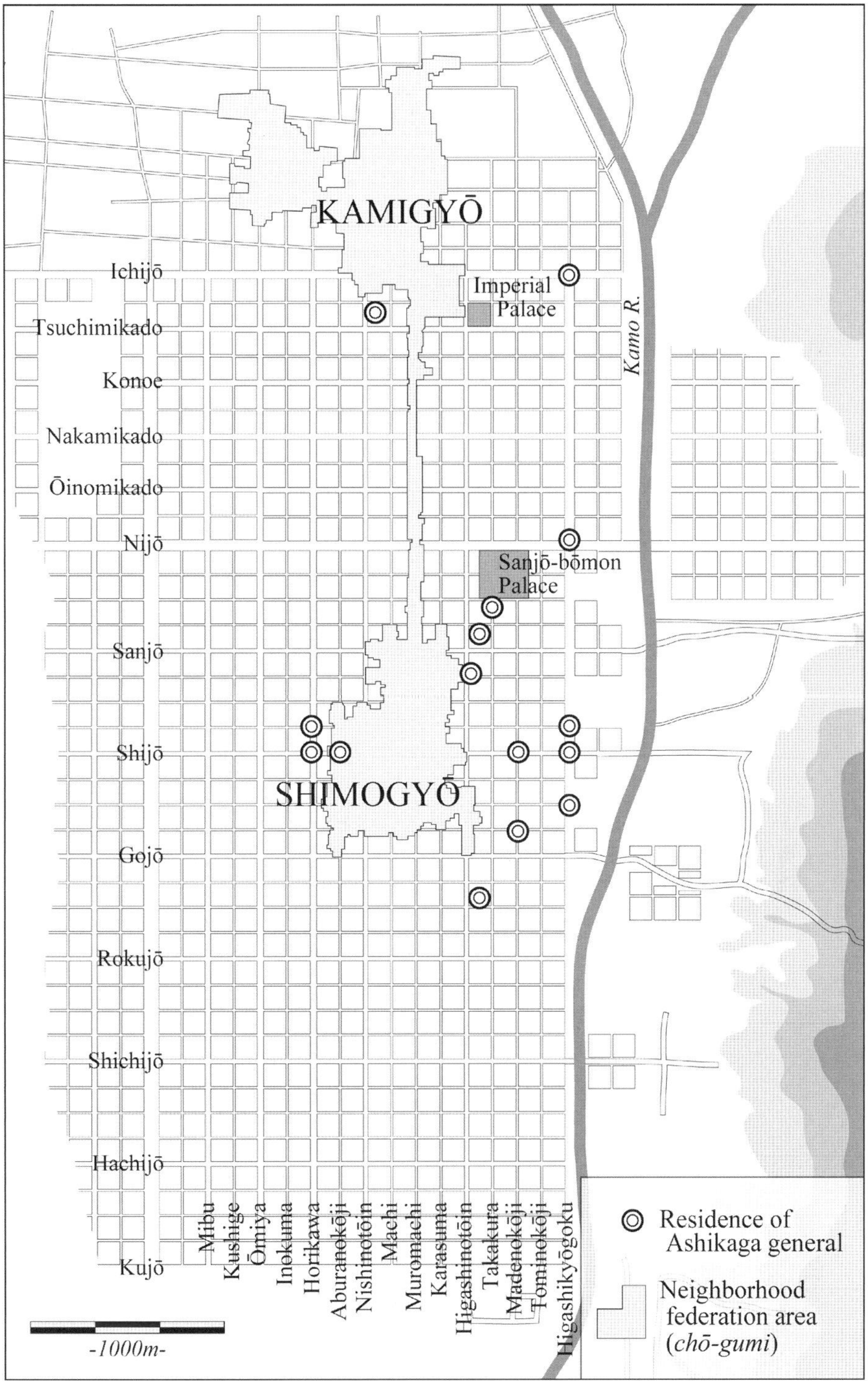
KAMIGYŌ
SHIMOGYŌ
Ichijō
Tsuchimikado
Konoe
Nakamikado
Ōinomikado
Nijō
Sanjō
Shijō
Gojō
Rokujō
Shichijō
Hachijō
Kujō
Imperial Palace
Sanjō-bōmon Palace
Kamo R.
Mibu
Kushige
Ōmiya
Inokuma
Horikawa
Aburanokōji
Nishinotōin
Machi
Muromachi
Karasuma
Higashinotōin
Takakura
Madenokōji
Tominokōji
Higashikyōgoku
-1000m-
Residence of Ashikaga general
Neighborhood federation area (chō-gumi)

marginalized Ashikaga leaders were during the 1350s (see Figure 5.1). Only one of the sixteen known residences was located within that central part of Shimogyō that, presumably because of its density and commercial importance, would retain its viability in the succeeding era. The rest were on the outside.

The shogunate's early policy objective of restoring and protecting land rights within the city meant, in certain cases, putting the claims of traditional landowners ahead of their own interests. The property dispute between Kogushi and Nakahara reminds us that much of the land in Shimogyō was actually under the proprietorship of members of the Kamigyō aristocracy. Their ability to successfully limit warrior residence in Shimogyō helped guarantee the district's continued commercial viability, a situation that benefited them and commoners alike. The above spatial analysis shows that whereas warriors did indeed settle in Shimogyō more than any other place in the capital basin, they did not penetrate the district's central area.

It is generally accepted that Yoshimitsu's decision to move to Kamigyō in 1378 was guided by an impulse to physically infiltrate the realm of high capital politics.[16] In a well-cited essay, Kurokawa Naonori wrote that the building of the Muromachi Palace (Muromachi-dono) put Yoshimitsu in a position to conveniently "host, house, and keep watch over the emperor."[17] While this assessment might be correct, it is critical not to assume proximity was of key political or even symbolic significance within the contemporaneous context. Indeed, if geography and location are to be read for their historical significance at all, the subtle spatial rules of the day must be considered with the utmost care. Kamigyō, for example, was the "elite district" to be sure, yet its status as such was purely informal. In fact, as a discrete entity, the enclave was little more than a cluster of dense development that from about the ninth century had been superimposed over the older and more formal northern boundary of the classical city's eastern half. In light of the evidence introduced in the previous chapter showing Heian-kyō's boundary still mattered at the time of the 1371 enthronement, it is notable that the Muromachi Palace, as well as each and every one of Yoshimitsu's other original projects in Kamigyō, were located north of Ichijō (see Figure 5.2). Having moved to the elite district, the shogun was indeed closer to the emperor and civil aristocracy. And yet, despite gaining the logistical and potentially symbolic advantages of proximity, he was unmistakably outside the formal boundaries of the capital.

5.2. Map of Kamigyō in the late fourteenth century. Asterisks indicate palaces of the civil aristocracy.

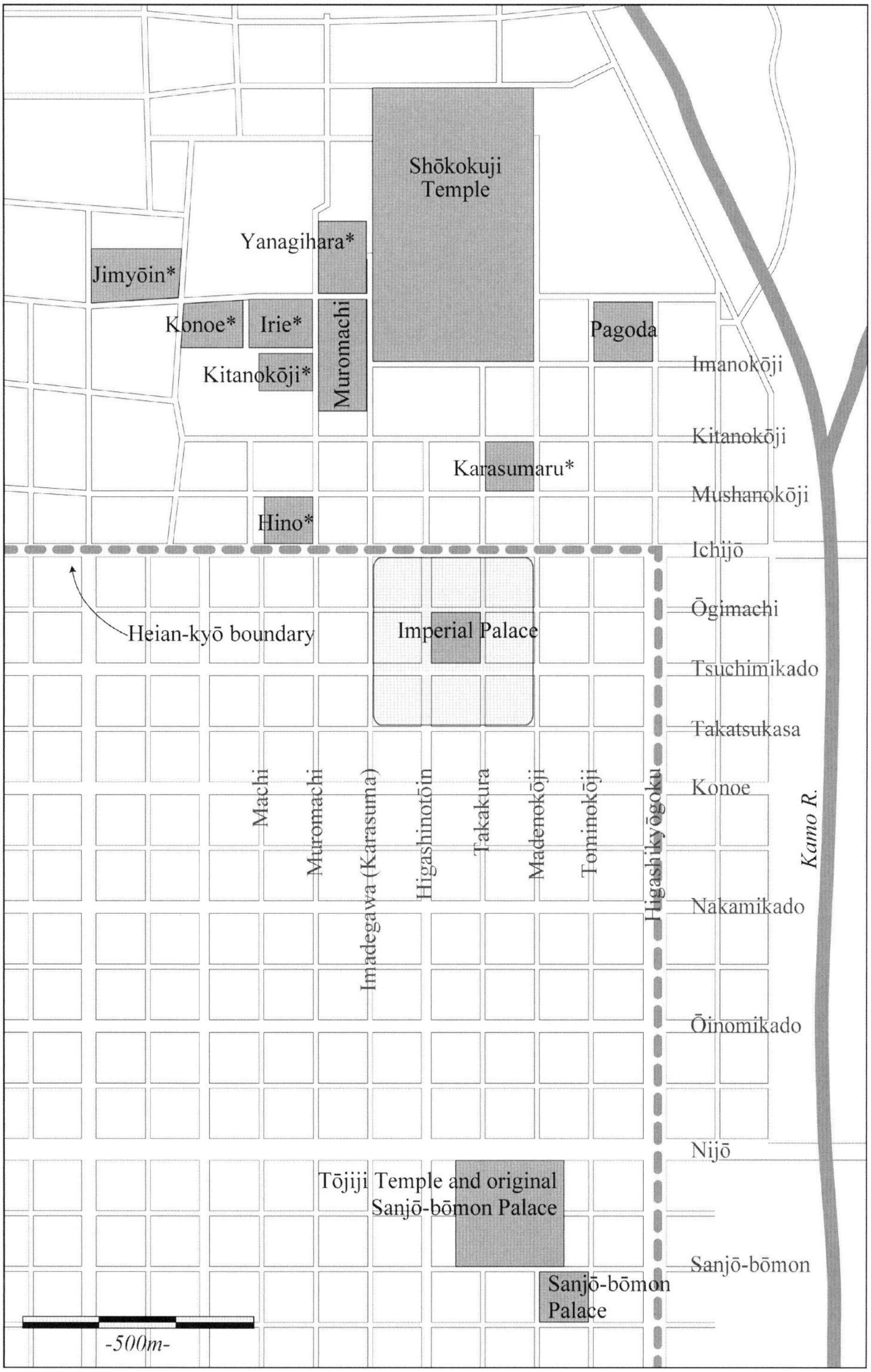

Shōkokuji Temple
Yanagihara*
Jimyōin*
Konoe*
Irie*
Muromachi
Kitanokōji*
Pagoda
Imanokōji
Kitanokōji
Karasumaru*
Mushanokōji
Hino*
Ichijō
Ōgimachi
Heian-kyō boundary
Imperial Palace
Tsuchimikado
Takatsukasa
Konoe
Machi
Muromachi
Imadegawa (Karasuma)
Higashinotōin
Takakura
Madenokōji
Tominokōji
Higashikyōgoku
Kamo R.
Nakamikado
Ōinomikado
Nijō
Tōjiji Temple and original Sanjō-bōmon Palace
Sanjō-bōmon
Sanjō-bōmon Palace
-500m-

Whether or not Yoshimitsu would have been able to build his Muromachi headquarters within the old city is a hypothetical question that cannot be answered with known textual and archeological evidence. The shogun might have preferred land north of Ichijō for the same reasons civil aristocrats did when they began living in the area from as early as the late ninth century: land on the outside was exempt from the strict codes and customs of the capital proper. There, people could build whatever they wanted, irrespective of status-based prescriptions that dictated architectural styles and property sizes.[18] The Muromachi Palace—covering nearly two whole city blocks in Kamigyō and possessing two complete and independent residential complexes (including a north and south *shinden*)—was massive by any standard. One wonders if a palace of this size and ostentation would not have been deemed unseemly, the loftiness of Yoshimitsu's formal status notwithstanding. Note too that while there were several other palaces in Kamigyō that were larger than a single block, not one was located south of Ichijō (see Figure 5.2). In this light, Yoshimitsu's move to Kamigyō begins to look more like an escape from the old capital than a move to be near the emperor.

Let us consider Yoshimitsu's two other major building projects in Kamigyō: the Zen monastery of Shōkokuji (completed 1382) and the seven-storied Shōkokuji Pagoda (completed 1399). The building of the former was a deeply disruptive affair for the residents of Kamigyō.[19] In his journal, nobleman Ichijō Tsunetsugu (1358–1418) lamented the seizure of more than twelve city blocks for the temple's construction: "There has been no greater case of a relocation of both the high and low of this scale since the capital was transferred to Fukuhara [in 1168]."[20] People were apparently not the only ones to suffer. The project placed a significant burden on the environment as well.[21] A contemporary diarist fumed in verse:

> In the capital
> Cypress and cedar exhausted
> Lamenting the building of Shōkokuji.[22]

We have no records of hardship caused by the building of the pagoda, but there can be little doubt that it too, occupying a whole block of prime Kamigyō real estate, was not a welcome newcomer. For as much strife as these two projects likely caused, it is important to note that both, like the Muromachi Palace, were located north of Ichijō. We can safely assume the Heian-era principle of temple exclusion remained in force well into the fourteenth century.[23] Yoshimitsu was either unable or unwilling to change it.

A sequence of events recorded in the journal of Sanjō Kintada provides further evidence of Yoshimitsu's deferent posture vis-à-vis the emperor and court when it came to capital land. In the summer of 1381, Kintada was trying desperately to acquire a taxable plot in Shimogyō to provide income for his financially strapped family. Written with stirring poignancy, the narrative requires no commentary; it illustrates with unusual clarity Yoshimitsu's reticence about impinging upon what he saw as the prerogative of the emperor. The entries likewise highlight the complexity of the relationships between the emperor, members of the aristocracy, and the shogunate:

> 12th day [1381/8]: There has been much impropriety on our provincial lands. . . . Because of this, we are up to our necks in poverty. I sent a messenger to the Lord of Muromachi [Yoshimitsu] with an appeal requesting that a block of land in Shimogyō at Shijō-bōmon be deeded to our family and that the surrounding roads be made into thoroughfares. The reply [from Yoshimitsu] was as such: "Capital land is the concern of the emperor.[24] I, therefore, cannot grant your request. Shall I convey your desires to court?"
>
> I sent another messenger to deliver a response. I wrote: "I am frightfully grateful to have received your reply. With this letter, I hereby request that you convey my desires to court."
>
> Some time passed before word was sent [from Yoshimitsu to the court]. Then, Lord Madenokōji, the court's shogunal liaison, delivered to me an imperial document that read: "So that there shall be no ambiguity, you must lodge your petition with the court personally."
>
> I sent my servant along with Lord Madenokōji accordingly. He is to go to court now and convey my desire for the block of land in Shimogyō.[25]
>
> 20th day: About the land: Because no reply had yet arrived from the court, I inquired again with the shogunate yesterday. I submitted a letter conveying my hope that Yoshimitsu press the court for a decision. My letter was forwarded to Lord

Madenokōji who took it to the [imperial] palace in the early evening. I expressed my hope that my concerns be conveyed quickly.[26]

22nd day: About the land: I have yet to receive the imperial reply via Lord Madenokōji. The emperor's will, however, has reached me discreetly through my daughter who is currently serving as an attendant in the Imperial Palace. I understand that the answer boils down to this: "In the end, the land within the capital is the business of the emperor (*kōke*). This goes without saying. Lodging your initial appeal with the shogunate was profoundly improper. Because there is someone [else] who has shown interest in this land before you, we must handle that request first. It has become necessary to explain this complication to the shogunate."

Appalling! The emperor is upset. Whatever can be done?[27]

24th day: About the land. Again, the emperor's will has been conveyed through my daughter: "In the end, because your appeal was initially made to the shogunate, it is now necessary to issue an imperial decree to address the matter. A scribe was commanded to write the letter on behalf of the emperor. The reason no action has yet been taken [i.e., the reason we have not simply rejected your appeal out of hand] is because it seems to go against the wishes of the shogun. Regarding the imperial attendant [your daughter], from now on, she shall no longer function as a go-between and shall no longer come face-to-face with the emperor."

How unfortunate this is! It was naturally absurd of me to have prevailed upon the shogun in a matter that is entirely the concern of the court. Nevertheless, it is not as if there is no precedent. But now, the entire situation is blown out of proportion. It is not as if I have turned my back on the emperor. And why should a child be blamed for a father's faults? The emperor's thoughts on this issue are beyond reason. Our family is dreadfully poor. I just wanted some good fortune via the shogun [i.e. by using a shogunal route to present the petition].[28]

11th month, 17th day: I requested that my petition for the property at Shijō be retracted. At any rate, I hear that the emperor will order that all land within the capital be returned to its original proprietors (*honshu*) in the coming days.

> All concerned officials have been notified. . . . Because of Yoshimitsu's intervention, the land of Nijō Yoshimoto and myself will be spared. Nevertheless, it is the emperor's wish that I give up the land anyway. If I do not retract my request, it will create a situation of bad timing for my daughter. She was the one who first urged me to submit a retraction. The Shimogyō plot is poor land anyway, inappropriate to someone of my status. Still, words cannot capture the sentiments of the emperor.[29]

"Building" Warrior Legitimacy

Cultural historians have long pointed to a dramatic transformation in the dominant style of elite residential architecture that took place during the period of Ashikaga rule. The standard narrative traces the displacement of *shinden* style by the newer *shoin* style (*shoin-zukuri*) in about the middle of the fifteenth century. Ashikaga shoguns are thought to have catalyzed this shift through their promotion of material culture and architecture inspired by a mixture of provincial rusticity and new continental influences.[30] Today, *shoin*-style architecture is so closely associated with medieval warriors that it is sometimes referred to as "warrior-style" (*buke-zukuri*) and its promotion in particular by the powerful and capital-dwelling Ashikaga is thought to have contributed to the undermining of classical building models.

The findings of this section show that the Ashikaga, rather than rejecting traditional building styles, actually embraced and celebrated them.[31] To be sure, up until the outbreak of the Ōnin War in 1467, each of the shoguns carefully maintained a core contingent of *shinden*-style structures at their official Kyoto residences. Doing so enabled them to fulfill their ritual duties as members of the Ritsuryō hierarchy. At the same time, however, they were also willing adopters of new architectural forms. Like their aristocratic counterparts whose building practices were touched on in previous chapters, Ashikaga shoguns created residential venues well suited to a variety of social and political intercourse entirely outside the grammar of Ritsuryō comportment. Therefore, while the Ashikaga may be accurately credited with having contributed to the proliferation of *shoin* style, they were by no means its early pioneers nor its sole promoters.

Ashikaga Takauji did not settle permanently in Kyoto until 1344. When he finally did, it appears that the residence he built adhered to

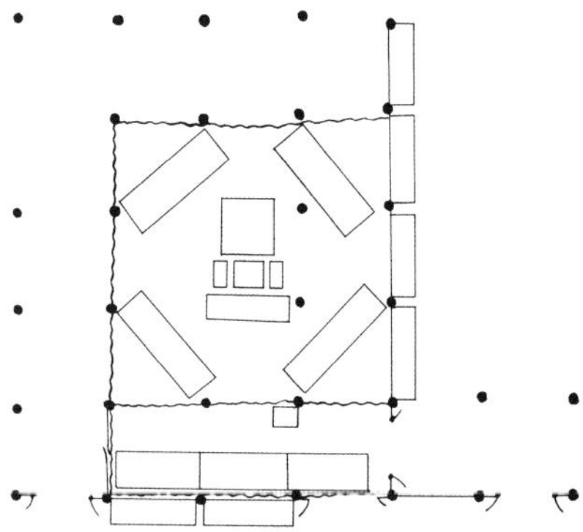

5.3. Central *shinden* at Ashikaga Takauji's Kamigyō residence, ca. 1346, in *Mon'yōki, zuzō* (vol. 11, 605). Top of image is east.

exceptionally traditional models.[32] A diagram of the central *shinden*'s plan drawn in 1346 shows that the building was a standard five bays (*ken*) wide and four bays deep (Figure 5.3).[33] Reticulating wooden shutters (*shitomido*) opened outward on the southern (front) and western sides, and an entrance corridor (*chūmon-rō*) extended to the south from the western side. All pillars were round and interior space was partitioned by a series of curtains alone. No permanent interior walls are apparent in the diagram and the accompanying text makes no mention of a *tsune-gosho*. In fact, the only known non-*shinden*-style structure on the property was a small Buddhist reliquary (*shari-den*), which was the centerpiece of a private oratory.[34]

The Sanjō-bōmon Palace, which was built by Ashikaga Tadayoshi (1306–1352) in about 1336 and served as the first functioning shogunal headquarters, likewise exhibited strong *shinden*-style traits.[35] Among them were a south-facing *shinden*, an opposing hall (*tainoya*), reticulating shutters, a cusped-gable roof (*kara-hafu*), and a hurdle veranda (*sunoko-en*) that opened onto a carriage port (*kuruma-dome*). A color illustration from the period confirms that the attached Ashikaga mortuary temple of Tōjiji possessed similar traits (Figure 5.4).[36] Its Buddha Hall (*Butsuden*) exhibited twin entrance corridors. While such a symmetry would have been typical of a temple or elite residence built in the eighth or ninth centuries, its implementation in the mid-fourteenth century was conspicuously reminiscent of a bygone era.[37]

Soon after Ashikaga Yoshimitsu completed construction of the Muromachi Palace in the early spring of 1381, he used the compound to formally receive and entertain his first cousin, the emperor Goen'yū. A detailed account of the imperial visit refers to a central *shinden*, an inner gate, eastern and northern opposing halls, a circular corridor (*sukiwata-dono kairō*), and a fishing pavilion. Peripheral chambers (*hisashi*) were surrounded by a hurdle veranda (*hashinosunoko*), and reticulating shutters opened wide to a front garden.[38] The diarist gives special attention to the central *shinden* and garden, where several formal rituals were performed:

> The palace, with its elevated connecting corridors (*sukiwata-dono*) and a fishing pavilion (*tsuri-dono*), is

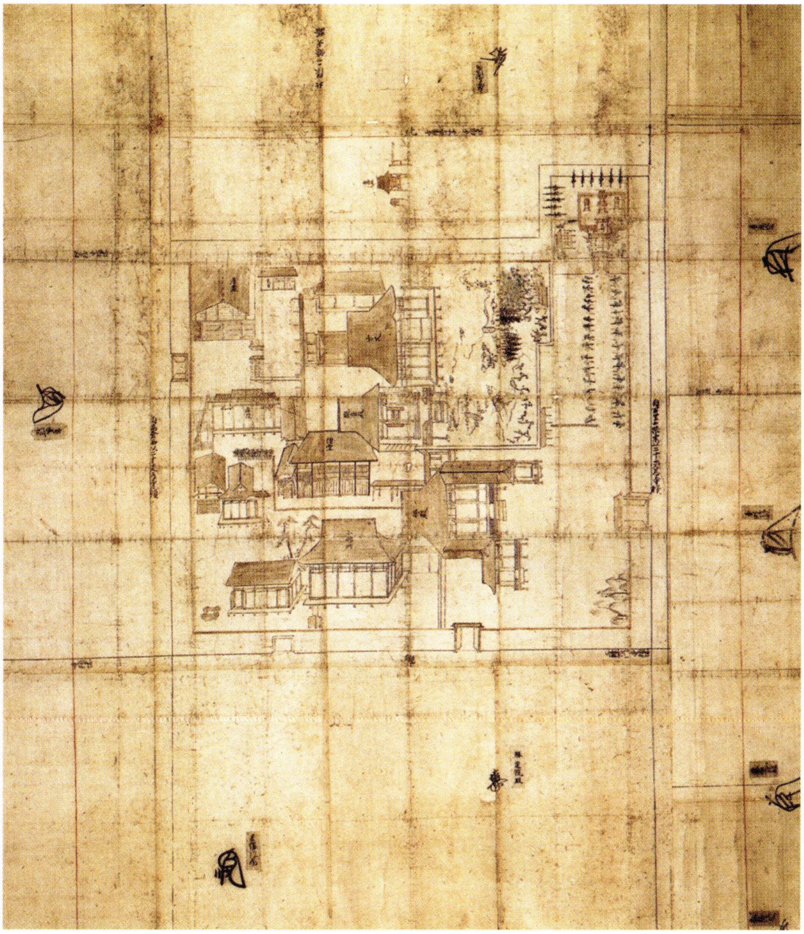

5.4. *Tōjiji-ezu,* depicting the Sanjō-bōmon temple-palace complex (including Tōjiji Temple). Inscriptions around the margins are the signatures (*kaō*) of successive Ashikaga shoguns. Courtesy of Tōjiin Temple, Kyoto

> surprising to the eyes. Water drawn from the Kamo River tumbles over rocks and babbles as it flows under the corridors. The sound, which blends with the wind in the pines, is most elegant. The ridgepoles of the central *shinden*, with their three and four-leaf decorations, are rumored to be newly crafted of cypress. This is all so very felicitous; the future indeed looks bright.

This account in *Sakayuku-hana* stands as a testament to Muromachi's adherence to *shinden*-style protocols. Indeed, the existence of a central *shinden* itself, augmented by opposing halls, a circular corridor, and an inner gate, demonstrates that careful attention was paid to the classical building model. Yoshimitsu's apparent preference for *shinden* style has been widely interpreted as having been related to the shogun's intent to cast himself as a man of status and refinement on par with his aristocratic counterparts.[39] The underlying assumption is that a warrior such as Yoshimitsu would have been expected to build in the "warrior style" of *shoin-zukuri.* This logic, however, is flawed in several ways. First, it is problematic to strictly categorize Yoshimitsu as a "warrior." By the time Muromachi was completed, he had attained the rank of chief councillor of state (*gon-dainagon*) and as such was a fully vested member of the imperial court.[40] Second, as pointed out, members of the Ashikaga leadership had been building in the *shinden* style since at least the founding of the shogunate. Finally, and most important, *shoin* style did not emerge as a discrete architectural genre until about the second decade of the fifteenth century.[41] Any assumption that Yoshimitsu should have built primarily in that style is therefore anachronistic.

But there is a more fundamental problem. The scholarship that treats Yoshimitsu's implementation of *shinden* style exhibits a misunderstanding about the genre's fundamental meaning. Its significance derived not from its conformity to subjective notions of opulence or fine living. Rather, it was its role as the prescribed venue of Ritsuryō ritual and performative statecraft that made it special and important.[42] Yoshimitsu's use of *shinden* style, therefore, should be read more as the result of a compulsion to fulfill the ritual demands of his official station than merely an attempt to impress his peers.

The distinction being made is of profound interpretive significance. The creation of the Muromachi Palace coincided with Yoshimitsu's court promotion to chief councillor and his assertion of political independence from the regent Hosokawa Yoriyuki (1329–1392). The *shinden*-style complex functioned as a stage—physical, not metaphorical—upon which the rising star could publicly comport himself in the manner of a ranking court official. It was in these structures that he held, for example, a grand ceremony (*haiga*) in the seventh month of 1379 by which he formally conveyed his gratitude to the emperor for a recent promotion. Other events that required a *shinden*-style setting include the formal hosting of Emperor Goen'yū in 1381 and another *haiga* marking his promotion to grand chancellor of state in 1395.[43] In each of these cases, great care was taken to ensure that both the necessary architectural infrastructure and décor (*shitsurai*) were in place to adhere to the strictest formalities of Ritsuryō pageantry and precedent. Muromachi's suitability as a venue of imperial functions is underscored by a decision made in 1401 that the palace should be used to house Emperor Gokomatsu (1377–1433) for an extended period while repairs were underway on the Imperial Palace.[44] Making the emperor comfortable was only part of the equation. Ensuring that he had the accoutrements necessary to fulfill his ceremonial duties as the sacerdotal head of state was paramount.

The several structures within the Muromachi complex that did not fit the *shinden*-style model have, to date, received more scholarly scrutiny than those that did. In particular, research has focused on the *kaisho* or "meeting place" that reportedly stood at the site.[45] While far too little information is available on this structure to examine its significance in full, there is one critical aspect that should not be overlooked: It was probably not built by Yoshimitsu. The structure first appears in documents from 1401, several years after Yoshimitsu moved to his retirement villa at Kitayama, thereby transferring both Muromachi and the post of shogun to his son, Yoshimochi (1386–1428).[46] The *kaisho* was Yoshimochi's preferred venue for social and political activity throughout the period. Indeed we have no evidence that he used the *shinden* at all prior to Yoshimitsu's death in 1408. Yoshimochi's avoidance of the Muromachi *shinden* might have been related to a perception that he should conduct business in a discreet, unofficial manner to avoid upstaging his father, who continued to wield ultimate power from retirement. For Yoshimochi, the *kaisho* constituted an ideal venue for low-profile social and political engagements, and it was his avid use of the structure that might help explain its later proliferation. Whatever the case, the observation that Yoshimitsu probably did not build the Muromachi *kaisho* throws into doubt the notion that the third shogun was a zealous proponent of new architectural styles.[47] We have no evidence, in fact, that he built any structures at Muromachi that departed from the *shinden*-style norm.

Yoshimitsu is well known for heavily patronizing the arts at his retirement villa in the northern hills of Kitayama during the opening years of the fifteenth century. The Golden Pavilion (Kinkaku shariden), which remained standing at the site until its destruction by arson in 1950, was an emblem of "Kitayama culture," a term used to describe forms of painting, performance, poetry, and tea connoisseurship that emanated from that period and place.[48] The Golden Pavilion's implementation of both *shinden* and *shoin* architectural styles (in addition to a Zen-inspired third floor) is often read as indicative of the way Yoshimitsu deftly straddled the courtly and warrior worlds while facilitating a transition in architectural aesthetics from the former to the latter (pictured in Figure 4.4).[49] And the Kitayama *kaisho*, within which Yoshimitsu so famously entertained the emperor in 1408, is regularly pointed to as the inspiration for the proliferation of that type of building in later shogunal palaces. But for all of Kitayama's contributions to the most celebrated features of the period's culture, there were deeply conservative elements to the site that should not be overlooked.

First, the move to Kitayama must not be read as a rejection of Kyoto politics. The villa was by no means a place where Yoshimitsu lost himself entirely in the cultural and religious pursuits for which the site is so well known. On the contrary, Kitayama was first and foremost a *betsugyō* designed to empower its owner to comport himself in the manner of a retired court official with sustained political influence.[50] Within the grounds of the greater Kitayama Villa, there stood not one but three independent *shinden*-style complexes. These were the "Northern Palace" (Kita no dai), the "Southern Palace" (Minami no dai), and an additional complex farther south within which lived Fujiwara no Nakako (1339–1427), who was the grandmother of Emperor Gokomatsu and Yoshimitsu's maternal aunt.[51] Most texts make only fleeting mention of the latter two complexes, and none include specific details about their appearances.[52]

Far more is known of Kitayama's Northern Palace. Textual accounts consistently indicate the compound's importance as a venue for public ceremony and Ritsuryō-style rituals. "Annual observances" (*nenjūgyōji*) and Shingon rituals for the protection of the state (*gokoku butsuji*) took place regularly, and it was there where in 1407 Yoshimitsu's wife began the prescribed set of court formalities (*judai girei*) related to her being made surrogate mother of Emperor Gokomatsu.[53] In 1408, when the emperor visited Kitayama, the Northern Palace's central *shinden* was used to hold a series of events in which Yoshimitsu ceremonially received the emperor and accepted his tacit agreement to swiftly promote his favored second son, Yoshitsugu (1394–1418). The structure was also used to lodge the emperor throughout the nineteen-day stay.[54]

Finally, and perhaps most dramatically, the Northern Palace was used to conduct international diplomacy. It was there where Yoshimitsu received envoys from both the Ming and Chosŏn courts on at least six occasions between 1402 and 1407.[55] Sources are explicit about the lengths to which he went to ensure strict adherence to Ritsuryō precedent in each case. In preparation for the most important visit by Ming ambassadors in 1402, for example, the head abbot of Daigoji Temple was retained as a protocol adviser for the planning of everything from the approach and seating arrangements to décor and clothing. Every detail was meticulously choreographed to follow precedent set out by "former sovereigns" (*senkō*).[56] Matters of precedent were critical to members of the imperial hierarchy, for whom familiarity with and attention to the grammar of official pageantry were markers of status. Maintaining the proper architectural setting was one of several performative necessities. Texts confirm that the Northern Palace exhibited all the fundamental elements of a *shinden*-style complex, including a central *shinden*, an opposing hall, an entrance corridor, a central gate, and a "four-legged gate" (*yotsu-ashi-mon*).[57] Detailed descriptions of the central *shinden* refer to a hurdle veranda, a south-facing staircase, and the use of curtains, folding screens, and bamboo blinds to partition interior space.[58] Each of these traits is characteristic of early *shinden* style. Archeological data collected over the course of seven excavations conducted between 1988 and 1993 make it possible to reconstruct the layout of the central *shinden*.[59] Most striking about the plan, as recreated in Figure 5.5, is its traditionalism in an era of architectural evolution.

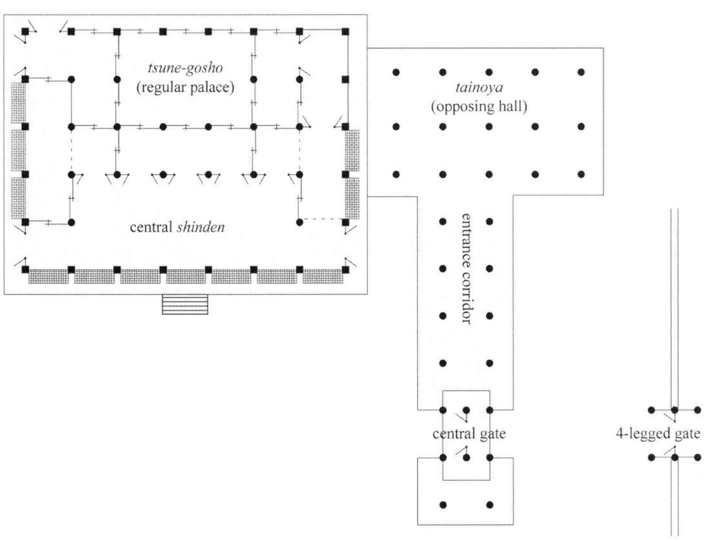

5.5. Central *shinden* at Kitayama Villa's Northern Palace (Kita no dai), ca. 1408.

Following Yoshimitsu's sudden and suspicious death in 1408, his son, Yoshimochi, moved from Muromachi to Kitayama. Almost immediately, however, he set into motion a plan to rebuild and reoccupy Sanjō-bōmon.[60] Completed in 1409, the reconstructed headquarters was used by successive shoguns Yoshimochi, Yoshikazu, and Yoshinori until 1431, when the latter rebuilt the Muromachi Palace and moved back to Kamigyō. The twenty-two years during which this Sanjō-bōmon Palace functioned without interruption as the shogunal headquarters was the single longest period of geographical stability for the regime during the entire era of Ashikaga rule.[61]

The latter Sanjō-bōmon Palace resembled Muromachi and Kitayama in the way it comprised two separate compounds, one consisting of a cluster of traditional *shinden*-style structures and the other several non-*shinden*-style structures. The former features prominently in documents that chronicle a succession of public events held between 1410 and 1430.[62] Accounts consistently describe a central *shinden* flanked to the west by a nobles' hall and a vassals' hall (*zuishin-sho*). An entrance corridor extending to the south opened onto a carriage port. East of the *shinden* was a large, nine-bay opposing hall. High aristocracy entered the property from the west through a four-legged gate. All the elements of a typical *shinden*-style complex were present.

Descriptions of the two *kaisho* and two *tsune-gosho* on the property feature prominently in studies tracing the emergence of *shoin* style.[63] These three freestanding structures functioned as dedicated residential facilities. They were private, personal spaces used for eating, sleeping, and bathing. Occasionally, they functioned as waiting rooms for guests attending formal events.[64] The new Sanjō-bōmon complex is the earliest confirmed case where a dedicated, freestanding residential structure stood within an Ashikaga shogunal palace. As far as can be discerned from extant sources, all previous shoguns had lived within their respective central *shinden*, most probably within internal "regular palaces" (*tsune-gosho*) fashioned on the northern sides of those structures. The creation of dedicated living space was a development of critical significance because it extricated private space from the *shinden* entirely.

The building changes described here should be understood as part of a broader trend leading to the creation of increasingly function-specific space within elite residences. As we have seen, in about the tenth century, members of the Kyoto aristocracy began building oratories at their residential compounds to accommodate private religious observances. Later, fountain pavilions (*izumi-dono*) and *kaisho* were introduced for entertainment and other informal functions. The necessities of private and daily affairs were accommodated through the creation of *tsune-gosho*, which again in their earliest forms were little more than rooms fashioned on the back sides of central *shinden*. Finally, as we see in the case of the latter Sanjō-bōmon Palace, living space eventually seceded from the *shinden* altogether with the creation of the freestanding *tsune-gosho* or perhaps a *shō-gosho* (minor palace).

This emergence of increasingly function-specific space should not be read as an abandonment of *shinden* style. On the contrary, it was a validation of its original significance. The creation of *kaisho*, *tsune-gosho*, and *shō-gosho* at Sanjō-bōmon, for example, restored that site's core *shinden*-style compound to its classical-era functional ideal as the exclusive and wholly dedicated venue for Ritsuryō rituals. Indeed, the documentary record confirms that the structures were used for those purposes exclusively.

In 1431, Ashikaga Yoshinori (1394–1441) abandoned Sanjō-bōmon in favor of a vastly upgraded Muromachi Palace. Although possessing a much larger and more opulent suite of *shoin*-style structures than its predecessors—including three *kaisho*, a *tsune-gosho*, and a *shō-gosho*—the new complex had at its core a cluster of *shinden*-style structures closely resembling those built by Yoshimitsu decades earlier (see Figure 5.6). It was within these that Yoshinori held, for example, the several formal celebrations (*taikyō*) that marked his successive promotions, first to the post of minister of the center and later to minister of the left.[65] Documents are explicit about how, on each of these occasions, ritual spaces were decorated in strict accordance with "noble precedent" (*kugyō girei ni shitagaubeku*).[66] In the case of the first *taikyō*, orders were given to intentionally imitate a similar investiture ceremony held in 1288 at a palace owned by the Konoe family of high aristocracy.[67]

In 1458, just prior to his promotion

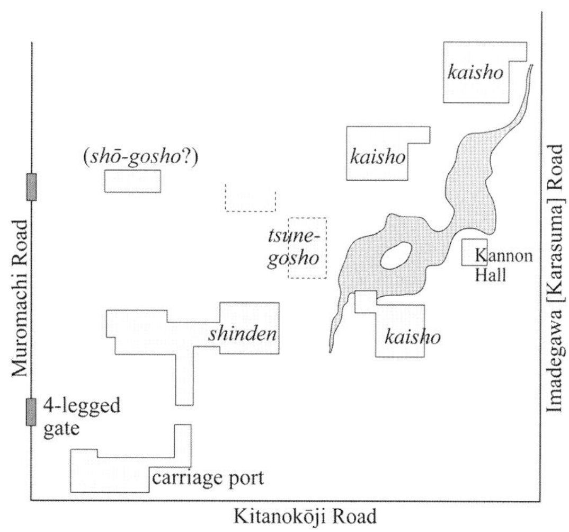

5.6 Grounds plan of Ashikaga Yoshinori's Muromachi Palace, ca. 1437. Karasuma Road was generally called "Imadegawa" north of Ichijō. After Nakamura, *Machiya no chashitsu*, 25

to minister of the center, Ashikaga Yoshimasa commissioned the production of a diagram of the Muromachi Palace as it appeared on the occasion of Yoshinori's 1432 *taikyō* (Figure 5.7). A full contingent of *shinden*-style structures is clearly visible, yet the illustration's most notable trait is how similar it is to a diagram of the Konoe residence dating from 1288 (Figure 5.8). Apparently, Yoshimasa sought to make his Muromachi Palace closely resemble that of his predecessor, Yoshinori (completed in 1431), which itself was a replica of a Konoe palace. The significance of this kind of architectural genealogy is in the identification of a conscious and sustained effort on the part of Ashikaga shoguns to adhere to traditional *shinden*-style models, irrespective of the contemporary proliferation of non-*shinden*-style structures.

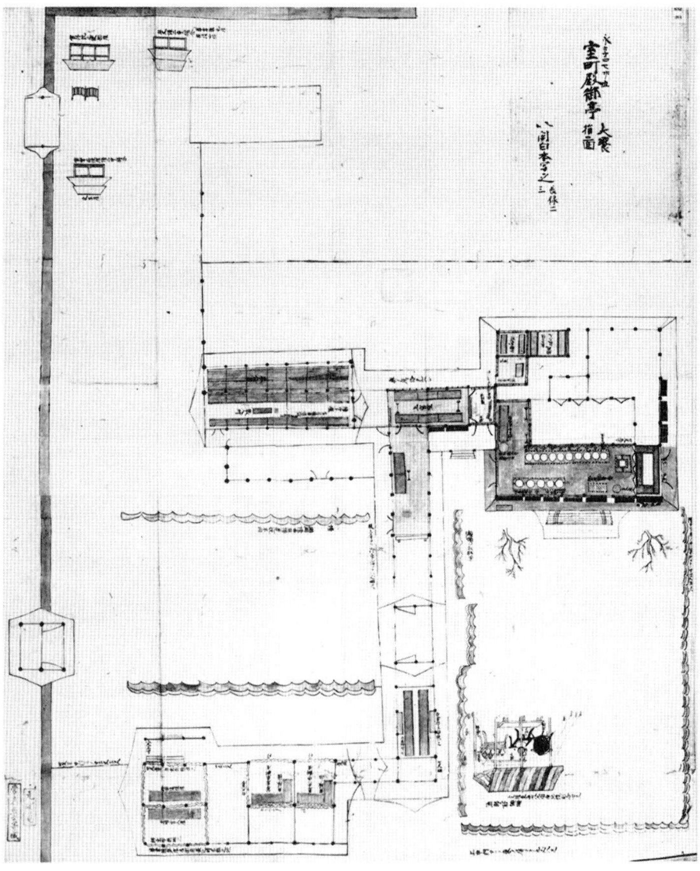

5.7. *Muromachi-dono gotei taikyō sashizu*, diagram depicting the Muromachi Palace on the occasion of Ashikaga Yoshinori's promotion to great minister of the center in 1432. National Diet Library, Tokyo

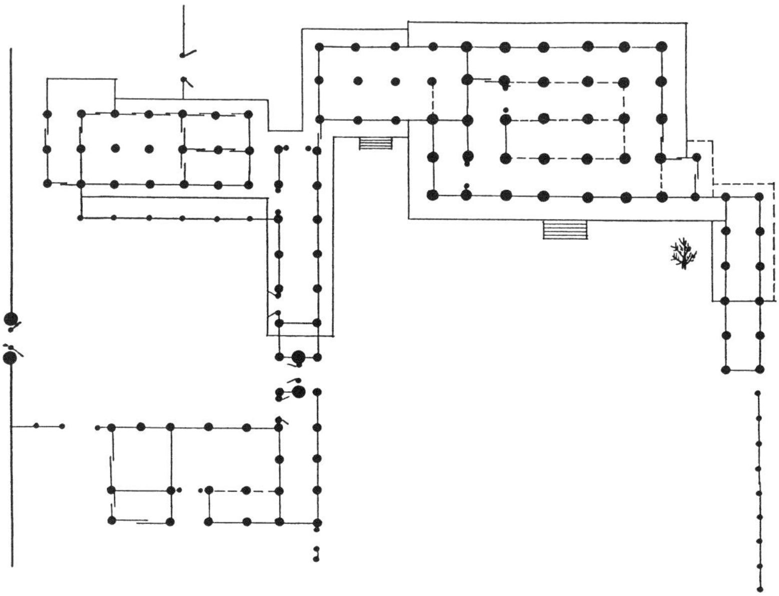

5.8. Grounds plan of the Konoe Palace in 1288. From Ōta Seiroku, *Shinden-zukuri no kenkyū*, 710

The ineluctable decline of the imperial state's efficacy (and the rituals it perpetuated) had not deterred Yoshimasa from perpetuating *shinden* style at Muromachi. Why he did so, however, is unclear. Whereas previous shoguns had used their palaces to engage in traditional rituals with some regularity, Yoshimasa did not. In fact, there is no documentary evidence he conducted any such functions at Muromachi until as late as 1464. In that year, the newly retired Emperor Gohanazono (1419–1470) paid an official visit and was ceremoniously received at the central *shinden.*[68] The next time that structure appears in texts is three years later when the outbreak of the Ōnin War caused both Gohanazono and Emperor Gotsuchimikado (1442–1500) to flee their homes and take refuge there.[69]

Despite his responsibility for the tensions that led to the outbreak of the war, Yoshimasa remained largely aloof of the conflict. In 1472, he took the tonsure and passed the post of shogun on to his son, Yoshihisa (1405–1489). The Muromachi Palace burned down four years later. Never again was an Ashikaga shogunal palace to possess a proper *shinden* or any of the standard ancillary structures. Yoshimasa retired to the Higashiyama Villa in 1483, where not a single *shinden*-style building was constructed. The Ashikaga, as a family and shogunate, never regained their former political influence.

As the frequency and perceived importance of Ritsuryō-style ritual waned during the medieval era, most *shinden*-style complexes were pared down while some were completely eliminated. In the Ashikaga shoguns, however, traditional elite architecture found a formidable ally. Not only did successive shoguns maintain the fundamental elements of *shinden* style, they went to great lengths to adhere to exceptionally retrospective models of form and function. By maintaining the style and using it to faithfully observe Ritsuryō customs, the Ashikaga continuously reaffirmed and authenticated their status as vested members of the imperial system.

In closing this section, it should be added that the use of architecture by Ashikaga leaders to "build" their legitimacy was not limited to the construction of their own palaces. To be sure, warrior patronage was instrumental in the commissioning of countless sites of imperial and religious importance both inside and outside the capital.[70] Within a decade of coming to power, for example, Takauji began advocating for the complete reconstruction of the Tsuchimikado Palace and the site's formal elevation to the status of permanent imperial palace.[71] To this end, blueprints were drawn up, a foreman appointed, and the site surveyed.[72] Construction was to be funded by taxes collected from rice-producing lands designated specifically for the purpose.[73] Although progress was delayed until 1401, when a fire made reconstruction inevitable, the clamor that preceded it bespeaks a powerful and sustained impulse on the part of successive Ashikaga leaders to provide for the material well-being of the emperor.[74] Providing a degree of amenity and perhaps luxury to a reigning sovereign had symbolic and sentimental ramifications. Creating an official imperial palace, however, meant much more. It guaranteed that the infrastructure of ritualized imperial statecraft was in place and reliably stable. Like the Fujiwara before them, who had provided so many emperors with *sato-dairi*, the Ashikaga recognized the central importance of imperial pageantry to the maintenance of the Ritsuryō hierarchy. Constructing the venues within which that hierarchy could be validated and perpetually reiterated was critical to Ashikaga success in infiltrating and eventually dominating the highest realms of authority.

Yoshimitsu's Urban Plan

The several monumental building projects commissioned by Ashikaga Yoshimitsu served to elevate the shogun's status and facilitate the long-term political success of his administration. As discussed, the reconstruction of the Imperial Palace made the shogun the primary guarantor not only of the emperor's living space but also of the most critical venues of imperial statecraft. The two temple projects of Shōkokuji and the Shōkokuji Pagoda constituted massive patronage of the Buddhist establishment. And finally, the Muromachi Palace, built in a grand, traditional style in the elite district of Kamigyō, undoubtedly elevated the profile of the warrior administration while providing the shogun himself with the formal and informal venues necessary to behave in the manner expected of a high-ranking member of the court.

A large body of scholarship has explored the styles and functions of these several sites individually. The significance of their locations, however, has only recently been examined.[75] That the historical relevance of location has been overlooked is a grave mistake in a city like premodern Kyoto, where notions of space, place, and orientation were deeply tied to pageantry as a function of status.[76] But there is an additional problem. It is assumed that because Yoshimitsu possessed the political and economic capacity to build what he wanted, anywhere he wanted, his decisions about what and where to build were arbitrary. Again, in a city such as this and with a man as political savvy as Yoshimitsu, we should assume quite the contrary. It would be more likely that the shogun carefully considered how certain structures and locations would be perceived as indicators of his status and role. A recent mapping exercise, made possible by new textual and archeological discoveries, showed precisely this, revealing that Yoshimitsu's several Kamigyō projects were not only strategically located, they were arranged according to a highly contrived matrix indicative of sweeping political objectives (Figure 5.9).[77]

It was first noticed that Shōkokuji's great Mountain Gate (*sanmon*) and the seven-storied pagoda were aligned perfectly along an east-west axis. This same axis, when extended to the west, bisected the northern half of the Muromachi property, the portion generally thought to have been used as Yoshimitsu's official residence.[78]

Drawing a north-south meridian on the map through the center of the Mountain Gate reveals yet another equally extraordinary configuration, one far too well constructed to be coincidental: Shōkokuji's Dharma Hall, Buddha Hall, and Mountain Gate were aligned along an axis that, when extended to the south, perfectly intersected the Imperial Palace's *shi-shinden*, the emperor's most important ritual structure

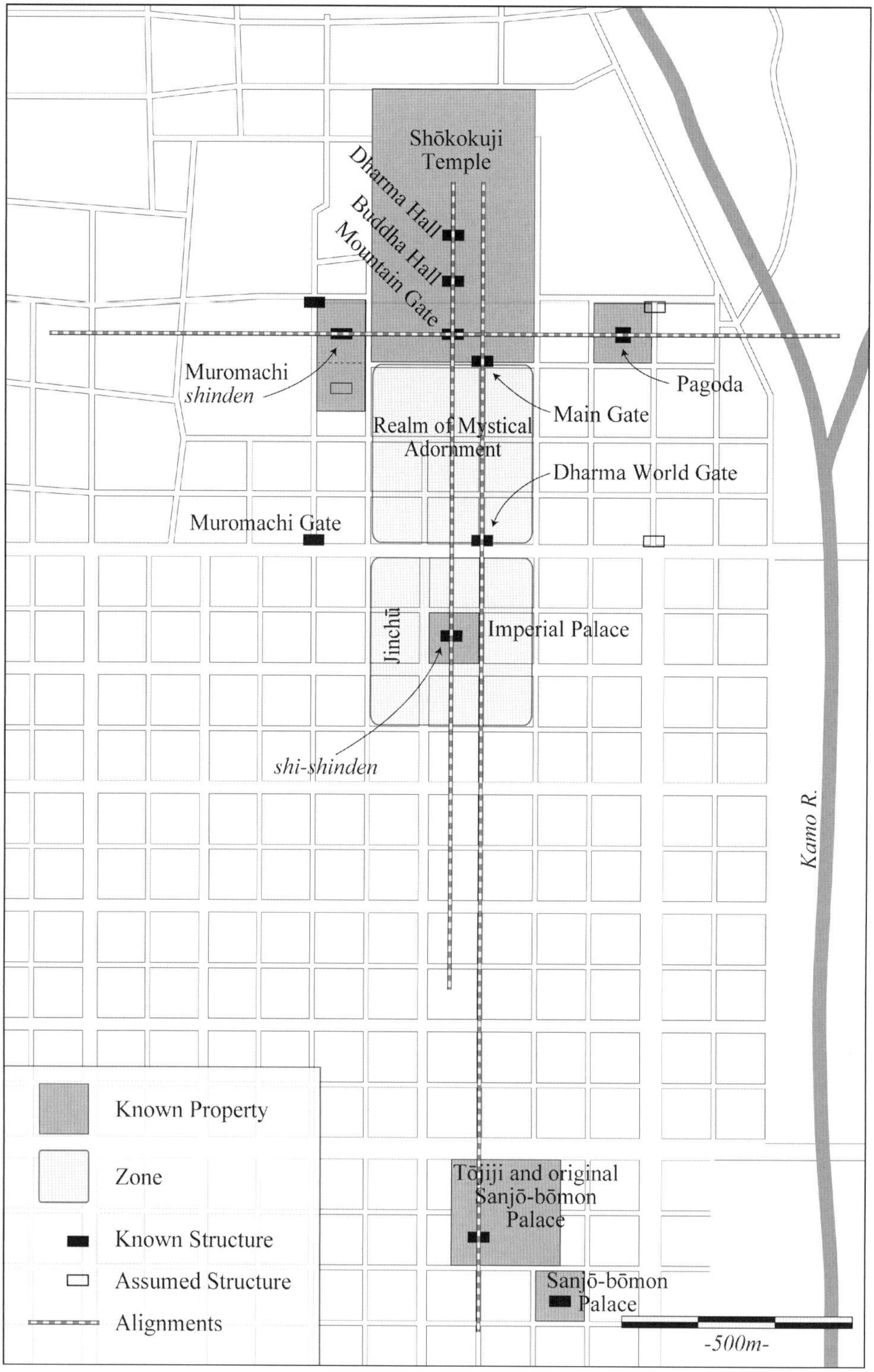

Shōkokuji Temple
Dharma Hall
Buddha Hall
Mountain Gate
Muromachi *shinden*
Pagoda
Main Gate
Realm of Mystical Adornment
Dharma World Gate
Muromachi Gate
Jinchū
Imperial Palace
shi-shinden
Kamo R.
Known Property
Zone
Known Structure
Assumed Structure
Alignments
Tōjiji and original Sanjō-bōmon Palace
Sanjō-bōmon Palace
-500m-

and site of the official throne room. Incidentally, this clean alignment of Shōkokuji and the Imperial Palace remains unchanged to this day, only slightly corrupted by several reconstructions.

Attention to the distance between the three east-west-aligned sites first mentioned leads to the discovery of a second north-south axis. Note how the Muromachi Palace's northern *shinden*, the Mountain Gate, and the seven-storied pagoda did not stand at an equal distance from each other. Rather, the Mountain Gate is offset slightly to the west of the point of equidistance. That point does, however, line up with another structure of significance: the monastery's functional outer gate, the *sōmon*, or "Main Gate." By drawing an additional north-south line through the Main Gate leading south, past the Imperial Palace, down into Shimogyō, an astonishing intersection emerges: Shōkokuji's Main Gate, the monastery's "front door," was aligned with the Ashikaga mortuary temple of Tōjiji and the original Sanjō-bōmon Palace, the first Ashikaga headquarters in Kyoto.

Textual sources frequently refer to what might best be characterized as buffer zones associated with each of Yoshimitsu's several projects.[79] The Imperial Palace, for example, was surrounded by a semiprotected area referred to as "Jinchū," meaning "within the encampment."[80] Guards were stationed at outer gates, and fires or crimes that occurred within were lamented for the danger or disrespect they posed to the palace. A similar though asymmetrical buffer was likewise attached to the Shōkokuji monastery. Bounded in the north by the monastery's Main Gate and in the south by another gate called Hokkai-mon (lit. "Dharma World Gate"), this so-called "Realm of Mystical Adornment" (Myōshōgon-iki), covered an area equivalent to a generous nine city blocks (more than thirty-two acres). Referred to in sources as an integral but not a core part of Shōkokuji, this "Realm" might be compared to the common medieval phenomena of *monzen-machi*, or "town in front of the gates," discussed in chapter 3. Similar associated spaces appear to have extended southward from both the Muromachi Palace and the seven-storied pagoda. Texts confirm that the former possessed a detached and wholly symbolic outer gate located on Ichijō Road near the intersection of Muromachi. Like the Hokkai-mon, also located along Ichijō, it too marked entry into a liminal space through which visitors would pass on their way to the respective primary structure three blocks to the north.

5.9. Map of Yoshimitsu's urban matrix, ca. 1400.

Although a similar detached gate for the pagoda has not yet been discovered, the robust symmetry of the overall plan strongly suggests one stood near the intersection of Ichijō and Higashikyōgoku. Had there actually been such a gate, the lining up of the three symbolic and detached egresses along Ichijō, Heian-kyo's northern boundary, stands as further evidence of Yoshimitsu's sensitivity toward the old city's spatial customs. While he relegated his warrior headquarters and major temple projects to the capital's outskirts, symbolic gateways leading to each provided perfect continuity connecting the latter to the former. Not only were Yoshimitsu's projects carefully arranged vis-à-vis each other, their locations took into account the classical city at a time when we might otherwise have expected such considerations to be long gone.

Interpreting Yoshimitsu's urban plan is difficult because many integral elements of the plan itself are likely buried under the modern cityscape. Indeed, much of the picture is yet to be revealed. Nevertheless, the evidence already uncovered makes it possible to propose that Yoshimitsu saw himself as a political unifier intent upon reversing the trend toward ever greater degrees of fragmentation that characterized the medieval status quo. Until his time, power in the capital was largely a matter of contest between the imperial court, various private interests (aristocratic and warrior alike), and each of the several powerful Buddhist sects. Throughout much of his career, even the imperial institution itself had remained divided. The urban plan introduced here suggests that Yoshimitsu sought to reimagine Kyoto as an integrated whole within which each of the powerful bodies of interest had a clearly defined place. The physical alignment of buildings reflected a more political, even philosophical, alignment of institutions that the hegemon was engineering through his strategic engagement in the workings of each. Yoshimitsu was, after all, not just shogun, the supreme leader of the military regime, he also became grand chancellor of state, the highest-ranking member of the imperial court. Not merely did he house, patronize, and protect the emperor, he negotiated the reunification of the imperial lineages in 1392, thus ending the civil war that had divided the institution for more than half a century. Besides being the pre-eminent patron of the Shōkokuji Pagoda when that structure was ceremoniously dedicated in 1399, he served as chief witness in the formal ritual, a role customarily filled by a cloistered prince acting in the guise of a Shingon priest. And finally, upon retirement, Yoshimitsu took the tonsure and became (at least ostensibly) a Zen priest affiliated most closely with the monastic community based at Shōkokuji.

Although profoundly different from its classical counterpart, medieval Kyoto under Yoshimitsu resembled Heian-kyō in one critical way: The city was once again a unified, largely symmetrical urban matrix, centered on the imperial palace. This urban plan can be easily read as a homology for the way this remarkable historical figure succeeded in unifying the capital's several bodies of authority. Yoshimitsu not only defined the interrelationships between these bodies—physically and politically—he effected a degree of unification among them. Besides the city itself, he was, after all, the one thing they all had in common.

Conclusion

The eventual success of Yoshimitsu and his immediate successors in dominating both the military and imperial realms of politics resulted in the creation of a stronger and more effective central governing apparatus. Even the challenges presented by religious establishments decreased leading up to the early fifteenth century, due in part to growing Ashikaga control over sectarian hierarchies through the strategic placement of shogunal offspring into positions of temple leadership.[81] Before becoming the eighth shogun in 1428, for example, Ashikaga Yoshinori himself had attained the lofty post of supreme abbot (*zasu*) of the Tendai sect on Mount Hiei. While the Ashikaga are well known for delegating authority over the provinces to their appointed deputies (*shugo*), the kind of full-spectrum dominance they came to enjoy in and around Kyoto resulted in a political and urban landscape more unified and centralized than it had been since perhaps the eighth-century reign of Emperor Kanmu.

Within this context, there was a further evolution in the discourse of capital space. Two centuries earlier, the distinction between Rakuchū and Rakugai had served to insulate a core portion of the city and assert the continued viability of capital institutions. In the late fourteenth century, however, as power became increasingly consolidated, the issue of exclusion became less relevant. No longer was it necessary to clearly define spheres of autonomy and jurisdiction in an environment in which the shogunate—now firmly based in Kyoto and functioning in unison with the imperial and religious establishments—had become the undisputed hegemon both within the capital and beyond. Such a circumstance helps explain why, from about the last decade of the fourteenth century, a wide variety of official documents began referring to the areas of Rakuchū and Rakugai as if in the same breath. Combined into a single compound word, "Rakuchū-Rakugai" became the most commonly used signifier for the capital basin, a broad area where taxes, policies, and central governance applied (more or less) uniformly.[82]

The rise of shogunal power had been made possible, in part, by the Ashikaga's demonstrated respect for traditional capital norms. After all, protecting the capital and its institutions was, ostensibly, the military regime's raison d'etre. Early on, such protection meant upholding the principles of capital exclusion by defending Rakuchū from the many and various invaders it faced, including rioting sectarians, rebellious warriors, and even rival claimants to the throne. Ashikaga shoguns went so far as to limit their own presence and prerogatives within Kyoto. Once the various threats were eliminated, however, capital institutions could return to an earlier status whereby they exercised direct control over an area that, although not the entire country, was much broader than the narrow confines of Rakuchū. The composition of capital institutions, however, had changed profoundly in the interim. Endowed with imperial ranks and posts as well as with the infrastructure necessary to engage in ritualized pageantry, the leaders of the warrior regime had infiltrated and co-opted the statutory state. In sum, Ashikaga shoguns had come to engender "capital authority" and in that capacity had greatly consolidated and expanded "Kyoto's" political reach.

6

Warring States Kyoto

Erasing the Classical City

THE SHŌKOKUJI PAGODA was destroyed by a lightning strike in the summer of 1403 and was never rebuilt at the original site.[1] Yoshimitsu died suddenly and suspiciously in 1408, and his successor, Yoshimochi, choreographed a triumphant return to Sanjō-bōmon followed by a dramatic and public demolition of Muromachi. In sum, within a few short years of Yoshimitsu's death, the neat alignment of disparate complexes that the former shogun had engineered over a lifetime had almost completely disappeared.

The physical breakdown reflected a parallel political disintegration caused in part by Yoshimochi's preoccupation with repudiating his father's legacy, not least of which included decoupling warrior and imperial institutions while distancing his administration from temple engagement.[2] In hindsight, Yoshimochi was a deeply flawed and distracted leader, haunted by the towering image of his father and harassed by growing challenges from the shogunate's regional officers. His successor, Yoshinori, was much more effective, governing in a style reminiscent of Yoshimitsu, although with a more autocratic penchant. He too, however, was beleaguered by growing problems in the provinces caused by struggles within and among vassal clans as well as peasant uprisings. The former weakened the solidarity of warrior government while the latter jeopardized a critical source of tax revenue. Yoshinori, in what is a supreme example of how fragmented shogunal rule had become (and in particular how disgruntled some were by his autocratic style), was assassinated by one of his own vassals in 1441. His seven-year-old son, Yoshikatsu (1434–1443) succeeded him, but he too died ignominiously after a fall from a horse only eight months later. Following that, the post of shogun remained vacant until 1447 when Yoshimasa, Yoshinori's second son, was chosen by secret ballot. Plagued by domestic strife and an apparent lack of political ambition, Yoshimasa was a weak leader whose lack of interest in public affairs—save those related to the gentle arts—had earned him the contempt of many prominent military houses. Yoshimasa was a politically detached aesthete, a role for which he was scorned in his own time and exalted in ours.[3]

A shogunal succession dispute that emerged in the twilight of Yoshimasa's career served as a pretext for rival warrior families to settle their differences through armed engagement. In the winter of 1467, armies aligned with the houses of Hosokawa and Yamana respectively clashed in the wooded area north of Shōkokuji, near Goryō Shrine. The ensuing conflict, which came to be called the Ōnin War after the imperial era name during which it started, raged in and around Kyoto for eleven years, devastating the capital and its political institutions. When organized fighting ended in stalemate in 1477, the shogunate and imperial court were both badly weakened. Continued unrest was inevitable. Besides the state of general lawlessness, conditions in Kyoto were exacerbated by two successive waves of large-scale violence: first during a period of debtors' uprisings around 1487 and then in the decade after 1527 when the city was embroiled in the wars between two rival shogunates and then a popular religious uprising lead by the Hokke or "Lotus" sect. The century following Ōnin was a time of such widespread political unrest and sustained conflict that historians refer to it as the Age of Warring States (1467–1580s). The Ashikaga shogunate, although surviving in name and titles until 1573, never regained its influence after Ōnin and the real-world efficacy of the emperor and imperial court dropped to an all-time low.

The dramatic physical and social changes that took place in Kyoto during the Age of Warring States have been studied extensively.[4] While the findings of earlier research are echoed strongly in this chapter, the discussion here glosses over the narrative of social and political rupture to focus instead on how the violence, fires, and lawlessness of the age conspired to decisively sever the tendrils—tenuous and sometimes imaginary—that anchored Kyoto to its classical past. Ōnin and the conflicts that followed destroyed the urban grid and key venues of aristocratic pageantry. *Shinden* style and the activities it facilitated became unsustainable, while an influx of warriors and temples erased all traditional notions about capital exclusivity. Commoners began buying, selling, and controlling land within a city whose boundaries became defined by walls and moats instead of laws and customs. Even burial within Kyoto, which had been considered taboo for its polluting effects, became accepted. Heian-kyō and all that the city was meant to represent—political centralization, public authority, functional purity, rationality, sacral and ritualized rule—was finally and utterly wiped away during the fifteenth and sixteenth centuries.

Urban changes reflected the disintegration of the bonds that had long tied public authority to private power. Political instability robbed the elite of their access to landed wealth and other forms of real-world influence. At the same time, the destruction of Kyoto deprived them of the infrastructure that had, until then, enabled them to engage in the prescribed repertoire of formal processions, annual observances, and religious ceremonies. The disappearance of *shinden*-style palaces and a cityscape that had been capable of facilitating Ritsuryō rituals left the traditional elite bereft of the infrastructure needed to nourish the idea that the statutory state still mattered. Under the circumstances, it was the old guard that was most adversely affected, those for whom rituals, ranks, and hereditary rights remained their primary, if not only, source of status and negotiable influence. The emperor and most members of the civil aristocracy had been in this category for centuries. After Ōnin, however, so too were the Ashikaga shoguns. With the final and irrevocable evisceration of classical ideas, the old order was all but finished. It is no coincidence that the individual who eventually began the process of national unification in the mid-sixteenth century, Oda Nobunaga (1532–1582), famously (and uniquely in premodern Japan) spurned public ranks and posts. To him, they no longer served as a meaningful pathway to orthodox legitimacy. And tellingly, when Nobunaga began the process of rebuilding Kyoto in the 1560s, his most important project, a castle fortress, in no way reflected the city's architectural heritage.

Losing the Venues of Classical Ritual

The documentary record of destruction and depopulation during the decade following 1467 paints a dire picture of urban devastation. Here are several representative examples:

> Holding aged parents in their arms, pulling along wives and children behind them, the townspeople fled the city in a roar of cries. And none was left to fight the blaze. The fires burned over one hundred blocks, from Nijō in the south to Goryō in the north, from Ōdoneri in the west to Muromachi in the east. About 30,000 residences—of aristocrats, military men, great and small alike—went up in flames. Everything is now ruined.[5]

> Across our charred land, all human traces have been extinguished. For blocks on end, birds are the sole sign of life.[6]

> Like hornets' nests, the sanctuaries of the eastern and western hills have all been burned and crushed.[7]

> The Capital of Flowers of myriad ages is now a lair of foxes and wolves.[8]

Figure 6.1 shows the extent of fire damage sustained during the Ōnin years. Over the course of the conflict, the elite district of Kamigyō was razed several times. Data for Shimogyō is conjectural due to a lack of documentation, although it is possible that that part of the city was purposefully spared. Not only was it bereft of the homes of key political figures, its commoners played a critical role in the war effort as the providers of food and fighting implements to armies operating in the area.[9]

Following the negotiation of a cease-fire in 1477, the Ashikaga shogunate spearheaded a large-scale effort to rebuild the city's most important venues of statecraft, including the Imperial Palace, the Muromachi Palace, and many of the homes of the civil aristocracy. They even attempted to reconstruct the urban grid, which had been compromised through the creation of an elaborate network of walls and moats.[10] Despite initial progress, long-term reconstruction efforts were hampered by the general state of political disorder and lawlessness. Financial woes were also a large problem. The emperor and aristocracy, as well as the shogunate itself, were finding it difficult to draw income from provincial estates, which fell increasingly under the control of renegade warlords. The Imperial Palace was partially restored around 1479, but we have no records of substantial repairs taking place after a succession of fires, floods, fighting, arson, and burglary visited the site over the next several decades.[11] So badly maintained was the Imperial

6.1. Map of fire damage during the Ōnin War (1467–1477), indicated with shaded areas and dots for major temples, shrines, or palaces destroyed.

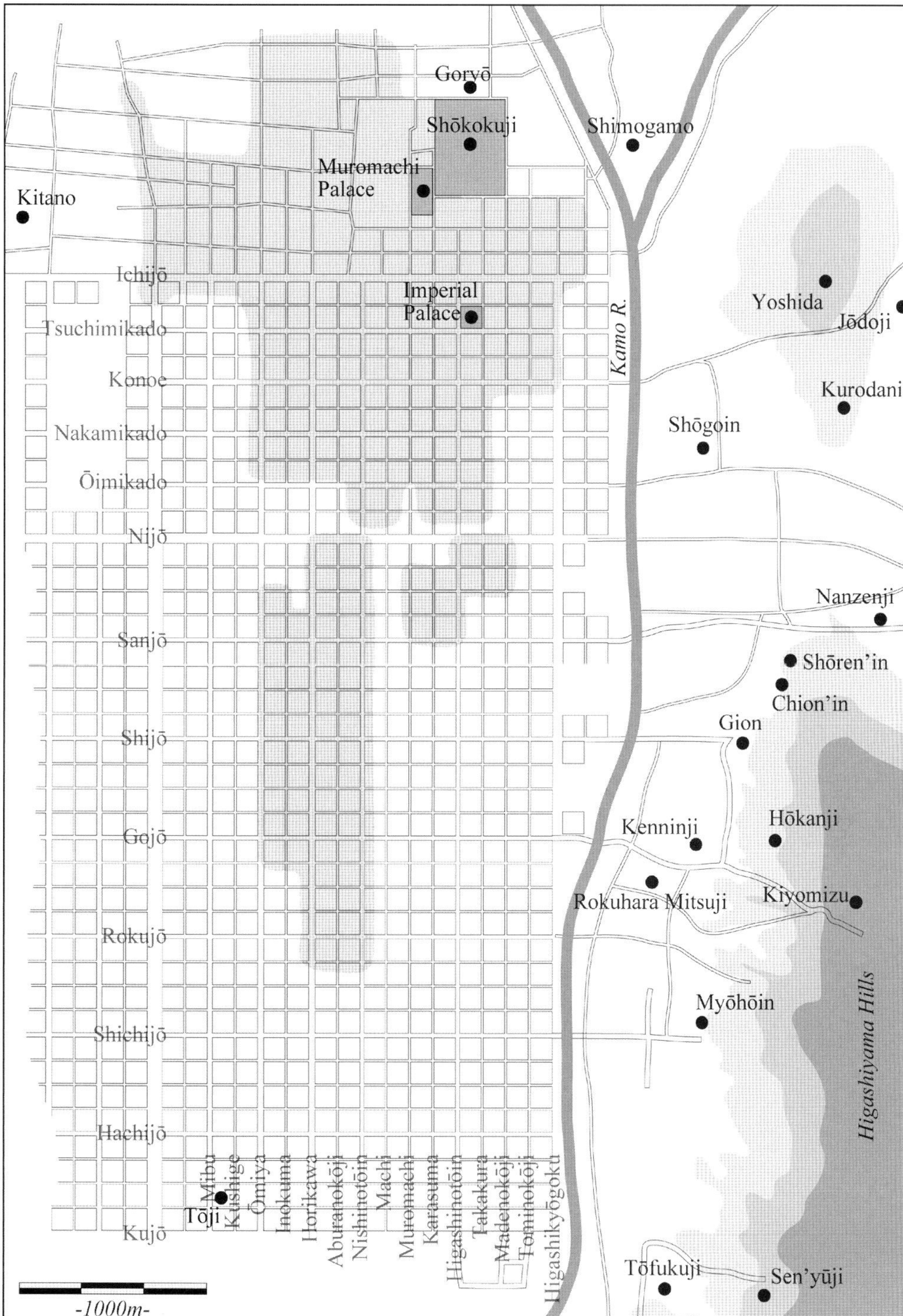
Goryō
Shōkokuji
Shimogamo
Muromachi Palace
Kitano
Ichijō
Imperial Palace
Kamo R.
Yoshida
Jōdoji
Tsuchimikado
Konoe
Kurodani
Shōgoin
Nakamikado
Ōimikado
Nijō
Nanzenji
Sanjō
Shōren'in
Chion'in
Gion
Shijō
Kenninji
Hōkanji
Gojō
Rokuhara Mitsuji
Kiyomizu
Rokujō
Myōhōin
Shichijō
Higashiyama Hills
Hachijō
Mibu
Kushige
Ōmiya
Inokuma
Horikawa
Aburanokōji
Nishinotōin
Machi
Muromachi
Karasuma
Higashinotōin
Takakura
Madenokōji
Tominokōji
Higashikyōgoku
Tōji
Kujō
Tōfukuji
Sen'yūji
-1000m-

Palace that one contemporary diarist deemed it "indistinguishable from commoner dwellings."[12] João Rodrigues, a Christian missionary who arrived in Japan in 1577, had this to say about Kyoto's venues of traditional authority:

> The palaces of the king and the *kuge* were wretched and made of old pine wood, while the walls were constructed of pine planks. The outward life of the *kuge* was extremely wretched and poor. The walls surrounding the king's palace were made of wood covered with reeds and clay, and were very old and dilapidated. Everything was left open and abandoned without any guards, and anyone who so desired could enter the courtyards right up to the royal palace without anybody stopping him, as we ourselves did to look around.[13]

The Muromachi Palace was partially rebuilt in 1479, yet the frequency of subsequent reconstructions suggests the site was either subjected to virtually continuous assault or that it was never rebuilt very well in the first place, or both. In 1527, Muromachi was abandoned as the shogun Yoshiharu (1511–1550) took refuge in Shōkokuji, the first of many examples of a wartime shogun either sheltering in fortified temples or remaining outside the city altogether. Several subsequent attempts were made to re-establish a sustained shogunal presence within Kyoto, but each was short-lived. In 1542, Yoshiharu moved into a restored palace, although he and his son, the future shogun Yoshiteru (1536–1565), had moved back into fortified temples by 1547 before moving yet again into outlying castles. A new shogunal headquarters was built in 1560, only to be destroyed in an attack five years later.[14] After that, a dedicated shogunal headquarters was not created in Kyoto until 1569.[15] Such locational instability demonstrates political and financial weakness, as well as the sustained threat of extreme violence. As we shall see, the inability to maintain a formal residence in the capital was not merely symptomatic. It hindered the shogun's ability to foster and regularly renew a connection with the statutory state.

Members of the court fared no better than the emperor and shogun. Their homes were likewise destroyed while many took refuge outside the city. When they finally returned, reconstruction was complicated by continued unrest, a lack of funds, and in some cases the presence of squatters who stubbornly occupied the ruins of their former palaces.[16] The shogunate's initial postwar reconstruction plan led to mass evictions of commoners and the successful construction of several Kamigyō palaces belonging to the Saionji, Kajūji, Takakura, and other aristocratic families. The documentary record from successive decades, however, suggests that progress was generally short-lived and, even where successful, limited in scope. Nobleman Kanroji Chikanaga (1425–1500), for example, was able to construct a palace substantial enough to be sought after by peers who wanted to borrow it to conduct certain rituals. Such was the case in 1488, when Ichijō Fuyuyoshi (1464–1514) held a *haiga* there to formally mark his promotion to the post of interior minister.[17] Indicative, however, of just how poor conditions were and how desperate the aristocracy had become, Chikanaga himself described his new abode with marked disparagement:

> The new structure has the *appearance* of a palace, yet it [certainly] is not. It's merely halfway completed. There's no gate and it's located at the end of a back alley. [The entry is so far back and the alley so narrow that] it's not even possible for me to board a carriage. That's why I lease a house on Ōgimachi [author's emphasis].[18]

Ichijō Fuyuyoshi was not alone in his need to borrow the homes of his peers. Yamashina Tokitsugu (1507–1579) insisted upon conducting formal meetings at the Kamigyō residence of a Lord Nakamikado. Otherwise, he refused meetings altogether while attempting to keep up appearances (and, presumably, defensive capacity) by spending what little money he had on maintaining the walls surrounding his house rather than patch a leaky roof.[19] Despite his best efforts, we know that Tokitsugu and at least several of his aristocratic colleagues ended up living in shacks built within the grounds of the Imperial Palace.[20] The architectural footprint of the traditional elite, as well as that of their commoner counterparts, was so profoundly eroded during the Age of Warring States that the poet Sōchō was moved to write the following in 1526:

> As I looked out over the city, I saw not one in ten of the houses that had been there formerly, either rich or poor. The sight of tilled fields around farmhouses, with the Imperial Palace in the midst of summer barley, was too much for words.[21]

When discussing the erosion of the courtly presence in wartime Kyoto, Mary Elizabeth Berry explained that the "destruction of the city signified . . . the destruction of civility and, one suspects, of identity itself." To the traditional elite, she argued, buildings represented order, secure social places, and coherent lives. The despair so clearly evident in their accounts "surely derived most acutely from fears of their own physical and social effacement."[22] Although accurate, Berry's wording can be easily misunderstood to mean that the sorry plight of the elite boiled down to a profound sense of humiliation borne of poverty and material privation. While humiliation was undoubtedly relevant, the old guard was haunted by a far more concrete and politically consequential affliction. Their inability to maintain *shinden*-style palaces, those built and decorated to meet certain status-specific prescriptions, meant the aristocracy were left incapable of properly engaging in official rites, rituals, and formalized activities. The efforts by some aristocrats to borrow the homes of their colleagues appear in hindsight to be feeble attempts to maintain a semblance of official conduct. Even Kanroji Chikanaga, who was apparently better off than most, was reticent about calling his own residence a "palace" at all. As Rodrigues wrote with perhaps more insight than he realized, war had indeed devastated the "outward life" of the aristocracy, a life that relied more than anything upon formalized ceremony and the scripted rituals of public pageantry.

The documentary record is replete with accounts of aristocrats lamenting their inability to conduct key public rituals.[23] The imperial house itself was apparently so bereft of funds it was unable to hold even the most essential ceremonies, including imperial enthronements and interments. The burial of Emperor Gotsuchimikado (1442–1500) was delayed forty-three days, while the enthronements of emperors Gokashiwabara (r. 1500–1526) and Gonara (r. 1526–1557) were postponed a staggering twenty-two and ten years respectively. When in 1502 the court requested help from warrior families to pay for Gokashiwabara's enthronement, not only did Hosokawa Masamoto (1466–1507) dismiss the appeal, the warlord's response called into question the very necessities of imperial government and ritual themselves:

> The prime minister is good for nothing. . . . For that matter, things like imperial posts and ranks are worthless. So what if someone gets a promotion? Even if you tell everyone about it, it has no effect. I shall make this statement to the throne:

> "The great enthronement ceremony at the Imperial Palace is worthless. Even if it *is* held, the common people will not know the king is king; and even if it is *not* held, I will know the king is king. All of the big ceremonies are, until the end of days, inappropriate" [author's emphasis].[24]

The failure to hold a formal enthronement ceremony kept Gokashiwabara from engaging in public events. Writing about royal banquets in 1506, nobleman Nakamikado Nobutane (1442–1525) decried the "abjection of imperial rituals" before, a few years later, explaining the cloistering effect of their abeyance:

> The emperor has not gone out [to participate in new year events] at all because his enthronement ceremony has not yet been held. The blinds are down. Even though he has been on the throne for seventeen years, [the ceremony has] not been held because there are not the funds. Why, oh why? This is leading to the end of days.[25]

Equating the abeyance of imperial rituals with the "end of days" is a common, though nebulous, refrain in noble diaries from the period. Yamashina Tokitsugu is more explicit about the relationship between ritual and the survival of his kind. After attending a fire festival (*sagichō*) in the first month of 1530, he was "heartbroken" by the palace's preparation of a meager twenty-six ritual pyres, far fewer than precedent dictated. To Tokitsugu, the lackluster showing was much more than mere anticlimax. Indeed, it signaled the "ruin of the aristocracy."[26]

With almost universal consistency, contemporary diarists blame a lack of funds for the problem. What they leave unexplained, however, is precisely what the funds were needed for. Following strict rules of status-based comportment and precedent was expensive. It required the procurement of numerous objects as well as the employment of many people. On the occasion of a promotion celebration, for example, an aristocrat of the fifth rank or above would be obliged to replace his formal wardrobes and procure for his guests sumptuous food, drink, and take-home gifts. To make the day's activities go smoothly, he would conscript a small army of minor officials, gardeners, attendants, craftsmen, cooks, menials, musicians, and chanters. Similar things would be required of an emperor preparing to be enthroned, in addition to a new oxcart with richly embroidered blinds. But for all this, by far the most expensive aspect of public events held by members of the imperial hierarchy would have been the manufacture, refurbishment, and decoration of the architectural environment.

Court rituals required specific structural and decorative elements that were more than merely fine. Many had to accord with prescriptions that governed comportment as a function of status. Recall, for example, that the styles of roofing tiles and walls, *tatami* edgings and entry gates (as well as where those gates were located), were all dictated by an aristocrat's formal status. Promotion to a higher court rank could easily necessitate a substantial refurbishment or replacement of many of these fixtures. For an enthronement, the Imperial Palace would gain a new raised dais (the Japanese equivalent of a "throne") and sleeping chamber. Paper doors, folding screens, and curtains would be meticulously mended, while the cypress bark tiles of the central palace structure, the *shi-shinden*, would also likely be replaced.

Needless to say, during wartime it became impossible for the traditional elite to maintain their palaces in conditions suitable to the continuation of rituals according to previous standards. Plagued by violence, lawlessness, and financial ruin, most were probably not even able to ensure that their respective residences had a central *shinden*, the most basic structural element of a *shinden*-style palace. When we read in the documentary record, therefore, of the dilapidation of the Imperial Palace, aristocrats living in shacks, or the disappearance of the shogun's headquarters, we are reading not merely of an effacement borne of disgrace. We are witnessing the disappearance of the infrastructure of classical pageantry. While the real-world efficacy of the emperor and statutory state had long been in decline, the destruction of Kyoto in the fifteenth century meant the loss of their means of asserting symbolic efficacy as well. War had rendered the traditional elite incapable of engaging in those acts of public pageantry that for centuries had served to validate and renew their status as members of the imperial hierarchy.

Losing the Grid and Its Taboos

Kyoto's urban grid, a perpetual reminder of the city's classical origins, was likewise destroyed during the Age of Warring States. By the time a measure of stability had returned following Ōnin, the populated portion of the city had contracted into two small and densely packed islands of fortified urbanization roughly corresponding to the most developed portions of Kamigyō and Shimogyō.[27] Connected by the singular artery of Muromachi Road and surrounded by a patchwork of walls, moats, and guardhouses, these small enclaves served as makeshift fortresses within which residents sought to secure a level of stability, safety, and commercial viability despite the violence and lawlessness of the age (see Figure 6.2). Politically, they organized into "neighborhood federations" (*chō-gumi*) through which they engaged in corporate defense and self-government.[28] They built internal defense apparatuses, carving up blocks and obstructing roads at seemingly random locations and angles. The creation of entirely new lanes and alleys, called "*zushi*," maximized land use while further eroding those few portions of the original grid that had remained. The largest, most populated portion of postwar Kamigyō stood north of Ichijō. Except for a small area around the Imperial Palace itself, this district, which had long been considered the center of elite Kyoto society, had come to exist almost entirely outside the boundaries of the original capital grid.

While most of the capital basin outside of Kamigyō and Shimogyō had been reduced to a virtual wasteland, small yet resilient islands of development existed in and around the many temples and shrines that had adapted to wartime conditions. Most of the old religious institutions that stood in the hills and plains surrounding the city survived, albeit in smaller and more fortified states. Closer to the city's core—in a formation roughly surrounding Shimogyō—stood twenty-one temples affiliated with the Hokke sect of Nichiren Buddhism. While many of these temples got their starts in the prewar city, it was not until the post-Ōnin era that they began to thrive by virtue of growing mass appeal as well as the absence of political capacity (and will) to exclude them.[29] Supported primarily by the patronage of wealthy Shimogyō commoners, the so-called "twenty-one headquarter temples" of the Hokke sect eventually grew in physical size and political influence to become the physical and philosophical nuclei of a broadly popular social movement that controlled Kyoto from 1532 to 1536.[30] The social and political implications of Hokke's postwar rise have been explored fully in earlier studies. Here, let us consider how the sect's success in establishing large sectarian temples within the old city signaled the nullification of classical proscriptions on temple construction.

In 1494, imperial regent Kujō Hisatsune (1469–1530) wrote with utter dismay about the construction of Hokke temples within Kyoto:

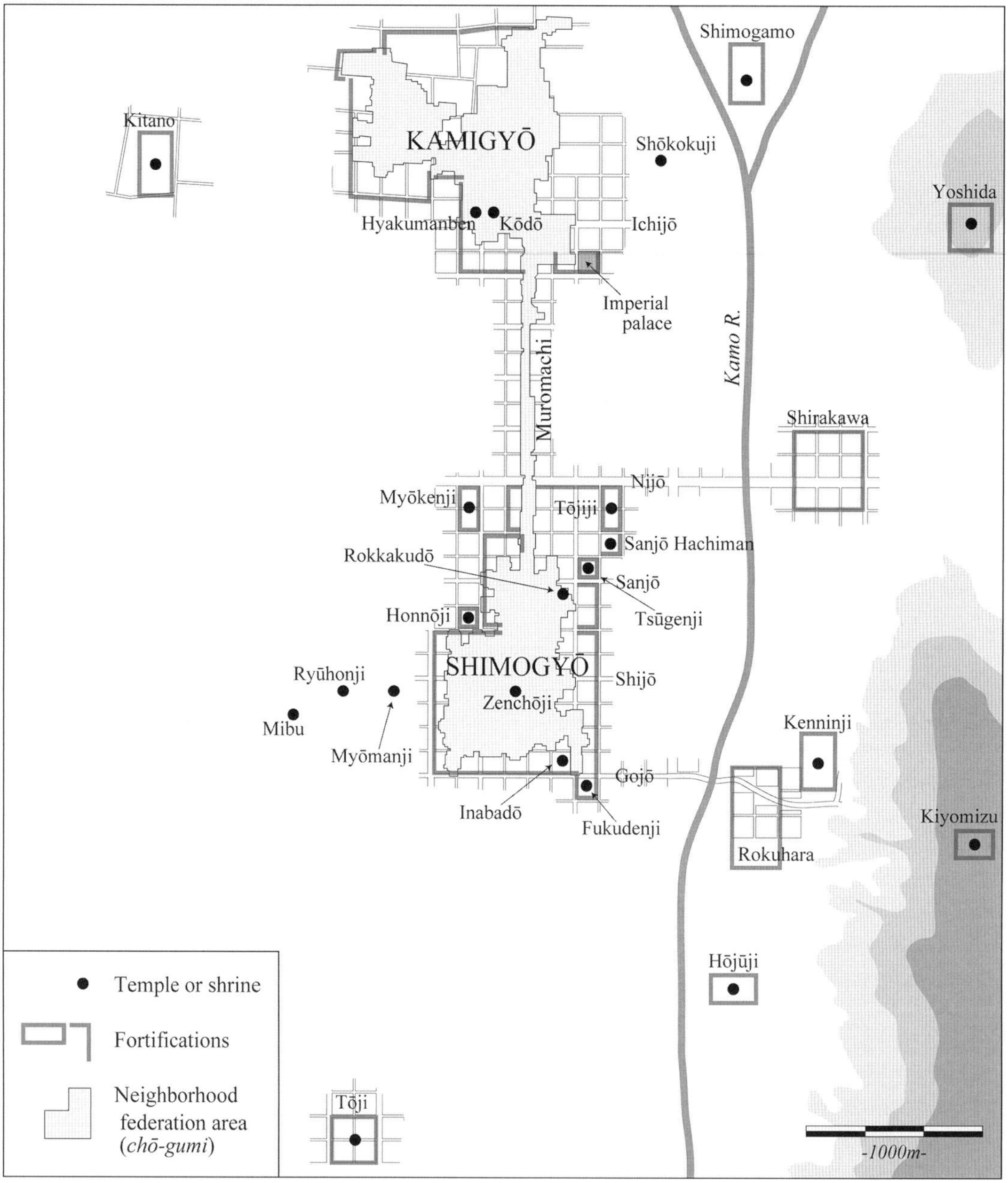
Shimogamo
Kitano
KAMIGYŌ
Shōkokuji
Yoshida
Hyakumanben
Kōdō
Ichijō
Imperial palace
Kamo R.
Muromachi
Shirakawa
Nijō
Myōkenji
Tōjiji
Sanjō Hachiman
Rokkakudō
Sanjō
Tsūgenji
Honnōji
SHIMOGYŌ
Shijō
Ryūhonji
Zenchōji
Mibu
Myōmanji
Kenninji
Gojō
Inabadō
Fukudenji
Kiyomizu
Rokuhara
Hōjūji
Temple or shrine
Fortifications
Neighborhood federation area (chō-gumi)
Tōji
-1000m-

> Temple construction was formerly prohibited east of Ōmiya Road. Nevertheless, since the end of the [Ōnin-] Bunmei War, the capital (*kyōchū*) is replete with Hokke temples. The reason for this eludes me.[31]

Hisatsune's mention of Ōmiya is significant because it shows a sustained sensitivity about the western boundary of Rakuchū, that portion of the capital the elite had been actively trying to insulate from temple and warrior influence since at least the thirteenth century.[32] Whether or not there had been a concerted effort to exclude temples following Ōnin is unknown. An entry from a chronicle written a few decades later, however, suggests that even if such an effort had been made, it had failed:

> Around the beginning of the Tenbun era [1532–1555], the Hokke sect was thriving in Kyoto. Each month would see the construction of two or three new temples. The capital was a town all chanting the Lotus sutra.[33]

The success of an upstart sect such as the Hokke, which had been started a mere two centuries earlier, attracted the scorn of the older Buddhist establishment. Their leaders protested Hokke's rise through numerous formal and informal appeals to civil and military authorities.[34] The Tendai monks of Enryakuji eventually spearheaded the violent campaign that crushed the Hokke army and led to the destruction of their temples and exile of their leaders from the region in 1536. Throughout the protracted ordeal, as far as we know from the extant documentary record, anti-Hokke rhetoric never drew on the discourse of capital exclusion. Perhaps the omission signaled a fundamental change indicative of the collapse of state institutions and traditional customs. Or maybe the monks of Enryakuji simply did not want to remind authorities of a rule that they themselves had long sought to subvert. Whatever the case, by about the mid-sixteenth century the classical taboo against temples had clearly become inconsequential as inner-city temples such as Kōdō (Seiganji), Rokkakudō (Chōhōji), Zenchōji, and Hyakumanben (Chionji) flourished.[35] The Jesuit missionary Louis Frois visited Hyakumanben in 1565 (Figure 6.3). His account illustrates that wartime Kyoto, for all its strife, was a place full of life and energy:

6.2. Map of post–Ōnin War Kyoto basin, ca. 1530. Tenryūji (not pictured) was also a fortified compound.

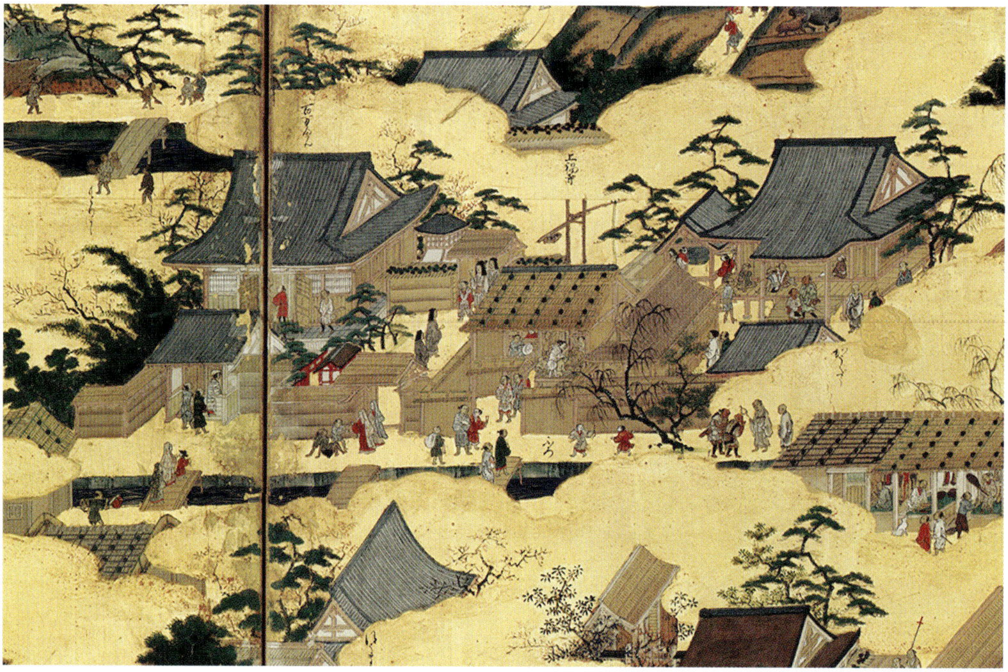

6.3. Hyakumanben (Chionji Temple) area, including public bath (*furo*), in the Uesugi version of *Rakuchū-rakugai-zu byōbu.* Courtesy of Uesugi Museum, Yonezawa

> At night in this neighborhood, the residents lock the gates at either end of the street. The area abounds with all manner of professional craftsmen, including some who weave silk and damask, and others who produce fans. The most popular destination for religious devotion in this neighborhood is a temple dedicated to the Buddha Amida called Hyakumanben, located in the middle of the various shops which crowd around it. At the end of each day, especially around dusk, the various craftsmen close their shops and, free from their work, go en masse to the temple to donate alms and pray to its idols. Men and women demonstrate their devotion by taking a rosary in hand and, while intoning the "Namu Amida Butsu," form a line and pace quickly around the exterior of the hall, bowing their heads and praying each time they pass before the entrance of the idol's hall.[36]

Eventually, Hokke temples were allowed to return to Kyoto in 1542, after which they rebuilt and again thrived. So successful were they that the most well fortified among them frequently served as de facto Kyoto headquarters for such key warlords as Oda Nobunaga and Toyotomi Hideyoshi (1537–1598) during the third quarter of the century.[37] Nobunaga, in fact, was in residence at the Hokke temple of Honnōji when he was ambushed and assassinated in the summer of 1582. By that time, temples had become a permanent fixture of Kyoto's urban landscape. The classical-era taboo had been well and truly swept away. As we shall see in the next chapter, there was to be one more occasion when authorities set policy regarding the location of temples in Kyoto. In that case, however, the guiding principle was related to social reorganization and defensive functionality, not classical ideas about exclusion.

The introduction of temples to the urban landscape shows that it was no longer possible or practical for authorities to think in terms of abstract boundaries that might govern who or what entered the old city. The much more narrow boundaries of fortified Kamigyō and Shimogyō were probably difficult enough to insulate. Under the circumstances, fighting men of the meanest origins and with absolutely no formal status became regular fixtures in wartime Kyoto. Frequently denounced as the worst perpetrators of arson, larceny, and murder, these so-called "Kyoto foot soldiers" (*kyōchū ashigaru*) not only occupied land within the city formerly considered off limits to men of their ilk, their leaders openly engaged in recruitment among the Kyoto townspeople.[38]

Perhaps it was the mixture of temples, warriors, and pervasive violence that led to the eventual acceptance of burial in Kyoto as well. The few documents that demonstrate official authorization, however, betray a sense that custom demanded reasonable justification. When in 1558, for example, the shogun Ashikaga Yoshiteru granted the temple of Amidaji permission to bury its parishioners within temple walls, he did so explicitly on the grounds that temple property was "unattached land" (*muen-jo*).[39] Although located within the old city, Amidaji was presumably considered outside the profane world and as such not subject its laws or customs. A document dating from just two years later shows that military authorities sought to reimpose and "strictly enforce a ban on new temple burials within Kyoto." That very same document, however, grants a blanket exemption to the temple of Chionji, saying that burial rituals "should be left up to temple law."[40] While it is reasonable to assume that burial had been taking place within Kyoto discreetly for many centuries, it was not until the sixteenth century that we find documentary evidence that this singularly polluting activity had become, if not favored, at least allowed.

A few remarks should be reserved for Kyoto's commoners who from about this period began appearing in documents as *machishū*, meaning the "neighborhood masses."[41] Although always more numerous than their elite counterparts, it was not until the Age of Warring States that their roles as agents of urban change finally became apparent. For this we have to thank the panoramic illustrations of the city known today as the *Rakuchū-rakugai-zu* folding screens.[42] These pictorial sources capture in vivid color the agency and industry of townspeople who began using neighborhood federations as the vehicles for asserting grassroots political organization.[43] Of course, the most dramatic example of commoner agency was the Hokke movement of 1532–1536, during which townspeople exercised de facto control over the city's defense and governance. Commoners were also to be credited for the creation of the walls, moats, and other fortified apparatuses that appear on the screens and together formed the framework of livable space in wartime Kamigyō and Shimogyō.[44] Dating to about 1570, the Uesugi version of the *Rakuchū-rakugai-zu* screens depicts several of these in striking detail. Note, for example, how in Figure 6.4 (left side) the gated opening in a

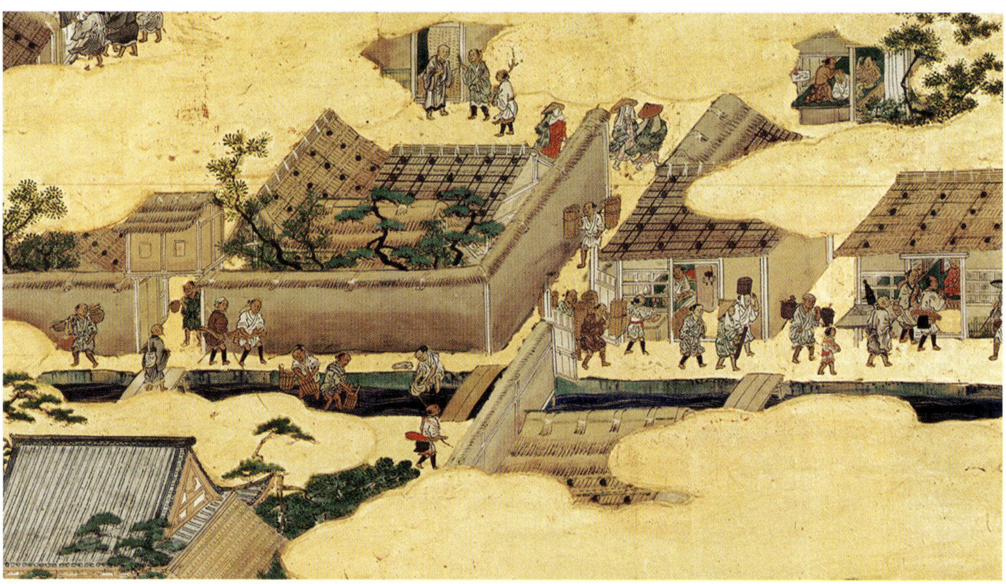

6.4. Guard house (*yagura*) over the gate of a walled neighborhood (left), and the gated entry to another neighborhood (right, *kuginuki*), in the Uesugi version of *Rakuchū-rakugai-zu byōbu.* Courtesy of Uesugi Museum, Yonezawa

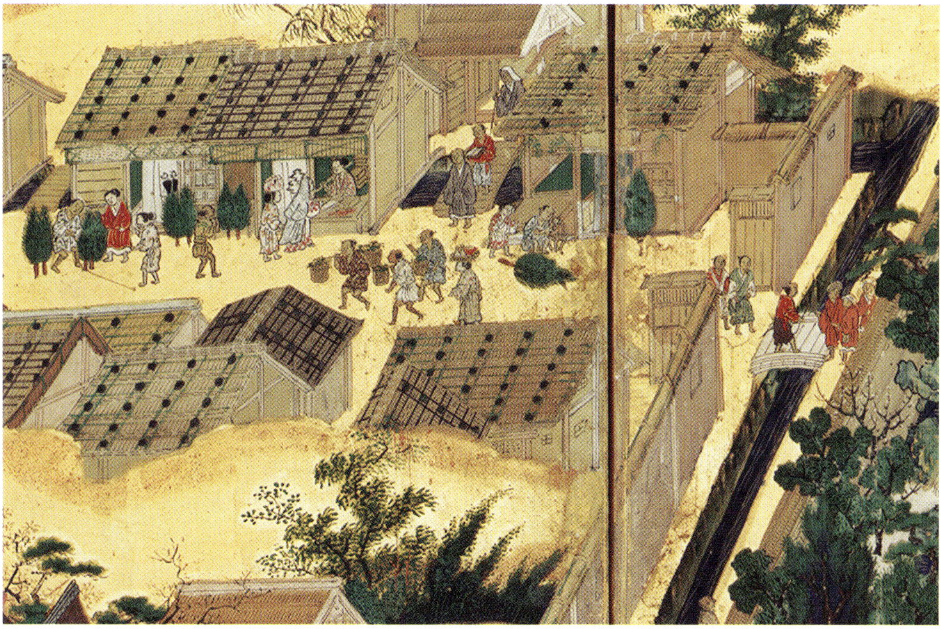

6.5. Walled neighborhood, in the Uesugi version of *Rakuchū-rakugai-zu byōbu.* Courtesy of Uesugi Museum, Yonezawa

high wall is surmounted by a guardhouse. Drums and bells were probably kept inside and used to warn of impending threats. Figure 6.5 shows another walled neighborhood and its entry gate, which, although less imposing than the first, is drawn taller than an average man.[45] The consistent juxtaposition of gates and urban streams is also noteworthy. It suggests a high degree of manipulation of the natural environment to maximize defensive capability.

Inside these fortified neighborhoods—due undoubtedly to the potent combination of rising wealth and political agency—townspeople began, for the first time, to buy and sell land.[46] The styles of the structures they built on that land adhered to a rustic, plebeian architectural aesthetic that grew in popularity over time to eventually inform the articulation of *suki* style. Perhaps most well known for its implementation in traditional Japanese tea houses, *suki* style entailed, among other things, the liberal use of bamboo and rough-hewn timber beams polished to a high-gloss finish.[47] The emergence of *machishū* as a force of substantial and long-lasting urban and architectural change in the late medieval period was indicative of much more than the failure of government and the rise of new wealth. It signaled the dawn of a new social environment, one in which formal status and pedigree no longer were the key requisites of political agency.

Conclusion

The classical ideal had been under siege for centuries prior to the outbreak of the Ōnin War. The early privatization of wealth and political power, followed by the so-called rise of warriors, had chipped away at the foundation of imperial government and transformed Kyoto's appearance and its venues of traditional statecraft. Nevertheless, throughout it all there had remained a sense among the capital elite that classical institutions mattered and that the capital city was a unique environment within which the trappings of imperial rule were perpetually renewed through the observation of certain rites, rituals, and rules. The Age of Warring States, however, changed everything in several key ways. First, persistent conflict and political chaos further eroded the real-world potency of capital institutions and the people who traditionally controlled them. Then, the devastation of the city itself robbed those people of the venues that had served to both underscore their status as public servants and reinforce the notion that the state remained relevant as a government and source of legitimacy. As the capital's grid pattern dissolved, so too did some of its foundational prescriptions and taboos. In the end, war had finally and irrevocably erased all traces of the classical city, its forms, its functions, and its exclusivity. In this environment, the agency of commoners grew to the point where they began having a major impact on the urban landscape and its politics.

Under the circumstances, it is remarkable that the imperial institution did not disappear entirely and that Kyoto kept its status as the center of the country. Not only did the city remain relevant throughout the age, its eventual occupation by Oda Nobunaga and Toyotomi Hideyoshi were prerequisites to each man's rise to hegemonic pre-eminence. And as we shall see in the next chapter, the urban transformation wrought by these two men signaled not just renewal but the dawn of a fundamentally new political order.

7

Castle-Town Kyoto

Cities are remarkably resilient social phenomena. In the wake of fires, wars, and natural disasters, they tend not merely to rise again; they do so in strikingly conservative ways. Even when authorities draw up plans to rebuild devastated cityscapes with ambitious aims to improve transportation or commercial infrastructure, these plans are often compromised by people reluctant to give up their land and livelihoods, even in the name of progress.[1] To them, restoring the status quo is the first priority. It is for this reason that postwar Kyoto, despite being utterly devastated by Ōnin and the century of strife that followed, came to roughly resemble its prewar self.

The similarities, however, were superficial. In fact, pre– and post–Warring States Kyoto were so profoundly different that it is possible to suggest the latter stood firmly on the far side of a divide that separated the premodern and modern cities. In this closing chapter, we explore Kyoto's rehabilitation under the successive leadership of Oda Nobunaga and Toyotomi Hideyoshi during the second half of the sixteenth century.[2] As we shall see, the key urban changes of this so-called "unification era" laid the foundations of Kyoto's modern appearance while also inspiring urban and architectural trends that shaped cities throughout the archipelago during the following century.

The first section examines how Nobunaga transformed Kyoto through the construction of the castle of Nijō in 1569. Built as the fortified residence of Ashikaga Yoshiaki, Nijō's creation—as well as its destruction—contributed significantly to Kyoto's postwar redevelopment. It also set several key material precedents that defined Kyoto's early modern appearance and informed broader national trends in urban planning and castle design. Most important among these was the installation of a fully fledged fortified compound, a castle, in the city center. Nijō was the first of three castles built in Kyoto, and each was a blunt reminder that warrior rule had become a permanent and unapologetic fixture of capital (and national) politics. Castles and castle-based cities proliferated throughout the country in the succeeding era, and many exhibited traits found first in and around Nijō. In this respect, Kyoto can be considered the prototype of early modern Japan's many castle-towns (*jōka-machi*), a stark indicator of just how much the imperial city had diverged from its classical model.[3]

The second section explores even more substantial changes that took place under Hideyoshi, who by all accounts was the most energetic and monumental builder of Japan's premodern age. Through either the creation or rehabilitation of several major architectural projects, Hideyoshi used monumentalism as a means of co-opting and manipulating Kyoto's traditional institutions. By moving to Kyoto, accepting imperial honors, and then taking up residence within a courtly palace, he signaled that his legitimacy was tied to public authority, not just military might. His subsequent decision to compel "great name" warlords (*daimyō*) to live in Kyoto further underscored his public profile, while also reconfirming the capital's status as the center of the postwar country. This section also explores several large-scale zoning projects and the creation of a wall around the entire city. In each of these cases, we discover unmistakable parallels between Hideyoshi's political vision and his urban planning. Finally, a theme that runs through the entire section is how Kyoto's reconstruction under Hideyoshi laid the foundations of the modern city's appearance and influenced the designs of early modern castle-towns that proliferated throughout the country during the succeeding age.

Nobunaga and Nijō Castle

Early in 1568, Oda Nobunaga marched into Kyoto in support of the beleaguered shogunal heir, Ashikaga Yoshiaki (1537–1597). Posing as a servant of the state and champion of the status quo, Nobunaga quickly drew up plans to repair the Imperial Palace and construct a headquarters for the newly appointed shogun.[4] In what might have served as an early unmasking of Nobunaga's disingenuousness vis-à-vis defending the old order, however, the shogunal headquarters he commissioned diverged sharply from all relevant architectural precedents. The resulting Nijō Castle did not resemble the Muromachi Palace in any substantial way, nor was it located anywhere near the traditional bases of Ashikaga influence either in Kamigyō or Shimogyō (see Figure 7.1).[5] In fact, it was a fortress of unprecedented size and military capacity, the first of its kind built in Kyoto and the first full-fledged castle to be built in an urban setting in Japan.[6]

Nijō's construction began early in the second month of 1569 along the eastern edge of Muromachi Road in the broad area between Kamigyō and Shimogyō that war had rendered largely vacant.[7] Nobunaga himself, with hoe and bamboo cane in hand, reportedly commanded every aspect of the castle's construction. Yamashina Tokitsugu was astounded by the pace of progress and noted in his diary that laborers were conscripted from eleven provinces.[8] No fewer than fifteen thousand workers occupied the site at any one time and sometimes there were as many as twenty-five thousand.[9] Luis Frois, a Jesuit missionary who witnessed the spectacle, commented that it was because of the enormous availability of manpower that the castle's construction, which "should have taken four or five years," was completed in a mere seventy days.[10] To hasten the move, many structures from the nearby Nichiren temple of Honkokuji were dismantled and transferred to the new site. Shogunal vassals followed suit, pillaging temple structures for raw materials to build their own residences in the vicinity.[11]

Frois visited Nijō shortly after its completion and described the grounds glowingly in a communiqué sent back to Portugal:

> Around the outside, a deep moat has been dug, filled with water and graced with various types of ducks. A suspension bridge hangs across the moat. Three large gates with mighty turrets punctuate a stone wall of six or seven *ells* in height, and a width of six, seven, or eight *ells*. Inside, there is a smaller moat and an amusement area. The inner grounds are luxurious and beautiful beyond words.[12]

Besides providing a glimpse of the compound's impressive fortifications and opulent décor, this entry is remarkable for its mention of a double ring of moats. As far as we know, such a trait was novel for the

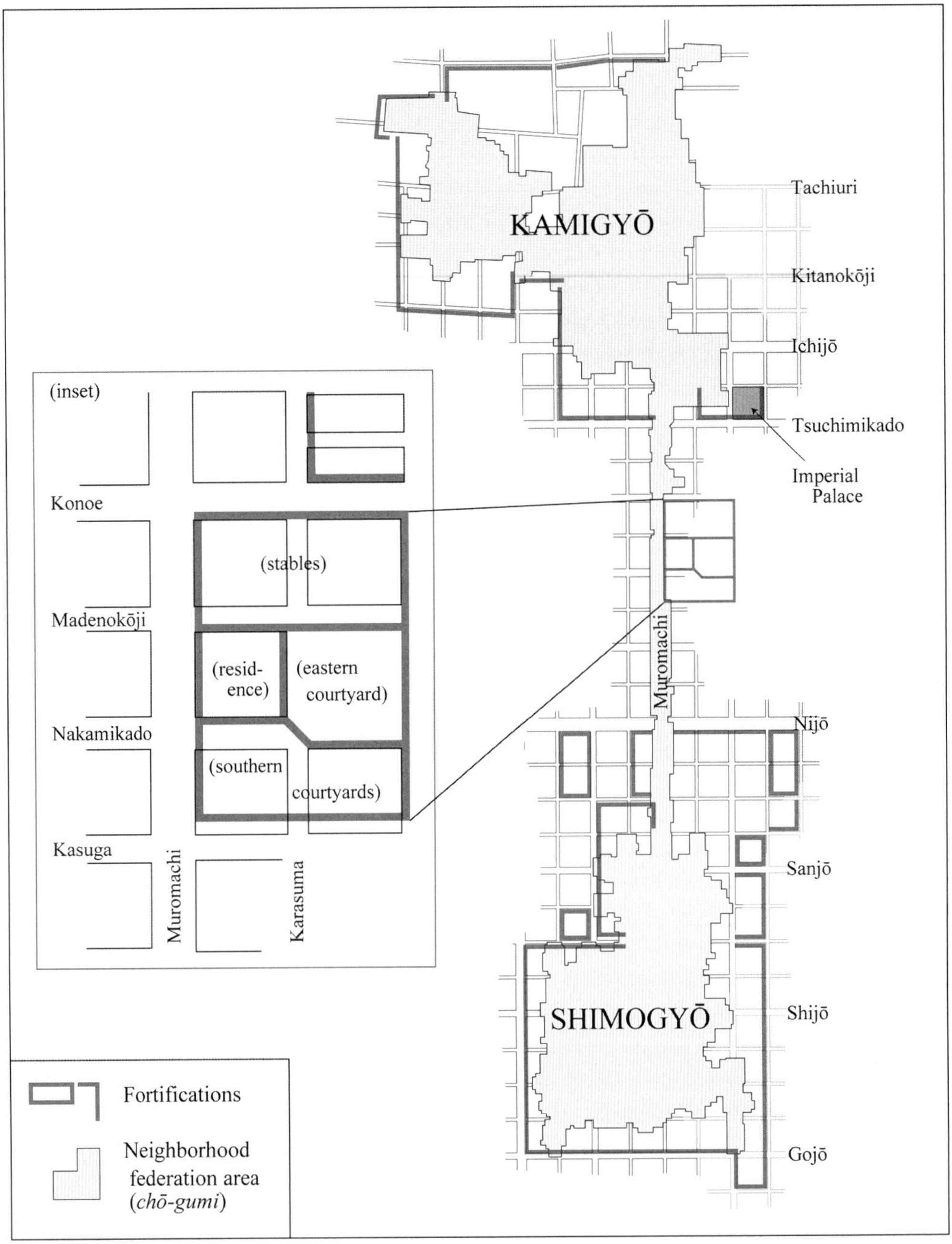
KAMIGYŌ
Tachiuri
Kitanokōji
Ichijō
Tsuchimikado
Imperial Palace
(inset)
Konoe
(stables)
Madenokōji
(resid-ence)
(eastern courtyard)
Nakamikado
(southern courtyards)
Kasuga
Muromachi
Karasuma
Muromachi
Nijō
Sanjō
SHIMOGYŌ
Shijō
Gojō
Fortifications
Neighborhood federation area (chō-gumi)

era and its implementation at Nijō suggests both a heightened level of danger and an unprecedented capacity to muster human and material resources. Yet another architectural innovation pioneered at Nijō was a *tenshu* castle tower, which reportedly rose three stories above a stone base that was itself eight meters high.[13] *Tenshu* castle towers (*tenshukaku*) became standard architectural features at virtually all castles built after this time. Their proliferation was tied to a rising tendency for *daimyō* to build fortresses on plains rather than hilltops, and increasingly amidst cities. Their height provided the outlook necessary to spot potential enemies approaching from afar.

The decision to build Nijō Castle along Muromachi Road between Kamigyō and Shimogyō made practical sense. Muromachi was a major thoroughfare, and land in the area had been cleared by years of war. There, Nobunaga could compel warriors to build homes in the castle's immediate vicinity without causing undue disruption. Several texts confirm that this is precisely what he did. *Shinchō kōki*, for example, explains: "At the front and back, left and right of the [shogun's] palace, *daimyō* from all provinces built, of their own free will, numerous homes in rows." Yamashina Tokitsugu describes the planning of residences for officials "in the service of the shogun."[14] And as we have seen, while the castle was still under construction, warriors had pillaged Honkokuji to build residences near their lord's new castle. Nijō, therefore, became the nucleus of a warrior enclave and in turn the catalyst of the first substantial urban development to occur between Kamigyō and Shimogyō in several generations.

By 1573, Yoshiaki's relationship with Nobunaga had deteriorated significantly. Nobunaga had refused to yield to the shogun's leadership and, indicative of his disdain for traditional authority, he generally resisted imperial promotions. He was a new kind of ruler who, as a matter of principle, derived his power from martial capacity, not state institutions.[15] Rejecting formal titles, ranks, and precedents, Nobunaga ruled the realm with an iron will and the backing of an almost invincible army. When Yoshiaki called on regional warlords to chastise Nobunaga in the spring of 1573, the latter became enraged. He surrounded Kyoto and began demanding tribute and other displays of servility in return for the staying of his hand. In the end, Nobunaga razed hundreds of villages and burned a large portion of Kamigyō. Shimogyō alone was spared because the rich merchants of that area lavished gold, priceless works of art, and other treasures on him.[16] As for Nijō Castle, it

7.1. Map of Ashikaga Yoshiaki's Nijō Castle, location and grounds layout.

sustained a massive assault on the twenty-third day of the third month. Although not immediate, the fall was inevitable. Rendered politically impotent and physically isolated, Yoshiaki was eventually "pardoned" and allowed to leave the capital for a life in exile. Nijō was subsequently overrun and most of its structures either razed or dismantled for use elsewhere.[17] Some were moved to the province of Ōmi for the construction of Nobunaga's own castle at Azuchi, which shared several key similarities with Nijō.[18] In 1597, Yoshiaki died in relative obscurity. He was the fifteenth and final shogun of the Ashikaga military regime.

Following Nijō's fall, Nobunaga ordered the townspeople of Kamigyō to fill in what remained of the moats, perhaps to ensure that an enemy did not take advantage of the favorable location and predug trenches.[19] By clearing the site and removing transportation obstacles, Nobunaga had also paved the way for subsequent urban redevelopment. *Rōjin zatsuwa* explains that "all that remains of the warlord's former edifice is a stone wall to the east. Homes now spread out to the west."[20] Some of the neighborhoods that grew up at the former site took names that reflected their respective relationships with the castle. The area south of the intersection of Kadenokōji and Muromachi, for example, became Bueijin-chō ("Warlord's Encampment" block). South of that was Daimon-chō ("Great Gate" block), and near the intersection of Konoe and Karasuma was Sakura no baba-chō ("Cherry-Blossom Horse Stables" block). And still further south was Horinouchi-chō ("Block Within the Moat").[21] While the creation of Nijō Castle had undoubtedly stimulated development in the former wasteland between Kamigyō and Shimogyō, so too did the castle's destruction. By the time Nobunaga was assassinated in 1582, Kyoto was well on its way to urban recovery. No longer was it a fragmented conglomeration of urban islands. It had once again become a whole and integrated city, albeit one very different from its premodern self.

Hideyoshi's Great Urban Reconstruction

Hideyoshi showed little interest in Kyoto during the first few years following Nobunaga's death.[22] His attention was much more on Osaka, which he sought to make his primary base of operations and, if possible, Japan's new capital. Luis Frois wrote of his ambition:

> [Hideyoshi] has set aside plots for the warlords of the various

> domains that he's conquered and ordered them all to build large palaces around his castle [at Osaka]. Also, if at all possible, he's determined to move the Kyoto markets to Osaka, and he's ordered the five main temples of the Gozan Zen sect and the temples of all the [other] sects to move their buildings to Osaka. He's also sent people to the Imperial Palace to implore [the emperor] to make the move to Osaka, saying he would build [for him] a palace even greater than that which stood at Nobunaga's Azuchi [castle].[23]

This was the first of two attempts by Hideyoshi to move the capital city. The second, hatched a decade later in about 1592, envisioned the Japanese sovereign engaging in a glorious, transoceanic imperial progress, concluding with his re-enthronement at the site of the Ming capital at Beijing.[24] As in the later case, the proposed move to Osaka was unsuccessful. Mired in a heated post-Nobunaga succession dispute and plagued by an ongoing rivalry with, among others, Tokugawa Ieyasu (1542–1616), Hideyoshi was simply not yet strong enough.[25] His loss to Ieyasu in the Battle of Nagakute in 1584 only underscored his weakness. It was precisely this weakness, however, that might explain what appears to have been a decisive shift in Hideyoshi's attitude toward Kyoto. Late in 1584, he turned his attention to the capital and began engaging with imperial institutions in new ways and in stark contrast to his predecessor, who had generally either ignored or dismissed them. This change in course profoundly impacted Hideyoshi's prospects. To be sure, in retrospect we can see that it was only after Hideyoshi moved to Kyoto and began accepting high imperial posts and governing—at least in form—within the framework of the imperial state that he was able to secure the vassalage of his long-time rivals and promulgate the famed "peace edicts" that solidified his hegemony.[26] When the *daimyō* of the various domains eventually gathered in Kyoto to take oaths of allegiance, they did so—again at least in form—as a matter of state policy put forward by Hideyoshi, who by then was acting in his capacity as imperial regent (*kanpaku*), not merely a conquering warlord.

Like many others who preceded him, Hideyoshi's entrée into the higher echelons of Kyoto society coincided with his sponsorship of several large building projects. In the third month of 1585, he was granted the high post of great minister of the center (*naidaijin*) as a reward for his restoration of the palace of the retired emperor (*sentō-gosho*).

Tenshōki describes the imperial appointment in a passage that captures how closely patronage was tied to public office and Hideyoshi's subsequent identification as an imperial advocate:

> The retired emperor's palace had wasted away from of old. Herewith, Hideyoshi presented himself at the former residence of the retired emperor and expressed his wish to reconstruct [the buildings] so that the enthronement ceremonies might be carried out and the retired emperor installed in his own palace. . . . An auspicious day was chosen and work began. At the same time, Hideyoshi was promoted and, as the chief supporter of the various offices, was an assistant to the Imperial Way. He was appointed Great Minister of the Center by the following proclamation: "To Taira no Ason Hideyoshi, Chief Councillor of State, Fujiwara Ason: Tsunemotosen presents the imperial decree; the above mentioned is graciously appointed to the post of Great Minister of the Center, Tenshō 13, 3rd month, 10th day." On that day, Hideyoshi visited the court and presented gifts of one thousand *ryō* of silver and a large sword.[27]

Clearly, rebuilding the *sentō-gosho* meant much more than simply providing an old man (however exalted) with a place to live (however luxurious). Indeed, it was that singular act that enabled the court to recommence the elaborate repertoire of rites and rituals surrounding imperial retirements and subsequent enthronements, all of which the war had rendered unfeasible for years. In this context, Hideyoshi's being hailed as "supporter of the various offices" and "assistant to the Imperial Way" can be interpreted as specific references to his role as a facilitator of imperial ceremony, not just a generous patron. And as we can see, he was richly rewarded through the granting of a high court post.

Hideyoshi's second major building project was closely tied to two subsequent and more substantial court promotions, first to the post of imperial regent in 1585 and then to grand chancellor of state (*dajō daijin*) the following year. Incidentally, it was from about this same time that he began using the family name Toyotomi. Meaning "bountiful minister," it suggested a filial posture toward the throne, indicative of his newly acquired status as a member of the imperial court.[28] Now a fully endowed courtier of unquestionable rank and status, Hideyoshi required a courtly residence. Thus, in 1586 he began building Jurakudai, a fortified palace-headquarters of unprecedented size and opulence. Covering a vast area of approximately 180 blocks or sixty-five acres at the former site of the Heian-era imperial palace enclosure (the Daidairi), Jurakudai was as sumptuous as it was forbidding (see Figure 7.2). *Taikōki* explains:

> The stone wall [stretched] for 3,000 *bu* on four sides like a mountain. As for the look of the residential entry gate (*sakura-mon*), its pillars were iron and its doors copper; the tower was decorated with stars. [Along] the joints of the tiles, jeweled tigers roared in the wind, golden dragons sang in the clouds. . . . The residential palace was thatched with cypress bark. By the entrance stairs there was a carriage port. A stage stood in the garden. . . . Even to the rear palaces, [the work] taxed the skills of the artisans and exhausted the hands of the painters. The splendor was exceedingly great.[29]

7.2. Jurakudai palace-headquarters of Toyotomi Hideyoshi, in *Jurakudai-zu byōbu*. Courtesy of Mitsui Memorial Museum

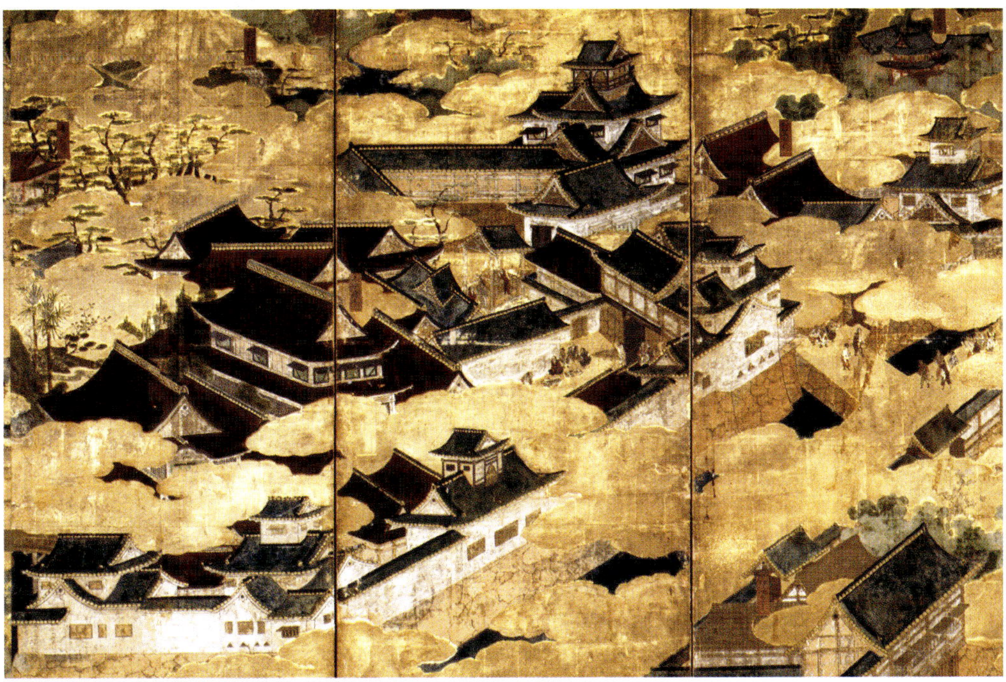

Much of what we know about Jurakudai comes from visual sources, including paintings and several grounds plans. Besides confirming the existence of the stone wall mentioned in this passage, the several sources also reveal that the property's interior was divided into fortified subcompartments.[30] In this respect, Hideyoshi appears to have followed the example set by Nobunaga at Nijō and Azuchi castles, both of which had two or more layers of interior defenses. Such a grounds plan maximized defensive capacity and partitioned space according to function. Within Jurakudai, for example, there were separate and dedicated areas for each of Hideyoshi's residence, the homes of his closest vassals, stables, kitchens, and storehouses. The centerpiece of the complex was a three-story *tenshu* castle tower. Although undoubtedly inspired by Nobunaga's earlier designs, the *tenshu* at Jurakudai, as depicted in *Jurakudai-zu*, appears more decorative than defensive (Figure 7.2). Adorned with gilded dolphin finials and end tiles, it had large latticed windows that opened on all four sides and a decorative veranda that might have been more useful as a moon-viewing platform than as a sentry perch. The walls were white stucco and the roofs ornately gabled.[31] The several palace structures that appear in the image around the base of the *tenshu* were equally fine. Although not adhering closely to *shinden*-style residential models, they exhibited some traits, such as cypress-bark roofing, suggestive of Hideyoshi's high court status. Jurakudai was completed in 1587, after which it was formally declared Hideyoshi's official residence, home to the imperial regent, his wife, and heir.[32]

Jurakudai served to further Hideyoshi's engagement with the court and assert his control over the *daimyō* in several concrete ways. The peace edicts of 1585 were promulgated in the name of the emperor by Hideyoshi, acting in his capacity as imperial regent. They outlawed violence as a means of redress and labeled intra-*daimyō* conflicts as "private wars" against the "public good."[33] As a sign of acquiescence, regional warlords were expected to travel to Kyoto, bow before Hideyoshi, take a formal oath of loyalty, and then leave their wives and heirs as hostages in the capital. At first, as was typical of Hideyoshi's policymaking style, orders were issued via personal letters addressed to *daimyō* individually. Following the completion of Jurakudai, however, the form and content of oath taking became more formalized and increasingly articulated within the framework of public authority. One of the main events to take place at Jurakudai was a five-day imperial visit in 1588 during which *daimyō* assembled, with great pomp and solemnity, before the sovereign and his regent, Hideyoshi, to take an oath of fidelity:

> Item: Each of us will strictly remonstrate should there be any lawless person who [impinges upon] the lands of the throne or the various investitures of the aristocracy and princely abbots (*monzeki*). We assert this for the present, needless to say, and unto [the generations of our] children and grandchildren without exception.
>
> Item: In all things, we will not violate in the least the orders of the Imperial Regent.[34]

The manner in which this oath was directed explicitly toward the throne and its interests is remarkable. It suggests that national unification was taking place within the context of a restored traditional order. Even the second item, which effectively solidifies Hideyoshi's hegemony over the *daimyō*, is directed not at the person of Hideyoshi but rather the office of imperial regent.

During the imperial visit, Jurakudai served as an eminently suitable venue in which Hideyoshi could play the role of courtier in the service of the emperor. Soon, however, the fortified palace was to acquire an even more central importance as Hideyoshi leveraged his public status to transform Jurakudai into the physical nucleus of an official policy that compelled *daimyō* to move to Kyoto permanently. Set out in 1589, *Tamon'in nikki* explains the terms of the new arrangement:

> All the various *daimyō* are to escort their wives and children to Jurakudai. It is ordered that they are [from now on] to reside in the capital. The Great Minister [Hideyoshi] himself has journeyed to the capital today with his wife and children [his heir]. . . . All tremble at this order.[35]

The implications of this decree were profound. First, Hideyoshi, the "Great Minister," was making *daimyō* submission a matter of blanket public policy.[36] No longer was it to be the domain of private correspondences or individual arrangements. Second, it conveys Hideyoshi's intent to sever the bonds that tied military leaders to their hereditary bases of landed wealth and feudal alliances in the provinces. The taking or exchanging of hostages was a practice common during the Age of Warring States. Forcing *daimyō* themselves, in addition to their heirs, to live alongside their lord, however, was novel and exhibited a new kind of influence, a power predicated firmly upon public authority (*kōgi*). While this policy is often pointed to as the antecedent of the alternate attendance system (*sankin kōtai*) of the following Tokugawa period, it was also deeply retrospective. As discussed in chapter 1, eight centuries earlier Emperor Kanmu had done something similar when he removed the aristocracy from the provinces, endowed them with public ranks and titles, and compelled them to live in his new capital. At the height of its power, the Ashikaga shogunate observed a similar though less formalized practice in which a vassal's sudden or unauthorized departure from Kyoto was interpreted as an unambiguous sign of revolt.[37] Clearly, Hideyoshi sought to remove potential rivals from their home bases while also keeping them close and easy to supervise. In Kyoto, it would be more difficult for them to engage in political intrigue or otherwise to plot rebellion.

The result was the formation of a warrior enclave surrounding Jurakudai (see Figure 7.3). So rapid and substantial was the resettlement process that Hideyoshi was forced to create more space for his vassals by forcibly evicting commoners from adjacent areas in 1591.[38] Reminiscent of what Hideyoshi would have seen surrounding Nijō and then Azuchi, the enclave he created enhanced Jurakudai's defensive capacity by creating a buffer zone through which would-be attackers would need to pass on their way to his headquarters. That so many *daimyō* were obliged to witness this plan firsthand perhaps helps explain why it proliferated, eventually becoming a trait found at each and every castle-town built after this time.

7.3. Map of Hideyoshi's Kyoto, late sixteenth century (including the Takase Canal, completed in 1614).

The twin objectives of separating potential rivals from their power bases while keeping them close likely informed yet another of Hideyoshi's major Kyoto projects. During the decade prior to 1592, he established two large temple enclaves on Kyoto's outskirts through the forced relocation of all but a few of the city's downtown temples.[39] The larger of the two enclaves, called Teramachi (meaning "temple-town"), was composed of more than a hundred temples assembled into a long row that ran the length of the city's eastern boundary. Most of these—many of which remain today where Hideyoshi put them—were associated

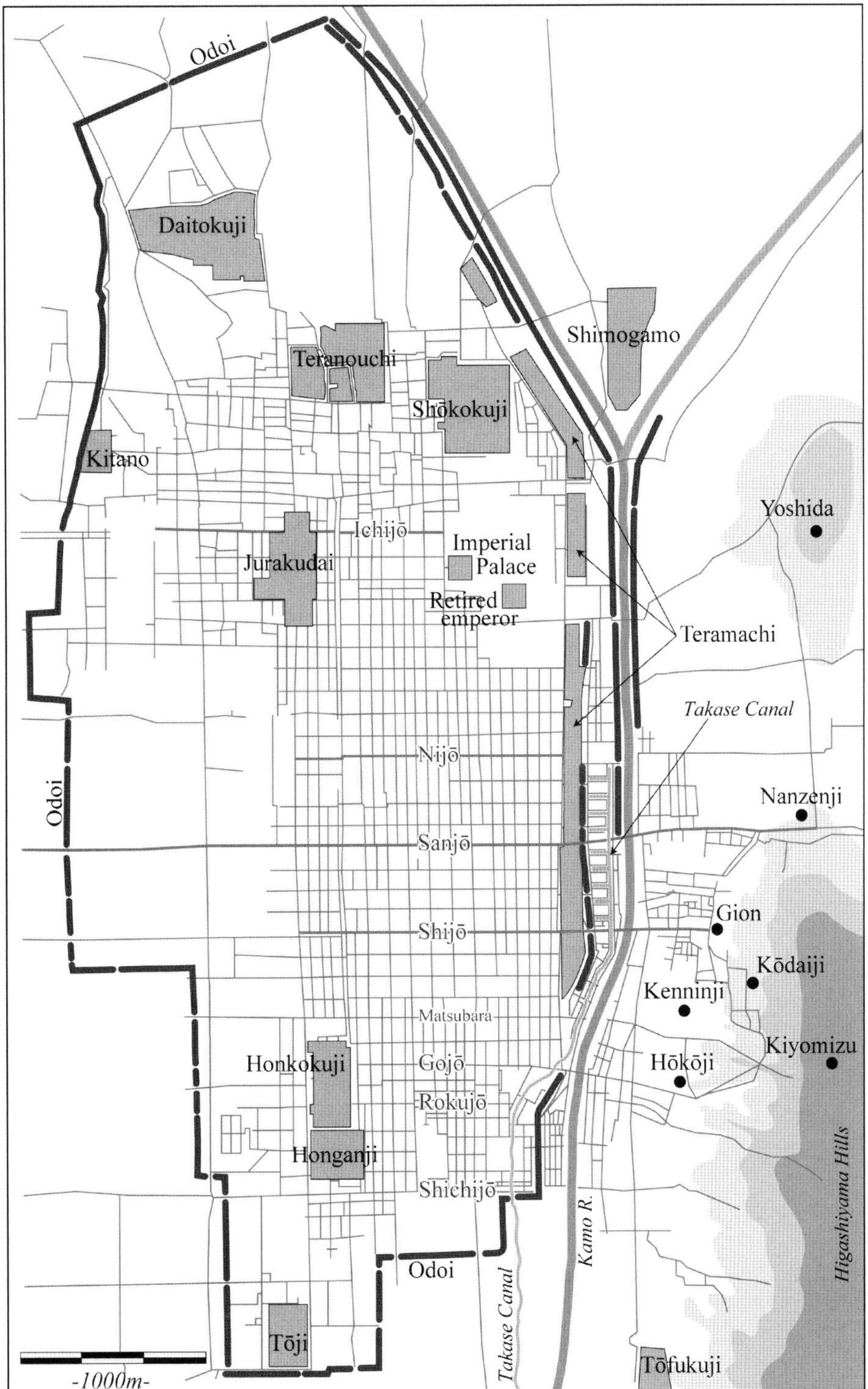
Odoi
Daitokuji
Shimogamo
Teranouchi
Shōkokuji
Kitano
Yoshida
Ichijō
Imperial Palace
Jurakudai
Retired emperor
Teramachi
Takase Canal
Nijō
Nanzenji
Odoi
Sanjō
Gion
Shijō
Kōdaiji
Kenninji
Matsubara
Kiyomizu
Honkokuji
Gojō
Hōkōji
Rokujō
Honganji
Shichijō
Kamo R.
Higashiyama Hills
Odoi
Takase Canal
Tōji
-1000m-
Tōfukuji

with the Nichiren and Jishū sects, both of which had histories of leveraging their strong relationships with Kyoto townspeople to organize mass, sometimes violent, sectarian movements.[40]

The second temple cluster, called Teranouchi, was located in the north. Earlier known as Agui, the area had a history of religious activity that long predated Hideyoshi. Since the beginning of the Kamakura period it had been an enclave of hermitages and retreats (*jūbō*), populated primarily by monks from the Tendai temple of Enryakuji.[41] After a century of vacancy following the Ōnin War, the area was suddenly revived when Hideyoshi allocated land there for the relocation of the Nichiren temples of Myōkakuji, Myōkenji, and Honpōji. In all, about sixteen temples made up Teranouchi, which, although much smaller than Teramachi, still dominated the city's northern flank.

Hideyoshi created one more "temple-town." Located in Kyoto's south, it was centered on the temple of Honganji, a headquarters of the True Pure Land sect (Jōdo Shinshū). This third case was fundamentally different from the first two in that it entailed the summoning of an important temple from the provinces rather than an eviction from the city center. Throughout much of the unification period, provincial True Pure Land temples had caused Nobunaga and other *daimyō* considerable grief through their armed opposition to unification policies. Sectarian "leagues" had successfully challenged warlords in several provinces by engaging in armed revolts called Ikkō-ikki. Broad support among commoners had enabled the True Pure Land sect to, among other things, turn its original Honganji headquarters at Osaka into a massive fortress capable of sustaining intermittent assaults by Nobunaga's forces for a staggering ten years before its ultimate surrender in 1581.[42] Hideyoshi's decision to "allow" the re-establishment of Honganji in Kyoto a decade later reveals something important about the aims of his temple relocation program in general.

It has been suggested that this program was designed to restore classical-era notions about capital exclusivity.[43] Such an objective, it is argued, would have underscored Hideyoshi's identity as a court official. But the fact that the three new "temple-towns" were located conspicuously within the boundaries of the newly emerging cityscape makes such an interpretation difficult. The relocation of Honganji makes it downright unsustainable. If, after all, Hideyoshi had sought to exclude religious institutions from Kyoto, why would he have gone to the trouble of actually introducing a new one, and one so large and influential?

A more feasible interpretation can be advanced by identifying similarities between this project and the *daimyō* relocation scheme. As in the earlier case, we see Hideyoshi attempting to use physical separation to sever the social, political, and economic bonds between potential rivals and their traditional sources of support. By creating Teramachi and Teranouchi, he plucked religious leaders from inner-city neighborhoods whose resident-adherents had long supplied the human and financial resources that made their institutions politically potent. In the case of Honganji, Hideyoshi was doing essentially the same thing by compelling the True Pure Land establishment, which had always derived its strength from the provinces, to migrate to the city.

A further similarity can be found in decisions related to location. In the cases of the *daimyō* and temples alike, Hideyoshi determined to cluster each group in ways that made them both easy to supervise and supplementary to defense objectives. The *daimyō* surrounded his palace while the temples virtually surrounded the city. It is from this perspective that the placement of Teramachi, Teranouchi, and Honganji on Kyoto's outskirts makes the most sense (see Figure 7.3). It was not so much about returning the city to a classical model as it was about creating a first line of defense along the city's north, east, and south faces. The functional advantages of clustering temples on the periphery did not go unnoticed by the many *daimyō* compelled to witness the relocation project. Such "temple-towns" became a ubiquitous trait of the many castle-towns of the Tokugawa period.

At about the same time Hideyoshi was finalizing his temple relocation project, he began constructing a wall around the city. Over the course of five months in 1591, a massive labor force consisting primarily of conscripts from *daimyō* armies built a stone and earthen rampart called the Odoi. Measuring, on average, 2.6 meters high and 9.5 meters wide at its base, the Odoi was augmented by an outer moat that ran around most of its twenty-three-kilometer perimeter. The top was covered with thick stands of bamboo. In his diary, nobleman Konoe Nobutada (1565–1614) described the work of the conscripts and provides insight on how the new wall was meant to function:

> From the first month of Tenshō 19 [1591], they have been made to dig a moat outside the city and bamboo has been planted [atop the earth dug out for the moat]. By the second month the work was more than half completed. . . . There are ten openings

> in this wall. As for the nature of the enterprise: when a malefactor appears, a bell can quickly be sounded, the ten gates will be closed at this signal, and [the criminal] will be encircled.[44]

The Odoi could hardly be considered a serious defensive apparatus. The gradual, sloping sides must have been easy to scale; it possessed no watchtowers or armories and was punctuated by multiple entry points, probably even more than the ten mentioned above. Hideyoshi ordered soldiers to patrol the perimeter on a rotating basis, but as Nobutada suggests, their role seems to have been about maintaining public safety more than deterring a military aggressor. In light of its inadequacy, Hideyoshi's motivation for building the Odoi has long puzzled historians. There are two widely accepted explanations. The first relates to a simple desire to better insulate the city from floods. The second, which does not negate the first, is more analytical. It sees the Odoi as a tool for demarcating the political boundaries of the postwar city. Having such a tool would have resolved or averted potential questions about law and jurisdiction in a place where boundaries had always been a sensitive matter. Such geographic clarification would have also corresponded closely with Hideyoshi's other policies, including his cadastral surveys and physical separation of warriors and peasants along occupational lines.[45] As we have seen in the cases of the *daimyō* and temples, he possessed a penchant for clustering people and institutions together based on identity and social roles. Wanting to create an unambiguous border that separated the city from the hinterland seems like a natural, physical extension of an underlying political impulse.

There is yet another way of interpreting the Odoi's significance: by recognizing the embankment's role as a corporate defensive apparatus, something that appears fairly frequently in contemporary primary sources as *sōgamae*.[46] In contrast to private or single-institution defenses—such as the walls or moats surrounding a private residence, a temple, or castle—corporate defenses were built by and for diverse associations of people seeking common solutions to shared difficulties. The earliest known examples include the walls and moats that surrounded and divided up Kamigyō and Shimogyō from the time of the Ōnin War. These were energetically constructed, maintained, and continually improved throughout wartime by the townspeople of Kyoto acting on their own volition, usually organized under the auspices of their respective neighborhood federations. Their first and foremost function was to protect lives, livelihoods, and property. In time, however, they also served to distinguish certain areas from others, thus creating a geographic basis for special treatment and privileges.

Corporate defense apparatuses eventually began appearing throughout the countryside during the Age of Warring States. Notable early examples included those built in the port town of Sakai as well as the many fortified communities that took shape around provincial Pure Land and True Pure Land temples. In each case, construction appears to have been part of a grassroots response to the violence of the age. At the original Osaka headquarters of Honganji, the agitation of parishioners seeking to extend temple defenses beyond the central sanctuary led to the creation of a "temple town" (*jinai-machi*) of substantial size and defensive capacity, enough, as we have seen, to formidably counter Oda Nobunaga's offensive.[47] There are cases in which *daimyō* surrounded their regional towns with forts as a way of improving defenses while also asserting control over the people within. More typically, however, the corporate defenses that appeared around provincial towns were built, albeit often with warrior assistance, at the behest of townspeople who energetically lobbied for their construction.[48]

Superficially, the Odoi can be considered an expansion and improvement of the corporate fortifications that had surrounded Kyoto's urbanized areas since the time of Ōnin. There was, however, a fundamental difference. The wall built by Hideyoshi was the product of top-down planning and executive authority rather than grassroots organization. By being the one who initiated the project, provided the military manpower to build it, and arranged for its ongoing patrols, Hideyoshi was signaling the dawn of a new era. No longer was defense meant to be the domain of commoners. It was the responsibility of the ruler. Hideyoshi had effectively relieved Kyoto's townspeople of the task of urban defense and taken on that duty for himself. The virtually simultaneous promulgation of policies aimed at disarming the populace and professionalizing military service only sharpen an interpretation of the Odoi as a monument to Hideyoshi's status as guarantor of peace and an embodiment of public authority.

Although less monumental than those projects discussed so far, a few more of Hideyoshi's building enterprises should be introduced, primarily for the sake of showing how they contributed to the formulation of Kyoto's modern appearance.

In 1589, Hideyoshi set into motion a plan to completely rebuild the Imperial Palace. As in the case of the *sentō-gosho*'s refurbishment, such an act was typical of a leader seeking to use imperial patronage to access public status. What made this case different was that it coincided with a series of policies that laid the groundwork for the later creation of an aristocratic enclave roughly surrounding the palace. Hideyoshi did not compel the civil aristocracy to move through a forced relocation regime. Instead, he catalyzed migration by attaching preferential conditions to land he deemed to have historical ties to the palace. While Hideyoshi was perpetuating long-held customs that protected the interests of the aristocracy, his method for doing so was novel in terms of its focus on geography instead of status. That is, he granted exemptions and privileges to the *land* rather than the aristocracy while, at the same time, making it clear that the aristocracy alone were welcome on land having a "special relationship with the palace."[49] The succeeding Tokugawa regime agreed with the principle of there being an aristocratic enclave in Kyoto, later defining the boundaries of a "noble village" that dominated the urban landscape right up to the dawn of the modern era. Today, its former area corresponds roughly to the vast space of the Kyoto Imperial Park (Kyōto gyoen). The Imperial Palace and *sentō-gosho* remain in their original locations.

Peace and political stability caused Kyoto's population to surge. People flocked to the city from the provinces and, although there is no solid evidence, we might safely assume there was a sudden rise in the birthrate, as is often the case following wars. Besides the top-down redevelopment projects discussed so far, townspeople themselves contributed greatly to Kyoto's regeneration through the construction of thousands of new homes, shops, and market places. In the process, they re-established many of the city's old neighborhoods. At some point, Hideyoshi began taking an interest in street-level redevelopment, eventually playing an active role himself. One of his key contributions was the decision to slice square city blocks, which had always been impractically large, in half through the creation of new north-south roads.[50] By maximizing residential exposure to roads and erasing "dead" space in the middles of former blocks, Hideyoshi was making official changes that commoners had been making themselves on an ad hoc basis for centuries. He was, in effect, making higher-density living and more user-friendly neighborhoods a matter of public policy. In the process, he changed one of the fundamental traits of the classical city. Early modern Kyoto continued to exhibit a grid pattern. That pattern, however, was (and continues to be) composed predominantly of rectangular rather than square city blocks.

Signs of higher-density living are evident in folding screens that document the appearance of two-story houses. With a few exceptions, prior to this era the only structures above two stories tended to be temple buildings and castle towers, both of which were nonresidential. The lively scene in Figure 7.4 depicts a rectangular block with numerous two-storied commoner houses. Several even sported verandas that hung out over the roads, indicative of more advanced building techniques. Evidence of permanence and greater wealth can be read in the implementation of improved roofing methods. The use of uniform tiles, made of both clay and timber, was a dramatic upgrade from the makeshift stone-anchored timber planks that are ubiquitous in earlier visual sources.

Last but certainly not least, Hideyoshi—for the first time in the city's history—built two permanent bridges across the Kamo River.[51] Located at Sanjō and Rokujō-bōmon, these new crossings replaced much smaller timber spans that had, through the centuries, proven susceptible to

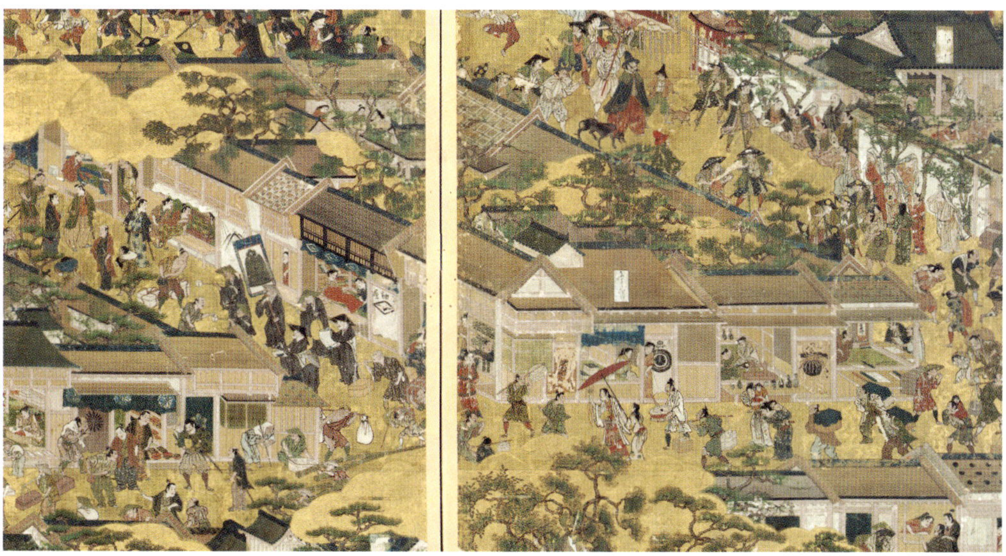

7.4. Two-story commoner houses, in Funaki version of *Rakuchū-rakugai-zu byōbu*. Courtesy of Tokyo National Museum

destruction by wind, fire, and, most frequently, floods. Completed in 1590, the "Great Sanjō Bridge" (Sanjō ōhashi) was the first river crossing to be built in Japan using granite pillars. Eight of the original columns continue to support the structure today, while another that stands on display nearby bears an inscription showing that it was quarried in 1589 from a site near modern-day Kobe. The depiction of the bridge in the Funaki folding screen shows polished bronze baluster caps (see Figure 7.5). Although they are now deeply tarnished and one is scarred by several sword swipes reportedly inflicted during the mid-nineteenth century, these baluster caps too remain in use on the bridge today (see Figure 7.6). Each is engraved with the following passage:

> The capital's Sanjō Bridge shall deliver those who cross it for generations to come. Five fathoms into the earth, foundation stones have been sunk. Upon these stand sixty-three carved stone pillars. This is the first stone pillar bridge in all Japan! First built during the Toyotomi reign by Masuda Nagamori. 18th year of Tenshō, 1st month.[52]

7.5. Great Sanjō Bridge, in Funaki version of *Rakuchū-rakugai-zu byōbu.* The small bridge in the top left spans the Takase Canal. Courtesy of Tokyo National Museum

The somewhat smaller bridge built at Rokujō-bōmon was never known by that road's name. Perhaps as a way of showing its importance,

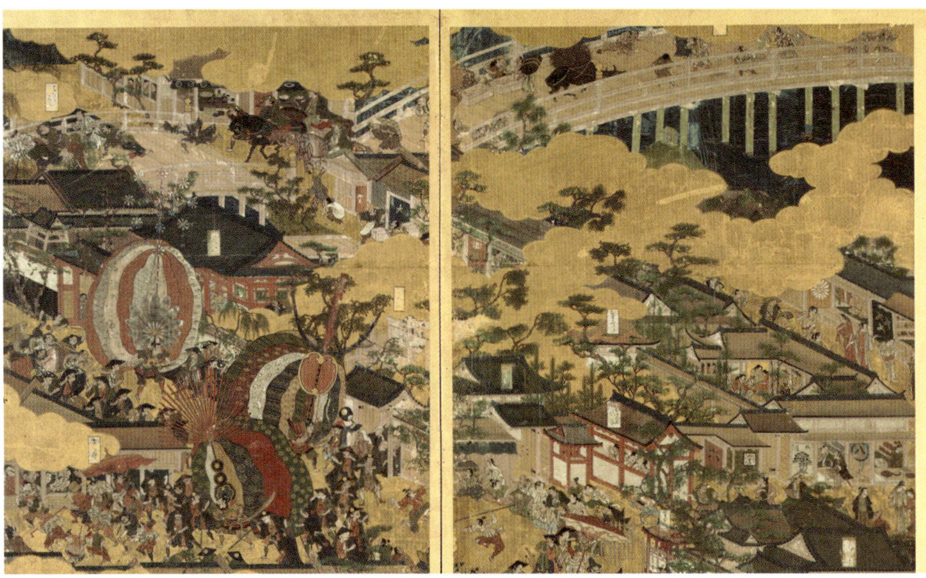

Hideyoshi dubbed it the "Gojō Bridge" and changed the name of the road to Gojō as well. In turn, the original Gojō Road was renamed "Matsubara" (see Figure 7.3). These name changes are the reason why today the distance between Rokujō and Gojō is shorter than those between the city's other major east-west roads. The new Gojō Bridge provided Hideyoshi easy access to the large temple of Hōkōji he had commissioned to the east as well as to the castle of Fushimi.[53] During the Tokugawa period, it was (anachronistically) eulogized in folklore and songs as the site of the legendary twelfth-century battle between Minamoto no Yoshitsune (1159–1189) and the warrior-monk Benkei (d. 1189).[54] Incidentally, Gojō Road today is a massive, eight-lane thoroughfare crossing the entire breadth of the city, while Matsubara—the original Gojō of Heian-kyō—has become a minor, narrow, and not entirely continuous byway with a single-lane bridge crossing the Kamo River.

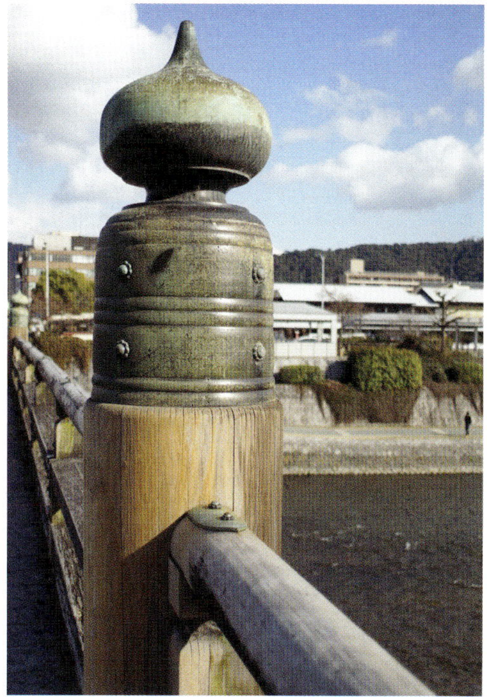

7.6. Bronze baluster caps on the Great Sanjō Bridge.

Conclusion

Late in 1591, the childless Hideyoshi formally retired from the post of imperial regent and quit the capital. Transferring his imperial titles and the Jurakudai Palace to his nephew and heir, Hidetsugu (1568–1595), he took up residence in Fushimi, about two hours' march to the south. Two years later, Hideyoshi's wife gave birth to a healthy son, thus setting off a succession dispute between Hidetsugu's supporters and those loyal to Hideyoshi's newborn, Hideyori (1593–1615). The deeply fraught affair ended in 1595 with Hideyoshi forcing Hidetsugu to commit ritual suicide, after which his entire family was, without ceremony, executed on the banks of the Kamo River, not far from the Great Sanjō Bridge. Jurakudai was thereafter systematically dismantled, with many of its structures transferred to castles in Fushimi and Osaka as well as several nearby temples and shrines. The land on which the once opulent palace-fortress had stood was hungrily absorbed by rapid urban development, soon becoming indistinguishable from its surroundings.

Although lasting well into the succeeding Tokugawa period, the Odoi embankment was another of Hideyoshi's major Kyoto projects that did not remain intact into the modern era. In one form or another, however, almost everything else did. In fact, whether we think in terms of the way roads are laid out in the modern city, where temples are clustered, or which of the many bridges now spanning the Kamo River are the most important, the artifacts of Hideyoshi's great urban reconstruction are ubiquitous.

While the dream and the ideals of Heian-kyō live on in art, literature, and the imaginations of many who walk Kyoto's streets, almost nothing remains of the classical city. Modern Kyoto traces its origins unambiguously to the late sixteenth century and the great urban reconstruction of Toyotomi Hideyoshi.

Epilogue

Bridge to the Modern

The dawn of the seventeenth century is a good place to end a book on Kyoto's premodern history. By 1600, Hideyoshi's great urban reconstruction had laid the foundations of the modern city, and political centralization under the succeeding Tokugawa shogunate (1603–1868) would soon bring in sweeping material, social, and political changes that moved Japan decisively into its early modern era. Just as important, with the military regime choosing Edo as its headquarters, Kyoto lost its status as the political center of the country, and by about 1630 ceased being Japan's largest city. To stop the narrative here, therefore, makes sense for both historical and historiographical reasons. Doing so, however, would be unfortunate in light of the lack of scholarship on the major buildings and urban projects of the Tokugawa period. Still visible in the city today, many stand as monuments to early modern advances in technology, changing architectural sensibilities, and, not least, warrior authority. This epilogue briefly introduces several of the most important of these, including Nijō Castle, the Kyoto Noble Village, and the Takase Canal. In closing, there is also consideration of the social and infrastructural factors that contributed to urbanization east of the Kamo River.

Nijō Castle

Tokugawa Ieyasu's 1600 victory in the Battle of Sekigahara essentially eviscerated the Toyotomi clan's political viability and paved the way for Ieyasu himself to become shogun. Whereas he, like several of his predecessors, had remained largely aloof of Kyoto and its institutions up to that time, hegemony meant engagement. A capital residence, even one that might be temporary or largely symbolic, was necessary to take part in the public pageantry expected of someone seeking imperial investiture and the trappings of formal legitimacy. Knowing this, Ieyasu began by ordering the removal of four to five thousand homes for the construction of a residential palace in the fifth month of 1601.[1] Six months later, local *daimyō* were ordered to begin sending financial contributions and corvée laborers to the capital for the construction of what began appearing in documents as "Nijō Castle" (Nijō-jō).[2]

The decision to call Ieyasu's official Kyoto residence "Nijō" could have been related to several factors. First, a similar name had been applied to the former compound of the late shogun Ashikaga Yoshiaki. Perhaps Ieyasu simply sought to mimic his predecessor. The other, and probably more likely, reason relates to simple topography. The new compound was built on a site that straddled and opened onto Nijō Road facing east (see Figure 8.4). As we have seen throughout this study, in premodern Kyoto, the names of people and buildings were frequently tied to their locations. While Ieyasu never adopted the toponym to become "Lord of Nijō"—presumably because he never actually lived there—his castle nonetheless did. Incidentally, the way the front gate opened directly onto Nijō Road might have had symbolic significance. Nijō, it will be recalled, was Heian-kyō's widest east-west thoroughfare and the southern boundary of the Daidairi imperial enclosure. As such, it was among the city's most important parade routes, second only to the great Suzaku Road. With Suzaku long gone, Ieyasu might have sought to leverage Nijō's historical association with the classical city. Having done so, each time he approached his Kyoto domicile, invariably traveling in a grand procession, the shogun would bolster his credentials as servant of the throne by evoking traditional modes of public pageantry.

Anyone looking at a map of Kyoto will notice that the fortress's silhouette sits slightly askew of the rest of the urban grid (see Figure 8.4). To be exact, it is tilted about three degrees clockwise. The reason for this misalignment long puzzled historians, and only recently has a possible explanation been proposed. Noticing that the castle's orientation corresponds closely to the location of magnetic north at about the time of construction, geographers have suggested that Nijō's planners used magnetic compasses in the initial planning stages.[3] Arriving from Europe with missionaries, sailors, and merchants in the late sixteenth century, the new technology was widely hailed by the Japanese of the day for its convenience and apparent reliability. Nijō's glaring skew shows that it was used for even the most important projects. It also shows, however, that the introduction of new technologies can be fraught with pitfalls. The urban grid laid out eight centuries earlier was noticeably more true to geographic north.

The first stage of Nijō's construction was completed in the third month of 1603, just in time to host a ritual celebration (*haiga*) by which Ieyasu publicly marked his appointment as shogun.[4] Corresponding roughly to the eastern half of the current castle's grounds, an area now called Ninomaru, the complex was composed entirely of structures built in the *shoin* style (see Figure 8.1).[5] The complete absence of *shinden*-style buildings at Nijō did not necessarily indicate an abandonment of classical, Ritsuryō rituals. The holding of a *haiga* there confirms this. Rather, it was probably more related to the fruition of a widespread trend that had, since the late fifteenth century, seen the usefulness of walls and dedicated rooms gradually trump the symbolic importance of ritual space.

Textual sources describing Nijō's earliest appearance are scarce and sometimes contradictory. Pictorial sources, however, confirm that the complex possessed a *tenshu* tower (*tenshu-kaku*), which by this time had become a common fixture at virtually all the many castles then being built around the country.[6] Perhaps the most noteworthy thing about the *tenshu* at Nijō is that, beside the moat and a low wall surrounding the property, it was the complex's only defensive apparatus. Indicative of the era's peace, Nijō, from the very beginning, was a poorly fortified fortress. Indeed, it was a "castle" in name alone. The *tenshu*'s lack of functional importance is underscored by the decision not to rebuild the structure after its loss to fire in 1750.

After his imperial appointment, the new shogun did not linger. At

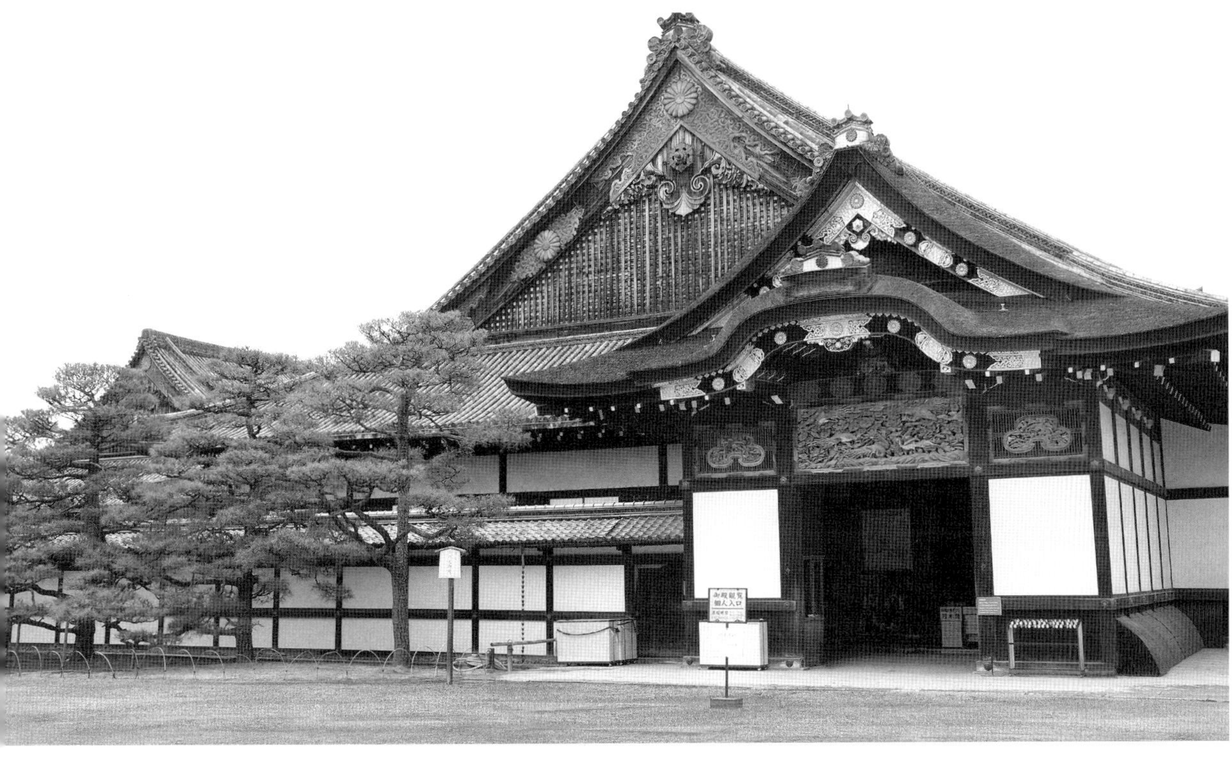

8.1. Nijō Castle's Ninomaru Palace.

the end of the fourth month, Nijō was vacated as Ieyasu traveled first to Fushimi and then further afield to Edo, where he began the task of establishing his military administration. He used the site on only two later occasions. The first was in 1611, when he attended the enthronement of Emperor Gomizunoo (1596–1680), and the second was in 1615 to celebrate victory in the "Winter" and "Summer" campaigns fought at Osaka Castle. In sum, the man who built Nijō Castle used the site only a handful of times and stayed only a few months in total.

Nijō received its first major upgrade in 1620 with the construction of an additional residential compound for Ieyasu's granddaughter, Masako (1607–1678).[7] To realize a lifelong dream of tying his family to the imperial line through marriage, Ieyasu arranged for Masako, the daughter of Tokugawa Hidetada (1579–1632), to enter the Imperial Palace as concubine of Emperor Gomizunoo. The new compound at Nijō served as the starting point of a grand and festive procession of civil aristocrats and warrior generals who, in the sixth month of that year, escorted the newly minted princess across town to the Imperial Palace.[8] Events such as this highlight the usefulness of building along Nijō Road. By traveling in a more-or-less direct route from the castle to the palace, the shogun and his vassals engaged in a mode of public pageantry unmistakably reminiscent of their classical (and aristocratic) counterparts.

The third Tokugawa shogun, Iemitsu (1604–1651), ordered a major expansion and refurbishment of Nijō in 1624. Over the course of two years, the grounds were nearly doubled in size through the creation of an entirely new cluster of connected structures west of the original Ninomaru. This "main keep" (Honmaru) was surrounded by double moats and graced with a newly refurbished (and relocated) *tenshu* tower. The most celebrated painters and craftsmen of the day were enlisted to fit out the new compound and refurbish the older adjacent structures. Together, they transformed Nijō Castle into what is today widely considered the finest and most sumptuous example of period art and *shoin*-style architecture.[9] Illustrated by a team of painters led by the luminary Kanō Tan'yū (1602–1674), the site's more than three thousand sliding-door paintings (*fusuma-e*) are now designated Important Cultural Properties (Jūyō bunka-zai). Many of the intricately carved and painted wooden moldings and transom grills are equally revered, and the whole of Ninomaru is itself a National Treasure (Kokuhō). While much has changed over the years due to damage and successive reconstructions, the current splendor of Nijō Castle is primarily the product of the work carried out by Iemitsu. Incidentally, the pretext for the upgrade was to host Emperor Gomizunoo for a five-day visit in the late summer of 1626. Carefully choreographed to mimic Emperor Goyōzei's (1571–1617) stay at Jurakudai in 1588, the imperial progress corresponded with Nijō Castle's zenith.

Following one additional visit by Iemitsu in 1634, something quite remarkable happened to the shogunate's official headquarters in Kyoto: it was virtually abandoned. Save for the presence of a skeleton crew of security guards and administrators charged with upkeep, Nijō Castle was left vacant for the next 230 years. During that long period, a succession of natural disasters took their toll.[10] The *tenshu* tower, for example, was destroyed by a lightning strike in 1750, and the great Tenmei fire of 1788, which also devastated a large portion of the city, claimed most of the Honmaru and parts of the Ninomaru.[11]

Nijō was not used in a meaningful way again until the 1860s, by which point it was clear that the military regime was doomed and that governing authority would soon revert to the emperor. Tokugawa Iemochi (1846–1866), the fourteenth shogun, visited from Edo briefly in 1863, followed a year later by his successor, Yoshinobu (1837–1913). It was during that stay that Yoshinobu both received the imperial appointment as shogun and, before the year was out, dissolved the shogunate. Upon Yoshinobu's retirement and subsequent departure from Kyoto in the last month of 1868, Nijō was converted into the imperial cabinet office. It served as such until 1871, when it became Kyoto's Prefectural Office. In 1885, ownership of the property was transferred to the Imperial Household Ministry, which turned it into a "detached palace" (Nijō rikyū). The city of Kyoto took possession in 1939, soon after which twenty-four buildings were designated National Treasures. Four more were added to this coveted list in 1944, and in 1950 the rest of the structures gained the designation of Important Cultural Property. In recognition of its value as a "masterpiece of human creative genius" and a cultural artifact of "universal value to humanity," Nijō Castle was made a UNESCO World Heritage Site in 1994.[12]

Kyoto Noble Village

As touched on in chapter 7, it was during Hideyoshi's reign that a series of policies catalyzed the creation of an aristocratic enclave surrounding the Imperial Palace. What had begun as a more-or-less natural congregation of the civil aristocracy—motivated by tax exemptions and promises of self-policing privileges—turned into a de facto relocation program under the Tokugawa. In 1615, the shogunate issued the Laws of the Imperial Household and Aristocratic Families (*Kinchū narabini kuge shohatto*), a document of breathtaking political audacity that limited the affairs of the emperor and aristocracy to the gentle arts, learning, and ceremony. Domestication was rewarded with stipends as well as pledges of financial assistance for palace construction and upkeep. Receipt of the latter was contingent upon construction taking place within a defined area close to the palaces of the reigning and retired emperors (see Figure 8.2). The result was the formation of what Mary Elizabeth Berry has aptly called a "royal ghetto."[13] Inscriptions on *Kyodai-ezu*, a map published in 1686, show that this "noble village," even at an early stage, encompassed the residential compounds of all the most esteemed aristocratic families.[14] These included the Konoe, Hachijō, Nijō, Fushimi, Yamashina, Reizei, Kujō, Takatsukasa, Arisugawa, Asukai, Ichijō, Karasumaru, Kanshūji, Kikutei, and the Hino. Interspersed among these in no apparent order were protector shrines (*chinjusha*) and the residential temples of princely abbots (*monzeki satobō*).

Numerous reconstructions over the course of the long Tokugawa period resulted in a general expansion and a better definition of the enclave's boundaries.[15] At some point in the early eighteenth century, it even gained a name, appearing in textual records alternatively as "Kuge-machi" (Noble town) or "Kinri," meaning more generally "the palace."[16] Maps such as *Dairizu* produced near the end of the period depict a densely urbanized, rectangular area covering about 245 acres, ranging from Karasuma in the west to Teramachi in the east, Marutamachi in the south to a block north of Imadegawa in the north (Figure 8.2).

8.2. *Dairizu*, depicting the Kyoto Noble Village, 1863. Courtesy of International Research Center for Japanese Studies (Nichibunken)

Following the emperor's move to Edo (which was thereby renamed Tokyo, meaning the "Eastern Capital") in 1868, the enclave was mostly abandoned. Only the former Imperial Palace and palace of the retired emperor were maintained, while over time all the aristocratic residences were removed.[17] In 1877, a wall was built around most of the former area to create the "Kyoto Imperial Park" (Kyōto gyoen). That large green space now dominates Kyoto's urban landscape and the palace is used regularly for imperial visits and major festivals.

The Takase Canal

In the autumn of 1610, the Kyoto-based merchant Suminokura Ryōi (1554–1614) conceived of a plan to divert water from the Kamo River to create a canal, connecting the capital to the region's primary waterways.

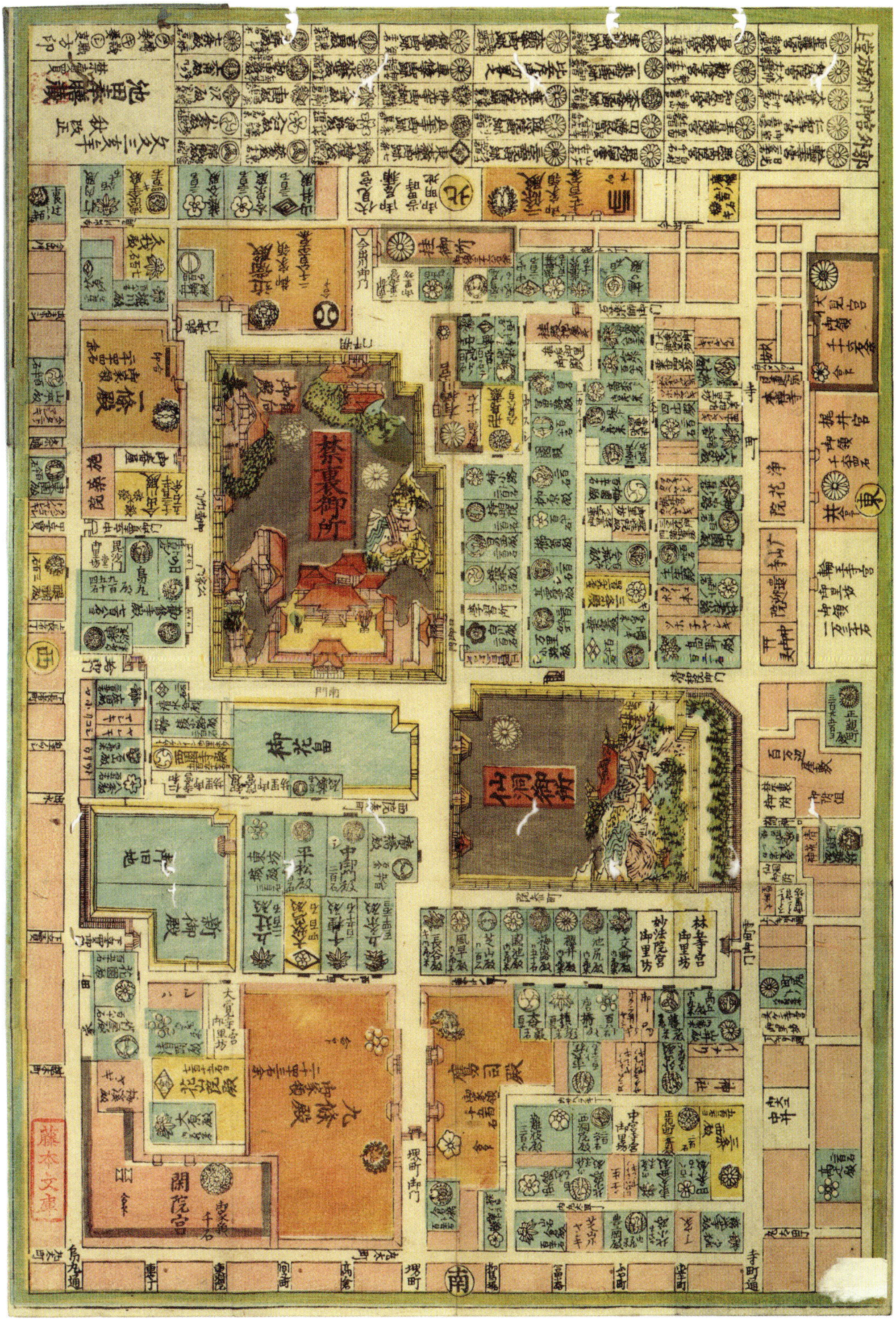

禁裏御所
一條殿
九條殿
閑院宮
新御殿
堺町御門
烏丸通
寺町通
北
南
東
西
藤本文庫

Because the Kamo River was shallow and its water supply unreliable, the transportation of goods to and from the provinces had always been a time-consuming and expensive overland affair. Peacetime reconstruction after 1600 only underscored the need for an improved supply chain. The proposition to create a manmade waterway was ambitious for the time, requiring considerable financial and technical resources, as well as imagination and foresight. Suminokura received permission from the shogunate to build the Takase Canal (Takasegawa) in 1611 and, having purchased the necessary land earlier, began excavation almost immediately. The plan called for a stone-lined canal that ran adjacent to the west bank of the Kamo River, just outside of the Odoi city wall, starting at Nijō in the north and rejoining the Kamo River at a point south of Kujō (see Figure 7.3).[18]

The laborious task of digging and lining the canal took three years. Eight meters wide and eleven kilometers long, the waterway was an immediate asset to the city, opening up the urban center to efficient shipments of such critical necessities as rice, *sake*, lumber, and coal. With as many as nine registered boat launches and numerous other loading docks, hundreds of vessels plied their way up and down the canal each year. Dealers of various commodities built storehouses along the shores and in time, aptly named districts such as Kiyamachi ("Lumber yard town"), Kamiyamachi ("Paper dealers' town"), and Ishiyamachi ("Stonemasons' town") were born. Besides the canal's utilitarian purposes, the spectacle of men shouting and towing long, cargo-laden boats upstream became something of a tourist attraction, regularly featured in popular tourist guidebooks (see Figure 8.3).

Eastward Expansion and the Disappearance of the Odoi

The Takase Canal was a resounding success, and its construction transformed the land-locked capital into one of the busiest port towns in the region. It also catalyzed robust urban development east of the Odoi city wall. In time, the shogunate recognized the need to fortify the banks of the adjacent Kamo River, thereby addressing problems with flooding and erosion that had plagued the area for centuries. The construction of stone-lined embankments between Nijō and Shichijō in about 1669 made the land there, for the first time in the city's history, safe for the building of permanent homes and businesses. A narrow road running parallel to the river's west bank between Sanjō and Shijō was created. As home to the most

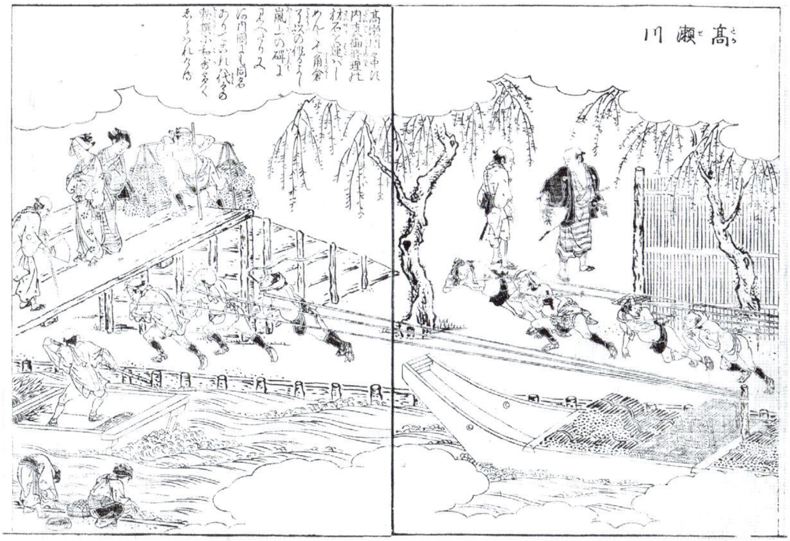

8.3. *Shūi Miyako meisho zue* (section), depicting people towing supplies up the Takase Canal for the reconstruction of the Imperial Palace. Courtesy of International Research Center for Japanese Studies (Nichibunken)

popular geisha houses, this "Pontochō," from the Portuguese word meaning "the point," would become early modern and modern Kyoto's most important entertainment district. The river basin itself became a popular destination, particularly during the fair seasons. The broad open areas where the river intersected with Sanjō, Shijō, and Gojō were particularly dynamic. There, stages were built to hold *kabuki* and *noh* performances, while numerous "amusement" booths offered more intimate encounters. It was from about this time that it became common for townspeople to engage in a summertime activity known as *kawara-nōryō* ("strolling by the river to cool off") and to drink *sake* and take meals on veranda-like platforms jutting over the water (*kawa-yuka*, or just *yuka* in Kyoto today). A scene of men enjoying the company of a *geisha* on one such platform is immortalized in *Shijō kawara yūryō*, a woodblock print by Utagawa Hiroshige (1797–1858).

Development eroded the Odoi physically while the persistent state of peace undermined the wall's function as a defensive apparatus. An illustration from 1676 shows numerous homes standing on land formerly occupied by the embankment just west of Pontochō. The accompanying caption, which refers to the area as Kawaramachi, or "Riverbank town," narrates the Odoi's disappearance and reveals the geopolitical implications of such change:

In former times, the land within the [Odoi] embankment was defined as the "inner-capital" (Rakuchū) while that beyond was the "outer capital" (Rakugai). In this area, later generations have built homes here and there, and the Odoi now lies beneath them.[19]

Development soon extended further east. The urbanization of the broad and gently sloping plain between the river and the Higashiyama Hills was only partially driven by the need for more space. The area's many temples, which thrived as the result of generous shogunal patronage, became popular destinations for pilgrims and tourists, as widely circulated guidebooks such as *Kyōwarabe*, *Kyōsuzume*, and *Kyōhabutae* extolled the area's wonders. A steady and seasonally heavy stream of visitors generated reliable demand for a variety of goods as well as lodging and leisure activities. There was an explosion in the number of shops, inns, and homes, resulting in the transformation of a disparate patchwork of "towns in front of the gates" (*monzen-machi*) into a more-or-less contiguous tapestry of urbanization. A popular gazetteer of the period published in 1686 reported that the roads east of the Kamo River are so well developed, "they differ not at all from those within the capital proper."[20] By the end of the Tokugawa period, westward expansion had also begun, putting Kyoto on track to eventually fill up a large portion of the Uta basin.

Following the emperor's relocation to Tokyo in 1868, it was feared that Kyoto would suffer the same plight of Nara, which after losing its capital status in the eighth century had become a virtual museum: a storehouse of priceless historical and cultural treasures with almost no political or economic relevance. True to the zeitgeist, modernization became the mantra, and in several respects the "old" capital became a beacon of progress. In 1890, for example, engineers succeeded in the technologically daunting task of drawing water from Lake Biwa via a tunnel (Biwako sosui) bored six kilometers through the Higashiyama Hills. Emerging at a site near the temple of Nanzenji, the water was harnessed to turn the turbines of Japan's first hydroelectric plant, opened in 1891. It also irrigated a large portion of the city via a carefully planned canal system (Shirakawa) that remains useful to this day. Electricity generated at the Keage plant, among other things, powered streetlights and a streetcar that, being Japan's first, served as the national model.

8.4. Kyoto's urban landscape through time. Heian-kyō grid (brown); neighborhood federations (*chō-gumi*) during Age of Warring States (yellow); Nijō Castle of Ashikaga Yoshiaki (blue); Jurakudai Palace (green); Nijō Castle of the Tokugawa period (blue and white); Imperial Palace (post-1336) and Kyoto Noble Village of Tokugawa era (purple); Odoi city wall (brown line).

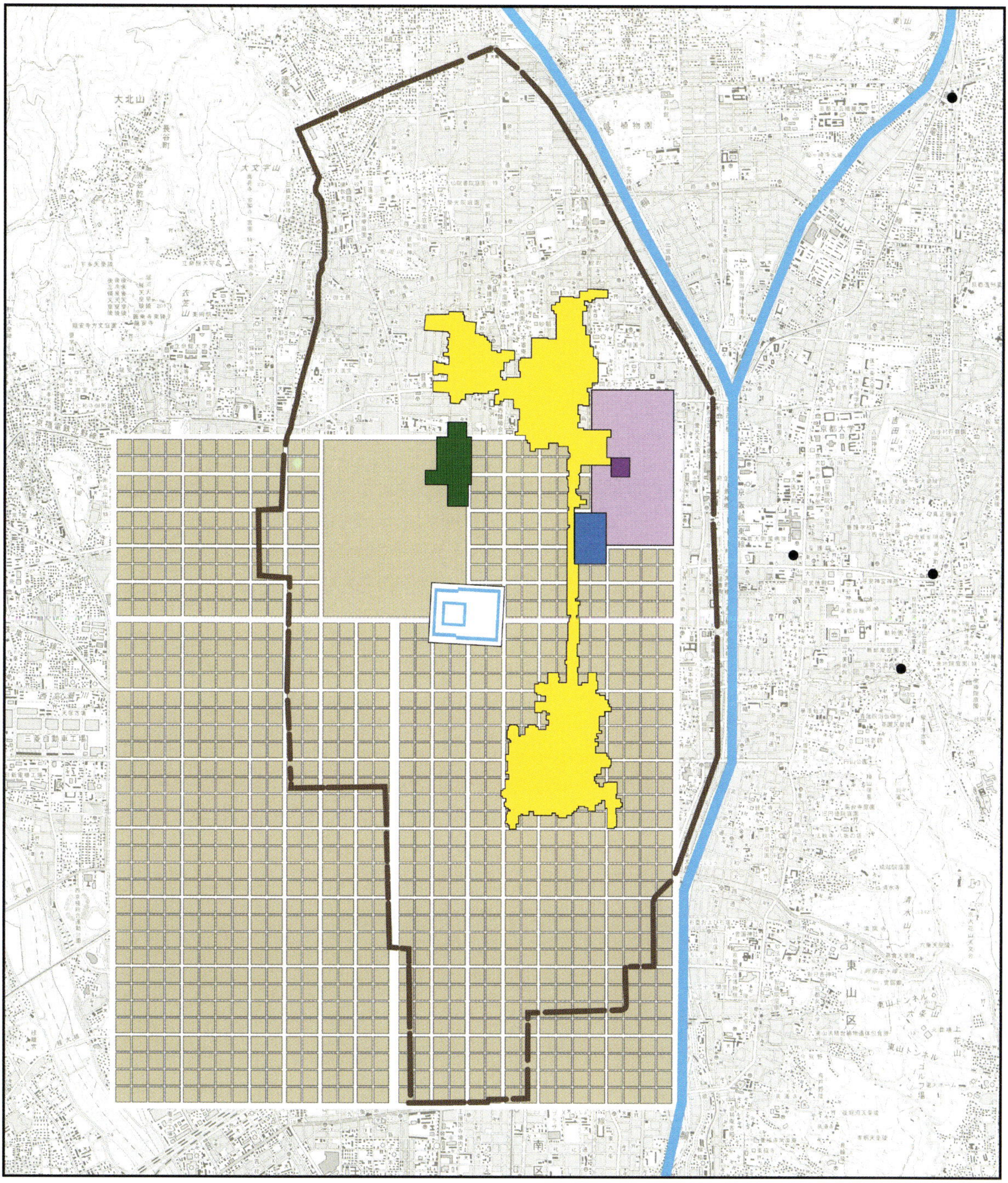
大北山
大文字山
三菱自動車工場
東山区

Modernization had a profound impact on Kyoto's architectural and urban heritage. With the Meiji Restoration, the Imperial Palace—the city's philosophical and cultural heart for more than a millennium—was left essentially vacant. Many Buddhist temples were vandalized due to an organized campaign that, until 1945, persecuted the "foreign" religion.[21] *Machiya* were dismantled at an alarming rate, usually replaced by ferroconcrete structures. Many roads were widened, paved, and bathed in neon. Despite all these changes, it is still possible to argue that modernity—with its relative political and economic stability, technologies, and robust preservation regimes—has, on balance, actually enhanced Kyoto's cultural legacy. It certainly made the city a more pleasant place to live. For all its cultural brilliance, premodern Kyoto was a dirty, dangerous, and perpetually unfinished place. Fires frequently wiped out large portions of the cityscape, and civil strife was common. The many famous temples and shrines so celebrated today were often poorly maintained, and the Kamo River was notoriously strewn with rubbish and rotting corpses.

Today, however, all that is a distant memory. Kyoto's countless temples and shrines stand as gleaming monuments to rich histories and living traditions. Seventeen UNESCO World Heritage Sites draw visitors from around the globe, and the city is the number one destination for Japanese domestic tourism. Aggressive preservation campaigns have stemmed the tide of *machiya* destruction, inspiring a trend to convert many into fashionable shops and restaurants. Even the built-up commercial areas have begun to take on more of a "traditional" appearance as new laws ban the construction of high-rises and the use of bright colors and gaudy signs. Purists will always lament the loss of old buildings, and they are right to do so. At the same time, however, it should be acknowledged that Kyoto today is perhaps more beautiful than it has ever been. It is truly one of the world's great historical cities.

Notes

Chapter 1: Heian-kyō: The Ideal

1. In English, see McCullough, "The Capital and Its Society," and Hall, "Kyoto as Historical Background." The most exhaustive examination of Heian-kyō (and Kyoto) in a Western language is Fiévé, ed., *Atlas historique de Kyoto*.
2. While numerous primary sources refer back to official and "original" codes banning temples, shrines, and warriors from the city, only burial receives explicit mention in the eighth-century Taihō and Yōrō codes, under the heading *sōsō-rei*.
3. McCullough, "The Capital and Its Society," 122.
4. A law mandating capital residence for anyone of third rank or higher and imperial princes was issued in 895. See *Dajōkanpu*, entry for Kanpyō 7 (895)/12/3, from *Ruiju sandai-kyaku*, in *KST* 25:620. This topic is also discussed in Hotate, *Heian ōchō*, 58.
5. See Toby, "Why Leave Nara?" The Versailles of Louis XIV served a similar function in centralizing authority, in part by severing the ties that bound the landed elite to their bases of influence.
6. Kostof, *The City Shaped*, 99–100.
7. One of the key motivations for establishing an "eternal" or stable capital was the abolition of the so-called dual capital system. On this topic and Nagaoka-kyō's history in general, see Van Goethem, *Nagaoka: Japan's Forgotten Capital*.
8. Van Goethem, *Nagaoka: Japan's Forgotten Capital*, 246–251.
9. *Nihon kiryaku*, entry for Enryaku 13 (794)/11/8, quoted in Tsunoda, ed., *Heian-kyō teiyō*, 63. Adapted from a translation by McCullough in "The Capital and Its Society," 101.
10. New research on the concept of *shijin sōō* ("befitting the four gods") shows that the topographic prescriptions applied to Heian-kyō and earlier capitals were probably limited to the existence of mountains and not, as is commonly held, streams, roads, and marshes. See Van Goethem, "The Four Directional Animals in East Asia."
11. The model is on display at Kyōto Asunii, a lifelong learning center operated by the Kyoto city government. For images, see Kyōto-shi, ed., *Yomigaeru Heian-kyō*, 17.

12. For details on the early Chinese urban model and how it was imported into Japan, see Steinhardt, *Chinese Imperial City Planning*, esp. ch. 5.
13. On the evolution of capital design, see the essay by François Macé in *AHK*, 41–46.
14. These and other details on the capital's physical traits are recorded in *Engishiki,* a tenth-century collection of court codes. Published in *KST*, vol. 15. In particular, see the section "Sayū kyōshiki: Kyōtei."
15. During the eighth century, the Japanese court received tribute-bearing missions from Korea on twenty-one separate occasions. For details, see von Verschuer, *Across the Perilous Sea*, 11–13.
16. See Heibon-sha, ed., *Kyōto-shi no chimei*, 33–34.
17. Several scholars have addressed this issue in English, including Toby in "Why Leave Nara?" 332, and Van Goethem in *Nagaoka: Japan's Forgotten Capital.*
18. Walls were so elemental to the composition of a city in classical China that the word for "city" itself, *chéng,* is synonymous with "wall" or "fortress."
19. Takahashi, "'Capitals' in Medieval East Asia," 71–72.
20. Murai Yasuhiko calls the building of Heian-kyō and the wars to pacify the Emishi the "two great projects" of Kanmu's tenure. See Tsunoda, ed., *Heian-kyō teiyō*, 64. Besides the war with the Emishi, the Japanese also felt threatened by attacks from the Korean kingdom of Silla. See *CHJ* 2:xviii, xx, and 89.
21. The current, albeit not universal, consensus among urban historians of Kyoto is to use the word "*machi*" to signify the physical space or the unit of a block. The word "*chō*" is used to signify a social unit or phenomenon that may or may not correspond to a physical block, as in "*chō-gumi,*" meaning "neighborhood federation." This topic is explored in more detail below.
22. For an overview of the problems with the block planning system in Heijō-kyō, see *KR* 1:260–261.
23. See chapter 2 of Akiyama and Nakamura's *Kyōto "machi" no kenkyū*, perhaps the single best study treating the material and social history of blocks in premodern Kyoto.
24. Mumford, "City: Forms and Functions," 450, recapitulated by Hall in "Kyoto as Historical Background," 13.
25. See the notes on conventions in the front matter for details on the use of the word "road" in this study. In Figure 1.3 and throughout this book, "*-kōji*" has been added to the names of roads only when not doing so might invite confusion.
26. Most roads in Heian-kyō were of two widths: sixteen meters and twenty-four meters. By way of comparison, Fifth Avenue in New York City today is about seventeen meters wide.
27. The official is Yoshishige Yasutane, author of *Chiteiki.* His tenth-century account of Heian-kyō will be discussed later in this study. For this anecdote, see Tsunoda, ed., *Heian-kyō teiyō*, 71. On the exact location of Yasutane's residence (called "Chitei"), see Tsunoda, *Ōchō no eizō.*
28. The Daidairi was expanded two blocks to the north in the ninth century,

thus extending the boundaries of the entire capital in the same direction and causing the creation of two more gates (to make a total of fourteen). While this topic is of profound significance due to its relationship to the consolidation of imperial authority and the rising wealth of the state, it is outside the scope of the current narrative. For discussion, see Tsunoda, ed., *Heian-kyō teiyō*, 120–121.

29. There was a major consolidation of imperial institutions in the ninth century resulting in some restructuring of the Daidairi. See Tsunoda, ed., *Heian-kyō teiyō*, 119–120.
30. The earliest and most reliable source of information on the appearance of the Dairi comes from scroll no. 2 of *Nenjūgyōji emaki*, a series of illustrated scrolls produced in the twelfth century. The Kyoto University Faculty of Letters has made its copy of the document available on the Internet at http://edb.kulib.kyoto-u.ac.jp/exhibit/index.html.
31. The early Japanese polity was different from China in two critical ways. The emperor was sovereign by right of divine descent, and public ranks and posts were generally bestowed based on birth and character rather than merit. In this latter respect, Japan was an aristocracy par excellence.
32. On these three sites, see corresponding entries in Heibon-sha, ed., *Kyōto-shi no chimei.*
33. Entry for "Kōrokan" in Heibon-sha, ed., *Kyōto-shi no chimei*, 987.
34. *KR* 1:384–386.
35. Eastern Market was "Higashi no ichi"; Western Market was "Nishi no ichi." On the alternating arrangement of the official markets (and how that arrangement mutated over time), see *Sankaiki*, entry for Jishō 3 (1179)/1/6, in *SKR* 4:117, doc. 26.
36. *Engishiki* includes details on how the markets worked and their appearances. For analysis, see Takahashi et al., eds., *Zushū Nihon toshi-shi*, 63, and Sugeta Kaoru's comments in Tsunoda, ed., *Heian-kyō teiyō*, 76, 359–372.
37. See Nishikawa and Takahashi, *Kyōto sen-nihyaku-nen, kami* (vol. 1), 24–27.
38. Several sources on Kūya's proselytism are in *SKR* 4:66, docs. 38–39. Also see Hori, *Kūya.*
39. *Nihon kiryaku*, entry for Enryaku 13 (794)/7/1, in *SKR* 4:64, doc. 31.
40. *KR* 1:366–373. Also see entries for Tōji and Saiji in Heibon-sha, ed., *Kyōto-shi no chimei.*
41. See NHK Special, "Yomigaeru Heian-kyō."
42. On the temple proscription, see Yamada, *Kyōto toshi-shi no kenkyū*, 151.
43. For maps showing the locations of *shoshi-kuriya-machi*, see Kyōto-shi, *Yomigaeru Heian-kyō*, 26–31.
44. Representative scholarship on *shinden-zukuri* includes Ōta, *Shinden-zukuri no kenkyū*, and Kawamoto, *Shinden-zukuri no kūkan to gishiki.* What is outlined here is discussed in more detail in Stavros, "Building Warrior Legitimacy in Medieval Kyoto."
45. Coaldrake, *Architecture and Authority in Japan*, 64.
46. For details and useful diagrams, see the essay by Fiévé in *AHK*, 85–88.
47. Kawamoto, "Kizoku jūtaku."

48. A useful source for visualizing the structure and décor of *shinden*-style palaces is Kyoto Costume Museum (Fūzoku hakubutsu-kan), ed., *Genji monogatari Rokujō-in no seikatsu.*
49. On gates as a function of status, see Kawamoto, "Kizoku jūtaku."
50. *Shōyūki*, entry for Chōgen 3 (1030)/5/14 (vol. 8, 176) cites a court order cracking down on *zuryō* building homes in Kyoto that did not follow status-based rules related to land sizes and gate orientations. Discussed in Oboroya, "Ōchō-ki no sumai," 128.
51. *Nihon kōki*, cited in Tsunoda, ed., *Heian-kyō teiyō*, 65. A second attempt to move the capital occurred in 810 during the "Kusuko affair," an attempted imperial coup in all but name.

Chapter 2: Heian-kyō: The Real

1. *Dajōkanpu*, entry for Kōnin 10 (819)/11/5, from *Ruiju sandai-kyaku*, in *KST* 25:485.
2. *Dajōkanpu*, entry for Tenchō 5 (828)/12/16, from *Ruiju sandai-kyaku*, in *KST* 25:642–643.
3. *Fusōryakki*, entry for Ōtoku 3 (1086)/6/26, in *KST* 12:326.
4. *Sandai jitsuroku*, entry for Jōkan 13 (871)/i8/11, in *KST* 4:293. For this interpretation, see Tsunoda, ed., *Heian-kyō teiyō*, 69.
5. Yoshishige, *Chiteiki*, 417–422. This translation is adapted from Watson, *Four Huts*, 25–26.
6. For a detailed discussion on the extent to which Heian-kyō was completed (and left incomplete), see Yamada, *Kyōto toshi-shi no kenkyū*, ch. 3.
7. For a selection of documents that refer specifically to "laws" governing land sizes as a function of status, see Oboroya, "Ōchō-ki no sumai," 129.
8. McCullough, "The Capital and Its Society," 120.
9. See Tsunoda, ed., *Heian-kyō teiyō*, 72–73, for discussion and an example of a *zuryō* named Ōe Kiminaka who possessed three one-block homes with a storehouse at one.
10. *Nihon kiryaku*, entry for Chōgen 3 (1030)/4/23, in *DNS* 2:29, 219.
11. *Shōyūki*, entries for Chōgen 3 (1030)/6/23 and 6/28, vol. 8, 180–182.
12. *KR* 1:494–497.
13. For an overview of population estimates, see *KR* 1:300–309.
14. Akiyama and Nakamura, *Kyōto "machi" no kenkyū*, ch. 2, parts 5 and 6. For diagrams, see Takahashi et al., eds., *Zushū Nihon toshi-shi*, 66.
15. There is some speculation inherent in consideration of premodern readings. The current explanation comes primarily from the fact that the word "*chō*" is still used in Kyoto today to describe a social unit bound by one or more shared streets.
16. Lamp-oil road: Aburanokōji; Brocade road: Nishikinokōji; Salt road: Shionokōji. See Akiyama and Nakamura, *Kyōto "machi" no kenkyū*, ch. 2, part 2. On the emergence of road names, see Takahashi, "Machi kara tōri e."
17. Takahashi, "Machi kara tōri e."
18. See, for example, discussion in *CHJ* 1, ch. 1.

19. See *KR* 1:526.
20. *Shoku Nihon kōki*, entry for Shōwa 9 (842)/10/20, cited in *KR* 1:526. Also discussed in Tsunoda, ed., *Heian-kyō teiyō*, 76.
21. On Parhae exchanges with Japan, see von Verschuer, *Across the Perilous Sea*, 20–21. On Heian foreign relations more generally, see *CHJ* 2:80–96.
22. See entry for "Rajōmon" in Heibon-sha, ed., *Kyōto-shi no chimei*, 34. The stones were excavated and moved to Hōjōji in 1023.
23. *Dajōkanpu*, entry for Jōkan 4 (862)/3/8, from *Ruiju sandai-kyaku*, cited in Heibon-sha, ed., *Kyōto-shi no chimei*, 529.
24. See entry for "Kōrokan" in Heibon-sha, ed., *Kyōto-shi no chimei*, 987.
25. On Kūkai's takeover of Tōji, see Abé, *The Weaving of Mantra*, 37, 60–61. As a Shingon sectarian temple, Tōji's name was changed to Kyōōgokokuji.
26. See entry for "Saiji" in Heibon-sha, ed., *Kyōto-shi no chimei*, 1003–1004.
27. McCullough, "The Capital and Its Society," 173–175.
28. Hall, "Kyoto as Historical Background," 15.
29. On the *sato-dairi* phenomenon in general, see Tsunoda, ed., *Heian-kyō teiyō*, 78–79.
30. The *sato-dairi* phenomenon is discussed in greater detail in chapter 3.
31. For more on this topic, see Stavros, "Building Warrior Legitimacy in Medieval Kyoto."
32. The *tsune-gosho* phenomenon is discussed in greater detail in chapter 4.
33. Oratories are discussed in greater detail in chapter 4.

Chapter 3: Making Kyoto Medieval

1. In his research, Yamada Kunikazu discussed Kyoto's urban medievalization in terms of a process by which the capital became a metropolitan "complex" consisting of numerous suburbs and exurbs. The nodal development explored in this chapter compliments Yamada's argument yet focuses more on the reasons for fragmentation instead of the results. Yamada, *Kyotō toshi-shi no kenkyū*, 181–186. Also see his essay in *AHK*, 157–162.
2. Contrary to popular understanding, no change in the city's name, formal or otherwise, occurred during the transition from the classical to medieval eras. See the explanation in the section on Conventions and Abbreviations.
3. Yoshishige, *Chiteiki*, 417–418.
4. See the Yūgao chapter of *Genji*. It is Ukon who appeals to Genji on behalf of princess Tamakazura, Yūgao's daughter.
5. Yoshishige, *Chiteiki*, 417–418.
6. These "outer markets" (read as either *gai-chō* or *soto-machi*) appear in several textual sources along with diagrams in *SKR* 4:64–66, docs. 33–36. For discussion, see Takahashi et al., eds., *Zushū Nihon toshi-shi*, 53. Another map, *Shōō go-nen kozu*, produced in 1292, shows substantial market expansion around the site of the Eastern Market. In Tsunoda, ed., *Heian-kyō teiyō*, 360.
7. Inscriptions in the *Engishiki* map identify these dark lines as "rivers," yet they are probably euphemistic. For analysis, see Kodera, "Heian-kyō no kūkan-teki hensen ni kansuru kōsatsu" (parts 1 and 2).

8. Yasutane is alluding to a poem in *Shih chi*, "Hereditary House of Sung," which describes the desolate appearance of the former capital of the Yin dynasty. Burton Watson has translated the phrase as "where only the 'ears of grain droop down,'" in his *Four Huts*, 37–38, n. 3.
9. For more on the sustained viability of Ukyō, see Tsunoda, ed., *Heian-kyō teiyō*, 179–184.
10. See *KR* 2:265. Fujiwara no Munetada also refers to fires in "*shimo-watari*" in a diary entry dated Gen'ei 2 (1119)/4/15. See *CYK(r)* 5:127.
11. The "capital" appears as 京中. "Upper and lower towns" appears as 上下町中. *Kanjingaku shōki*, cited as *Shien shōnin ichigogyōshōki* (*sic*) in *KR* 2:265.
12. *Chiteiki* refers to the bogs in the east and the chronic flooding problem in the northeast. On Heian topography, see Tsunoda, ed., *Heian-kyō teiyō*, 42–48.
13. Other factors included proximity to Shimogamo Shrine, Enryakuji Temple, and the Kamo River, the last from which many elites diverted water to irrigate their palace grounds.
14. For a full study on urbanization north of Ichijō, including discussion of retreat palaces, see Takahashi, *Kyōto chūsei toshi-shi kenkyū*, ch. 1, parts 2 and 3. For images, see Takahashi et al., eds., *Zushū Nihon toshi-shi*, 65.
15. Takahashi, *Kyōto chūsei toshi-shi kenkyū*, ch. 1, part 5. For an image, see Takahashi et al., eds., *Zushū Nihon toshi-shi*, 55.
16. This overview of elite household enterprises and *karei* is based on the work of G. Cameron Hurst III in "The Structure of the Heian Court," 46–49.
17. For reference to a "northern storehouse block" see *CYK(r)* 5:193, entry for Hōan 1 (1120)/1/2. In addition to "storehouse blocks" surrounding Fujiwara no Tadazane's palace, the source *Shissei shoshō* refers to an office of construction (*shūri-sho*), a provisions office (*sakumotsu-sho*), a kitchen office (*nie-dono*), and dedicated storage facilities (*osame-dono*). Discussed in *KR* 1:512.
18. Documents refer to storehouses filled with fine silk, gold, silver, family heirlooms, and countless other tangible monuments to their owner's private wealth. See *Heian ibun*, no. 2614, and *Hyōhanki*, in *SKR* 4:117, doc. 25. Other related documents are in *SKR* 4:115–117.
19. For the authoritative research on *mikura-machi*, see Kitamura, *Heian-kyō*, ch. 4. *Chiteiki* refers to several tens of retainer families that clustered around an aristocratic palace in Ukyō.
20. On the topic of aristocratic marriage practices, see McCullough, "Japanese Marriage Institutions in the Heian Period."
21. On Fujiwara domination of the *sesshō* and *kanpaku* offices, see *CHJ* 4:64–74.
22. Purpose-built *sato-dairi* of outstanding size and opulence included Ichijōin (built 1010) and Kayain (built 1060). For details, see Hashimoto Yoshihiko, *Heian kizoku*, ch. 6. For a map showing the locations and sizes of *sato-dairi*, see Kyōto-shi, ed., *Yomigaeru Heian-kyō*, 110.
23. *Eiga monogatari*, book 2. In English, see McCullough and McCullough, trans., *A Tale of Flowering Fortunes*, vol. 1, 114.
24. See Fujiwara, *Midō kanpakuki*, entry for Kankō 6 (1009)/10/19, vol. 2,

24–25. Michinaga named his *nishi-no-tai* "Seiryōden" and central *shinden* "Shishinden."

25. Oboroya Hisashi has written that the object of imitation was to ensure the emperor "did not feel disoriented." See his "Ōchō-ki no sumai," 132.
26. On the medieval economy, see Hongō, *Chūsei-jin no keizai kankaku*, and Gay, *The Moneylenders of Late Medieval Kyoto.*
27. See chapter 2 for discussion on how officials attempted in vain to save the Western Market. Also, *KR* 2:487.
28. For documents that refer to several fires, see Tsunoda, ed., *Heian-kyō teiyō*, 76.
29. The places where roads were turned into something else—usually cultivated fields or shops—were called *kōsho.* On this phenomenon, see Umada, "Tōji-ryō kōsho."
30. On the topic of *kōsho* as "unaffiliated space" or *kugai*, see Takahashi, "'Capitals' in Medieval East Asia," 76–77. On *kugai* in general, see Amino, *Muen—Kugai—Raku. Engishiki* mentions taxes being levied on squatters settled near official markets. *SKR* 4:4:64, doc. 31.
31. See chapter 2 of this book and the maps in Takahashi et al., eds., *Zushū Nihon toshi-shi*, 88–89.
32. See the topographic map in Takahashi et al., eds., *Zushū Nihon toshi-shi*, 50. The road names "Machi" and "Muromachi" are toponymic. They derive from the fact that both ran through major "dormitory blocks" (*kuriya-machi*) in Kamigyō during the Heian period. See chapter 1 of this book and Takahashi, *Kyō machiya*, 27–28.
33. On the emergence of *machiya*, see Takahashi, *Kyō machiya.* It should be noted that 町家 was far more common in premodern sources than 町屋, which is standard today.
34. Tsunoda, ed., *Heian-kyō teiyō*, 77. Takahashi, "'Capitals' in Medieval East Asia," 76–77.
35. Fujiwara, *Meigetsuki*, entry for Bunryaku 1 (1234)/8/5, vol. 3, 422.
36. On *dosō* and *sakaya* functioning as financiers, see Gay, *The Moneylenders of Late Medieval Kyoto.* Enryakuji on Mount Hiei exercised a large degree of control over most of Kyoto's moneylenders until 1333, at which time Emperor Godaigo sought to sever that strong tie. Then, from about 1441, the Ashikaga shogunate sought to wrest control of financial outlets from temples and the aristocracy. See *KR* 3:231–268.
37. *KR* 3:231–234.
38. *Byōsō-shi*, paraphrased in Tsunoda, ed., *Heian-kyō teiyō*, 77. For image of the obese *kashiage*, see Kyōto-shi, ed., *Yomigaeru Heian-kyō*, 168.
39. *Kitano tenmangu monjo*, entry for Ōei 33 (1426)/2/16, in *SKR* 4:257–262, no. 27.
40. See Kawashima, *Gion-matsuri.*
41. *KR* 2:264–66.
42. On land ownership in Kyoto, see Wakita, *Nihon chūsei toshi-ron*, ch. 2. On premodern land ownership more generally, see Watanabe and Gomi, eds., *Tochi shoyū-shi.*
43. For example, the great shrines of Kitano and Gion (Yasaka) were both under the control of Enryakuji for much of their histories.

44. Itō, *Toshi no kūkan-shi*, 90.
45. The Gion shrine today is called Yasaka Shrine.
46. Itō, *Toshi no kūkan-shi*, 89–90.
47. On church-state relations with respect to Buddhism, see Bowring, *The Religious Traditions of Japan, 500–1600*, esp. chs. 3 and 7.
48. On commendation, see *CHJ* 3:261–264. On the role of *zuryō* in particular, see Hurst, "*Kugyō* and *Zuryō*," 94.
49. On religious demonstrations and activism during the medieval era, see Adolphson, *Gates of Power*. This topic is discussed in more detail in the next chapter.
50. On Zen temple structures, sub-temples, and their populations, see Collcutt, *Five Mountains*, ch. 5.
51. Urban character means that the occupants were engaged in occupations other than primary industries (agriculture in this period).
52. Strictly speaking, in the documentary record, the word "*monzen*" was much more common than *monzen-machi*. On the topic of *monzen-machi*, see Itō, *Toshi no kūkan-shi*, ch. 1.
53. For work on medieval temple boundaries and jurisdictions, see Itō, *Toshi no kūkan-shi*, ch. 1.
54. On temple law (*jihō*), see Itō, *Toshi no kūkan-shi*, 3–4, and *KR* 2:55–56.
55. For leading research on Hosshōji's appearance, see the work of Tomishima Yoshiyuki, including "Hosshōji garan keitai to sono tokuchō" and "Hosshōji hakkaku kyūjū no tō no fukugen ni tsuite." From the outside, the Hosshōji's pagoda appeared to have ten stories. The first tier of roofing, however, is an attached roof (*mokoshi*) with no relationship to internal construction. The six temples of Shirakawa are referred to as Rikishōji or Risshōji.
56. Evidence of various officials and others relocating to Shirakawa is in *Honchō seiki*, entry for Kyūan 4 (1148)/3/10, in *KST* 8:659–660.
57. For detailed treatment of Shirawaka's composition, see Inoue, "Insei-ki ni okeru shin-toshi no kaihatsu."
58. Horiuchi, "Shirakawa gaiku ni okeru chiwari to sono rekishi-teki hensen." Yamada, *Nihon chūsei no shuto to ōken toshi*, ch. 2, part 1 (map on 136).
59. *Heike monogatari*, book 7.
60. For the most recent scholarship on Shirakawa and Toba, see Yamada, *Nihon chūsei no shuto to ōken toshi*, ch. 2. Yamada summarizes his findings in French in *AHK*, 113–116. Other work includes Inoue, "Insei-ki ni okeru shin-toshi no kaihatsu" and "Insei-ki no Kyōto" and Mikawa, "Toba-dono to insei."
61. *Fusōryakki*, entry for Ōtoku 3 (1086)/10/20, in *KST* 12:326–327.
62. On Hōjūji, see Oboroya, *Heian kizoku to teidai*, 120–169.

Chapter 4: Rakuchū-Rakugai

1. Amino, *Igyō no ōken*, esp. 226–246.
2. Onjōji Temple (also known as Miidera) is located in the neighboring Shiga Prefecture (premodern Ōmi) and Kōfukuji Temple is located in Nara Prefecture (premodern Yamato).

3. Adolphson, *Gates of Power*, 5.
4. *CYK(i)* 1:228, entry for Kanji 7 (1093)/8/26.
5. On the content and form of demonstrations, see Adolphson, *Gates of Power*, esp. ch. 6.
6. *CYK(i)* 2:278, entry for Kahō 2 (1095)/10/26.
7. *CYK(r)* 3:340–341, entry for Tennin 1 (1108)/3/30.
8. *Honchō seiki*, entry for Kanji 1 (1087)/8/29, in *KST*, 9:282.
9. On oratories (appearing in documents as *midō*, *odō*, or *jibutsu-dō*), see Tsunoda, ed., *Heian-kyō teiyō*, 82–84, and Takahashi, "'Chōdō' to 'sentō' to hitobito," 38.
10. On the distinction between 堂 and 寺, see Yamada, *Kyōto toshi-shi no kenkyū*, 151, and Tsunoda, ed., *Heian-kyō teiyō*, 84.
11. Morozane refers to the principle of "self restraint" (*habakari*) as the only hindrance to the covering of a house with tiles (the symbol of a certain status) and building "temple bells within Rakuchū." See *Hyakuren-shō*, entry for Kahō 2 (1095)/6/18, in *KST* 11:43. The dedication ceremony is detailed in *CYK(i)* 2:229, Kahō 2 (1095)/6/18.
12. Customarily, the imperial regalia included a sacred mirror, curved jewel, and sword.
13. From *Kikki*, entry for Jishō 4 (1180)/11/10, cited and discussed in Takahashi, *Chūsei no toshi to bushi*, 110.
14. Jien, *Gukanshō*, entry from about Juei 2 (1183)/8/20, discussed in Kuroda, "Nihon chūsei no kokka to tennō," 8, 12.
15. *GMK* 2:14, entry for Ōan 4 (1371)/3/24.
16. The image of Kiyomori as a "despot" might be the result of a postdeposal propaganda campaign, which includes the narrative in *Taiheiki*.
17. *Hyakuren-shō*, entry for Kanji 5 (1091)/6/12, in *KST* 11:41. Yoshiie eventually regained repute and moved back to Kyoto.
18. *Hyōhanki*, entry for Hōgen 1 (1156)/7/5, vol. 19, 114–115.
19. *Hyakuren-shō*, entry for Hōgen 1 (1156)/11/18, in *KST* 11:72.
20. *Shōki mokuroku*, entry for Chōgen 1 (1028)/6/1, in *DNS* 2:27, 164–165.
21. For discussion, see Gomi, "Shichō no kōsei to bakufu."
22. Saionji, *Kinhira kōki*, entry for Enkei 4 (1311)/3/25, vol. 3, 244–245; also discussed in Gomi, "Shichō no kōsei to bakufu."
23. On the Jōkyū Disturbance, see *CHJ* 3:66–73.
24. Ibid.
25. *Azuma kagami*, no. 4494, entry for Katei 4 (1238)/6/10. Discussed in Heibon-sha, ed., *Kyōto-shi no chimei*, 45.
26. On the Rokuhara tandai(fu), see Takahashi, *Chūsei no toshi to bushi*, esp. part 1.
27. Taira no Kiyomori maintained a residence in the Hachijō area, the city's far south. A warrior who owned a house at the intersection of Oshinokōji and Horikawa wrote, "It is customary, past and present, to have someone else live in your Kyoto residence." In other words, a warrior might *have* a Kyoto residence, but someone else would generally live in it. See Takahashi, *Chūsei no toshi to bushi*, 111, n. 36.

28. Widely referred to as *Shōgen ninen in rakugaki*, this document is included in *SKR* 5:147.
29. *Shibukaki*, entry for Tenpuku 1 (1233)/5/19, in *GR* 27:160–161. Tokiuji's tenure was from 1224 to 1230.
30. Several mentions are in *Kamakura bafuku tsuika-hō*, such as in no. 136, in Satō and Ikeuchi, eds., *Chūsei hōsei shiryō-shū, vol. 1, Kamakura bakufu-hō.*
31. Ibid., no. 100. For discussion on the destruction of criminal property, see Takahashi, *Chūsei no toshi to bushi*, 112.
32. *Azuma kagami*, no. 2767, entry for Kenpō 3 (1215)/4/18.
33. Hurst, "The Kōbu Polity."
34. See Conventions and Abbreviations at the front of the book for discussion on the city's name.
35. Kuroda Jun'ichirō says that the capital was a critical element of medieval kingship. See his "Nihon chūsei no kokka to tennō," 8–12.
36. Kamo no Chōmei, *Hōjōki*, segment 19.
37. *Taiheiki*, book 9.
38. This finding is based on statistics accumulated through word-frequency surveys conducted on the full-text databases of the University of Tokyo's Historiographical Institute as well as the following primary sources (scanned and processed for optical character recognition): *Chūyūki*, *Shōyūki*, *Gunsho ruijū*, *Zoku gunsho ruijū*, *Meigetsuki*, *Azuma kagami*, *Noritoki kyōki*, *Nochikagami*, *Entairyaku*, *Moromoriki*, *Gogumaiki*, *Goshinshin-in kanpakuki*. The words queried include 京中, 上京, 京内, 在京, 入京, 洛中, 上洛, 洛内, 在洛, 入洛.
39. Seta, *(Zōho) Rakuchū-rakugai no gunzō*, 252–256.
40. For example, see the case above where Kamakura officials were required to consult with relevant *kenmon* before destroying the homes of criminals located outside the city.
41. An early distinction between *hare* and *ke* made by Yanagita is found in his *Shokumotsu to shinzō* (published in 1940). Also see Yanagita's folklore encyclopedia, *Minzokugaku jiten*, 449. Modern scholarship on this topic includes Masuda, "Heian no waka-shi de 'hare' to 'ke' towa nanika," and Ihara, *Nihon chūsei no kokusei to kasei.* The author is grateful to Mikael Bauer and several other participants in a discussion related to this topic carried out on PMJS.org.
42. Kawakami, *Nihon chūsei jūtaku no kenkyū*, 6–15. All citations refer to the 2003 edition. For further analysis, see Iibuchi, "Heian-ki shinden-zukuri ni okeru 'rei' oyobi 'hare' ni tsuite."
43. See discussion in chapter 1.
44. Kawakami, *Nihon chūsei jūtaku no kenkyū*, esp. 6–12, but also discussed throughout the book. Also see Stavros, "Building Warrior Legitimacy in Medieval Kyoto," 15–17.
45. On *shoin* style in general, see Gotō, *Nihon kenchiku-shi*, 148–155.
46. See the cases in chapter 3 of *zuryō* being punished for building palaces that covered too much land. Even the highest members of society were censured. According to *Ōkagami*, Fujiwara no Kaneie was called "preposterous" by his

peers for, among other things, building a wing of his Higashisanjō palace to resemble the Imperial Palace's Seiryōden. McCullough, *Ōkagami: The Great Mirror*, 162. Also see *KR* 1:462.

47. See chapter 3 for discussion of Fujiwara creation of *sato-dairi.*
48. Yoshie Akio, in his "Chūsei zenki no toshi to bunka," 213–214, refers to a phenomenon he calls "*sumi-wake*" (divided living), yet does not provide a systematic analysis.
49. See Shimizu, "Hōjōji no garan to sono seikaku," and Suematsu, "'Ōkagami' hōjōji shodō junkan ni miru ōidono Michinaga." *A Tale of Flowering Fortunes* (*Eiga monogatari*) gives detailed accounts of Hōjōji. See the English translation by McCullough and McCullough.
50. Stavros, "Locational Pedigree and Warrior Status in Medieval Kyoto."
51. On Higashiyama-dono's grounds plan and architecture, see the special issue of *Nihon-shi kenkyū*, no. 399, Nov. 1995. Yoshimitsu's "Golden Pavilion" was formally considered a reliquary (*shari-den*) while Yoshimasa's "Silver Pavilion" (Ginkaku kannon-den) was a Kannon Hall. To clarify names, it should be mentioned that Yoshimitsu created "Kitayama-dono," within which stood the structure known as the "Kinkaku reliquary" (Kinkaku shari-den). After his death, the site became the temple of "Rokuonji," and today it is customarily, yet only informally, called "Kinkakuji." The "Ginkaku Kannon Hall" was only one of many structures at Yoshimasa's Higashiyama-dono. Today, the site is the Rinzai sectarian temple of "Jishōji," informally called "Ginkakuji." Both Rokuonji and Jishōji are institutionally part of the Rinzai sublineage led by Shōkokuji.
52. On the topic of patterns, it is worth noting that Yorimichi's central religious structure at Uji was a "phoenix hall," topped by two bronze phoenix figures. The Golden Pavilion and the Silver Pavilion were both also topped by phoenixes. The significance of this similarity has yet to be explored.
53. See the second definition for "*betsugyō*" in *Nihon kokugo daijiten.* Inoue Mitsurō problematizes the meaning of the word in "Insei-ki no Kyōto," 142.
54. Kyōto-shi maizō bunka-zai kenkyū-sho, ed., *Insei-ki no Kyōto: Shirakawa to Toba.*
55. Hanazono (Emperor), *Hanazono tennō shinki*, entry for Bunpō 1 (1317)/4/19, vol. 2, 125–126.

Chapter 5: Warriors in the Capital

1. On Godaigo's imperial restoration and its failings, see Goble, *Kenmu: Go-daigo's Revolution.*
2. See Uwayokote, "*Taiheiki* no shakai," 220.
3. On the era of northern and southern courts ("Nanbokuchō" 1336–1392), see Varley, *Imperial Restoration in Medieval Japan*, and two books by Satō Shin'ichi and Itō Kiyoshi, both titled *Nanbokuchō no dōran.*
4. Strictly speaking, the Ashikaga shogunate was not established until Takauji was formally appointed shogun by the emperor in 1338. The institutional framework, however, was in place by 1336.

5. For the *Kenmu Formulary* in English, see Grossberg and Kanamoto, *The Laws of the Muromachi Bakufu*. In Japanese, see Satō and Ikeuchi, eds., *Chūsei hōsei shiryō-shū, vol. 2, Muromachi bakufu-hō.*
6. *Taiheiki*, book 12.
7. Documents on *shitaku tenjō* are in *Takeuchi Fumihira-shi shōzō monjo*, in *Gunma-ken-shi, shiryō hen,* vol. 6, no. 603. For comments on the severity of the quartering policy and its role in turning the population against Godaigo's regime, see Satō, *Nanbokuchō no dōran*, 150.
8. See the section on Shimogyō in chapter 3.
9. This dispute over the property at Sanjō–Madenokōji is chronicled in the diary of Moroshige's son, Nakahara Moronao. See *MMK* 10:172, entry for Jōji 6 (1367)/9/26.
10. *MMK* does not confirm victory, but we know with some certainty that Kogushi never succeeded in constructing a residence at the location in question.
11. On warrior movement into Shimogyō, see Takahashi et al., eds., *Zushū Nihon toshi-shi*, 86–87; Yamada, *Kyōto toshi-shi no kenkyū*, 171–180; Niki, *Kūkan, ōyake, kyōdōtai,* 49–54. Also, *KR* 2:528–531.
12. Commoner land ownership began during the Age of Warring States. On this, see Wakita, *Nihon chūsei toshi ron*, and Seta, "Kinsei toshi seiritsu-shi josetsu."
13. For a more detailed exploration of this topic, see two articles by Stavros: "The Sanjō bōmon Temple-Palace Complex," 17–18, and "A Dis-Integrated Urban Landscape."
14. Figure 5.1 was produced by synthesizing maps by Takahashi Yasuo (*Zushū Nihon toshi-shi*, 89) and Tasaka Yasuyuki ("Muromachi-ki Kyōto no toshi kūkan to bakufu," 50).
15. See discussion of commercial development in chapter 3.
16. Hayashiya with Elison, "Kyoto in the Muromachi Age," 19–20; *KR* 3:45; Hall, "Kyoto as Historical Background," 28; Takahashi et al., eds., *Zushū Nihon toshi-shi*, 86–87.
17. Kurokawa's essay, "Chōtei to bakufu," is in *KR* 3:46–47.
18. See discussion in chapter 3.
19. See Stavros, "Locational Pedigree and Warrior Status in Medieval Kyoto," 14–15, and Tomishima, "Shōkokuji shichi-jū no tō."
20. *Kōryaku*, entry for Eitoku 2 (1382)/11/2, quoted in Imaeda, *Chūsei Zenshū-shi no kenkyū*, 476. The entry for Eitoku 2/10/3, also in Imaeda, refers to the forced relocation of elite palaces, temples, and commoner homes.
21. Some structures were culled from local temples and aristocratic residences: the *hattō* was taken from the *hattō* of Tōjiji; the *hōjō* was originally the *shinden* of the residence of Hatakeyama Motokuni. See entry for "Shōkokuji" in Heibon-sha, ed., *Kyōto-shi no chimei*, 563. Also, discussed in Imaeda, *Chūsei Zenshū shi no kenkyū*, 476.
22. *Gyokujin*, quoted in Heibon-sha, ed., *Kyōto-shi no chimei*, entry for "Shōkokuji," 563.
23. *KR* 1:220–242, and Hall, "Kyoto as Historical Background," 10.

24. "京都ノ地ハ公家ノ御計ライナリ." *Kōke* can be translated variously as "emperor," "court," or the "statutory state." I do not believe that this mention refers to *kuge*, generally meaning "the aristocracy" or "nobility."
25. These several entries are from *GMK* 3:34–35.
26. *GMK* 3:40.
27. Ibid.
28. *GMK* 3:40–41.
29. *GMK* 3:46.
30. For representative literature, see Varley, "Ashikaga Yoshimitsu and the World of Kitayama"; Varley, "Cultural Life in Medieval Japan"; Hashimoto, *Architecture in the Shoin Style;* Hashimoto, ed., *Shoin-zukuri;* Itō with Novograd, "The Development of *Shoin*-Style Architecture;" Nishi and Hozumi, *What Is Japanese Architecture?*, 74–77.
31. The findings of this section are discussed in greater detail in Stavros, "Building Warrior Legitimacy in Medieval Kyoto."
32. The sum of our knowledge on this site comes from *MMK* 2:133, 3:82, 5:117, and 119–120; *Mon'yōki*, entry for Jōwa 2 (1346)/2/8 (vol. 73, myōdō-kyō 10), vol. 11, 605; Tōin, *Entairyaku*, vol. 3, 99–100.
33. *Mon'yōki*, entry for Jōwa 2 (1346)/2/8 (vol. 73, myōdō-kyō 10), vol. 11, 605.
34. Sanbōin, *Kenjun sōjō nikki*, entry for Jōwa 2 (1346)/03/01.
35. For a full discussion on the Sanjō-bōmon Palace, see Stavros, "The Sanjō bōmon Temple-Palace Complex." Also, Hosokawa, *Kyōto no jisha to Muromachi bakufu*, part 1, ch. 1, and Tomishima, "Tōjiji butsuden to Shōkokuji hakkō-dō."
36. *Tōjiji-ezu*, ink on paper, 148 cm x 177.5 cm. Property of Tōjiin Temple, Kyoto. Sometimes called *Tōjiji-kozu.* Reproduced in *DNS* 6:5, 602 (leaf) and in color in Museum of Kyoto, ed., *Kyōto: gekidō no chūsei—mikado to shōgun to machishū to*, 30–31.
37. Nakamura Masao, in *KR* 3:384; Sawamura et al., *Shin kenchiku-gaku taikei*, vol. 2, 267– 281.
38. *Sakayuku-hana*, in *GR* 3:514–522. The imperial visit took place on 1381/3/11.
39. See Nakamura, in *KR* 3:388. In English, see Hayashiya with Elison, "Kyoto in the Muromachi Age," 19.
40. Yoshimitsu was promoted to chief councillor of state on 1378/3/10. See *GMK* 2:261.
41. Hashimoto, ed., *Shoin-zukuri.*
42. On the centrality of ritual to *shinden-zukuri*'s function ideal, see the research of Kawamoto Shigeo, especially his *Shinden-zukuri no kūkan to gishiki.*
43. The *haiga* for promotion to chief councillor of state was held on 1379/7/25. The imperial visit was on 1381/3/11–3/16. See *Buke nendaiki*, 109, and the same date entry in Konoe, *Goshinshin-in kanpakuki.* The promotion to grand chancellor of state took place on 1394/12/17. See *Ashikaga-ke kan'iki*, in *GR* 4:270–281.
44. Gokomatsu lived in the Muromachi *shinden* for a year and nine months (1401/2/29 to 1402/11/19). See *DNS* 7:4, 914, and *Ashikaga-ke kan'iki. KR* 3:47 suggests that this stay shows Yoshimitsu's strength. It might, but the

very candidacy of Muromachi as an imperial residence in the first place unquestionably shows that the palace adhered to *shinden*-style models.

45. See, for example, Yokoi, *Higashiyama bunka*, 17–21.
46. Yoshimitsu moved permanently to Kitayama following the death of his wife in the fifth month of 1399. The exact date is unknown.
47. See Varley, "Ashikaga Yoshimitsu and the World of Kitayama."
48. Ibid.
49. This claim is almost ubiquitous. See, for example, Akamatsu and Kawakami, *Kinkaku to Ginkaku*, 74–83.
50. See Stavros, "Locational Pedigree and Warrior Status in Medieval Kyoto." On Yoshimitsu's imperial aspirations, see two works by Imatani: *Muromachi no ōken*, and "Not for Lack of Will or Wile."
51. Fujiwara no Nakako can also be read Fujiwara no Chūshi and often appears in documents as Sūkenmon-in.
52. The texts in which we find the most substantial descriptions of the Kitayama property are *Kitayama-dono gyōkōki; Kōryaku* (excerpted variously in *DNS*); Mansai (Daigoji zasu), *Mansai jugō nikki;* and Yamashina, *Noritoki kyōki. Mon'yōki* also includes several important diagrams as well as descriptive text. Archeological findings confirm that the grounds plans of both followed *shinden*-style models. See Kyōto-shi maizō bunkazai kenkyū-jo, ed., *Tokubetsu shiseki, tokubetsu meisho Rokuonji (Kinkaku-ji) teien, bōsai bōhan shisetsu kōji ni tomonau hakkutsu chōsa.*
53. The event's official record is *Kitayama-in on-judai-ki*, in *GR* 29:690–704. Also see *Kōryaku*, entries for Ōei 14 (1407)/3/5–23, in *DNS* 7:8, 822–826.
54. Gokomatsu was at Kitayama during the period 1408/3/8–28. See *Kitayama-dono gyōkōki*, and Yamashina, *Noritoki kyōki*, vol. 2, 216–236.
55. Yoshimitsu received envoys from the Ming on 1402/9/5, 1403/2/19, 1404/5/16, 1405/5/1, 1405/8/3, 1406/6/11, 1407/8/5, and from Chosŏn on 1403/10/29. See, respectively, *Mansai jugō nikki*, vol. 2, 576; *Yoshida-ke hinamiki*, quoted in Rokuonji, ed., *Rokuon*, 24; *Sanenobu kōki*, in *DNS* 7:6, 700; *Tōji ōdai-ki*, 96; Yamashina, *Noritoki kyōki*, vol. 2, 102–103; and *Yoshida-ke hinamiki*, in *DNS* 7:6, 348.
56. Mansai, *Mansai jugō nikki*, vol. 2, 583–584.
57. Four-legged gates (which actually had six "legs") were an architectural element reserved exclusively for aristocracy with a status of great minister (*daijin*) or higher.
58. See accounts cited in note 55.
59. The reconstruction of the Northern Palace in Figure 5.8 was created by the author based on the archeological findings reported in Kyōto-shi maizō bunkazai kenkyū-jo, ed., *Tokubetsu shiseki, tokubetsu meisho Rokuonji (Kinkaku-ji) teien.*
60. On the location, size, and orientation of Yoshiakira's "new" Sanjō-bōmon Palace, see entries from *Daigeki-shi natsuki* in *Nochikagami*, vol. 1, 700.
61. Even after Yoshimochi moved away from the palace at Muromachi, contemporary authors continued to refer to him and all successive shoguns eponymously as "The Lord of Muromachi" (Muromachi-dono).

62. For details, see Stavros, "Locational Pedigree and Warrior Status in Medieval Kyoto."
63. Representative work includes Hashimoto, *Architecture in the Shoin Style*, and Akamatsu and Kawakami, *Kinkaku to Ginkaku*, 139.
64. For the uses of the *tsune-gosho* and *shō-gosho*, see Fushiminomiya, *Kanmon nikki*, vol. 5, 116–117; Mansai, *Mansai jugō nikki*, vol. 2, 4–5; and *Kaei sandaiki*, in *GR* 26:66–142.
65. The promotion to great minister of the center took place on Eikyō 4 (1432)/7/25. See *Fukō-in dono nin-daijin sechie no shidai*, in *GR* 2:47; Fushiminomiya, *Kanmon nikki*, vol. 4, 75–78; and Mansai, *Mansai jugō nikki*, vol. 2, 407. His promotion to great minister of the left took place on 1432/8/28. See Fushiminomiya, *Kanmon nikki*, vol. 4, 90–91, and *Fukō-in dono sadaijin go-haiga no ki*, in *GR* 22:174–175.
66. Mansai, *Mansai jugō nikki*, entry for Eikyō 4 (1432)/7/25, vol. 2, 407.
67. See Ōta, *Shinden-zukuri no kenkyū*, 710.
68. *Inryōken nichiroku* reports that the reception was modeled after Yoshinori's entertainment of Gohanazono in 1437. Entry for Ōnin 1 (1464)/11/7, in vol. 1, 506.
69. Gohanazono and Gotsuchimikado first took refuge at Muromachi on 1467/1/18. See *Munetaka kyōki*, in *DNS* 8:1, 49.
70. Of equal importance was the Ashikaga construction of Tenryūji Temple in 1339 and the 1345 advent of a nationwide program to construct one official temple and pagoda in every province (*ankokuji/rishōtō* system). Tenryūji and the *ankokuji/rishōtō* system are discussed in Collcutt, *Five Mountains*, 103–109.
71. Takauji presented a proposed diagram for the new palace in 1345. See Tōin, *Entairyaku*, entry for Jōwa 1 (1345)/7/3, in vol. 1, 299. The following year, he forced the matter upon the court's high council for debate. See Tōin, *Entairyaku*, entry for Jōwa 2 (1346)/5/15, in vol. 1, 529.
72. *Moromoriki*, entry for Jōji 4 (1365)/2/21, in *DNS* 6:26, 731. The matter was again taken up by the high council on 1365/3/8. See *Moromoriki*, entry for this date in *DNS* 6:26, 743. Neither entry is in *MMK*.
73. Rice land in Mino Province was set aside. See *Sanbōin monjo*, entry for Jōwa 3 (1354)/1/24, in *DNS* 6:18, 706–707.
74. Tsuchimikado remained the Imperial Palace from 1336 to 1868, the single longest period of locational stability in Japanese imperial history.
75. The collaborative research of the author and Takahashi Yasuo has been published in Takahashi's "Muromachi-ki Kyōto no toshi kūkan." The findings of this section are explained in greater detail in this article.
76. On location as a function of status, see Stavros, "Locational Pedigree and Warrior Status in Medieval Kyoto."
77. What is discussed here on Yoshimitsu's urban plan is an overview of a much more detailed forthcoming study by the author. Also, see the map produced by the author in Takahashi, "Muromachi-ki Kyōto no toshi kūkan."
78. Excavations have uncovered foundation stones thought to be from Yoshimitsu's northern *shinden*. See Sukigara, *Chūsei Kyōto no kiseki*, ch. 3.
79. Detailed in forthcoming publication by the author.

80. On the topic of "buffer zones" around the Imperial Palace, see Momozaki, *Chūsei Kyōto no kūkan-kōzō to reisetsu taikei*, chs. 4 and 5. Also see Nakamachi, "Heian jidai chūki no sato-dairi kūkan." Iibuchi discusses similar earlier notions of space surrounding the palace during the Heian period in *Heian jidai kizoku jūtaku no kenkyū*.
81. For details on the placement of shogunal offspring into positions of religious influence, see *KR* 3:52–53.
82. On this change in general, see Seta, *(Zōho) Rakuchū-rakugai no gunzō*, 251–256.

Chapter 6: Warring States Kyoto

1. Orders were immediately issued for the pagoda to be rebuilt at Kitayama. The new edifice, however, was still unfinished when a storm destroyed it in 1416. It was apparently rebuilt in 1425, but then burned down again in 1470. See Rokuonji, ed., *Rokuon*, 26.
2. Grossberg, *Japan's Renaissance*, 39–43.
3. Donald Keene suggests that Yoshimasa's patronage of the arts contributed to the creation of "the soul of Japan," an expression he uses as the subtitle of his book *Yoshimasa and the Silver Pavilion*.
4. Takahashi Yasuo has written the definitive works on Kyoto's wartime urban landscape. On the period explored in this chapter, his *Kyōto chūsei toshi-shi kenkyū* is most instructive and informs the narrative on urban change described by Mary Elizabeth Berry in her *Culture of Civil War in Kyoto* (59–69). In this chapter, the author relies heavily on Takahashi's foundational work while borrowing from Berry's rich interpretations and reliable translations. For excellent visual materials on wartime destruction, see *AHK*.
5. *Chronicle of Ōnin* (*Ōninki*), entry from early in the sixth month. Translation adapted from Berry, *Culture of Civil War in Kyoto*, 29.
6. Berry, *Culture of Civil War in Kyoto*, 29.
7. Ibid., 61.
8. Ibid., 29 (translation amended).
9. On Shimogyō's plight during the war, see Ashikaga, ed., *Kyōto rekishi atorasu*, 60–61.
10. On the initial reconstruction campaign of 1477 see Takahashi, *Kyōto chūsei toshi-shi kenkyū*, 293–296. Page 295 includes a relevant quote from *Haretomisukuki* (Bunmei 9/3/15) about the plan to reconstruct the grid.
11. From Berry, *Culture of Civil War in Kyoto*, 61, who cites the chronology in *KR* vol. 10.
12. *Rōjin zatsuwa*, in *SKR* 4:272, no. 33 (no year indicated).
13. Rodrigues, *This Island of Japon*, 115.
14. The shogunal headquarters built by Yoshiteru in 1560 was a substantial structure with castle-like characteristics. Despite being short-lived, its location (in the middle of a city) and composition (fortified and surrounded by vassal residences) have led to suggestions that it was a prototype of the early modern castle. For details on this structure, see Takahashi with Stavros, "Castles in Kyoto at the Close of the Age of Warring States," 43–51.

15. The description outlined in this paragraph draws upon the chronology in Berry, *The Culture of Civil War in Kyoto*, 312 n. 32.
16. Takahashi, *Kyōto chūsei toshi-shi kenkyū*, 294.
17. Ibid., 295.
18. Kanroji, *Chikanaga kyōki*, entry for Chōkyō 2 (1488)/3/26, vol. 3, 43.
19. Yamashina, *Tokitsugu kyōki*, entry for Tenbun 17 (1548)/4/28, vol. 2, 395.
20. *Tokitsugu kyōki* and *Nisuiki*, in *SKR* 5:264, nos. 16 and 17.
21. *Sōchō shuki*, entry for Daiei 6/3/28. From Horton, trans., *The Journal of Sōchō*, 104.
22. Berry, *Culture of Civil War in Kyoto*, 61.
23. See, for example, the documents included in *SKR* 5:262–256, several of which are discussed here.
24. *Daijōin jisha zatsujiki*, entry for Bunki 2 (1502)/6/16, in *SKR* 5:253, no. 24. The way Hosokawa refers to the sovereign can be construed as a double insult. First, he broke with custom by referring to the emperor in an extremely direct manner. Second, calling him a "king" (*ō*) instead of one of the more common terms applied to a Japanese sovereign (*kimi*, *shukun*, *tennō*, etc.) would have likely been considered disrespectful.
25. On the "abjection of imperial rituals," see Nakamikado, *Nobutane kyōki*, entry for Eishō 3 (1506)/1/1, vol. 2, 88–89. For this longer quote by Nobutane, see *Nobutane kyōki*, entry for Eishō 14 (1517)/1/1, vol. 2, 251.
26. Yamashina, *Tokitsugu kyōki*, entry for Kyōroku 3 (1530)/1/18, in *SKR* 5:254, no. 28.
27. "Two thirds of the capital has been fortified by trenches." From *Sōchō shuki*, entry for Daiei 7 (1527)/2/12, cited in Niki, "'Odoi' e no michi," 48.
28. For foundational work on *chō-gumi*, see Akiyama and Nakamura, *Kyōto "machi" no kenkyū*, ch. 6. On their profile during wartime, see Takahashi, *Kyōto chūsei toshi-shi kenkyū*, ch. 4, part 3. We cannot know the contemporaneous reading for the characters used for "*chō-gumi*." Recently, scholars have begun using *chō-gumi* instead of *machi-gumi* due to an impulse to more accurately capture the social nature of the phenomenon. See discussion on the difference between *machi* and *chō* in chapter 2.
29. On the re-emergence of Hokke after Ōnin, see Itō, *Toshi no kūkan-shi*, 21–24.
30. On the Hokke uprising, see Imatani, *Tenbun Hokke no ran*, and Berry, *Culture of Civil War in Kyoto*, 153–156.
31. Kujō, *Nochi no jigenin donoki* (1494/10), quoted in Imatani, *Tenbun Hokke no ran*, 36–37.
32. Although not the original western boundary of Sakyō, which was actually Suzaku (later called Senbon), Ōmiya was the western limit of urban development throughout the Muromachi era. See Takahashi et al., eds., *Zushū Nihon toshi-shi*, 86.
33. Excerpt from *Sekijitsu hokka-roku*, quoted in Fujii, "Saikoku o chūshin toshita Muromachi-ki Hokke kyōdan no hatten," 1. Also see *KR* 3:547.
34. See Imatani, *Tenbun Hokke no ran*, and documents in *SKR* 4:283–284.
35. On Kōdō, Hyakumanben, and Rokkakudō, see Takahashi, "'Chōdō' to 'sentō' to hitobito." On Zenchōji, see Ashikaga, ed., *Kyōto rekishi atorasu*, 50–51.

36. This English translation (from the Japanese) of Frois' account is adapted from McKelway, *Capitalscapes*, 115–116.
37. Honnōji and Myōkakuji were used by Nobunaga frequently between 1568 and 1582. See usage graph in Ashikaga, ed., *Kyōto rekishi atorasu*, 66–67.
38. On the activities of *ashigaru* in wartime Kyoto, see *KR* 3:341–344.
39. *Amidaji monjo*, entry for Eiroku 1 (1558)/10/27, in *SKR* 3:369–370, no. 36.
40. *Chionji monjo*, entry for Eiroku 3 (1560)/8/20, in *SKR* 3:370, no. 37.
41. The agency of commoners in premodern Kyoto is treated broadly in Hayashiya, *Machishū*.
42. In English, the authoritative work on *Rakuchū-rakugai-zu* is McKelway, *Capitalscapes*.
43. During the Age of Warring States, *chō-gumi* paid tax and tribute to the shogun on behalf of their constituent neighborhoods.
44. One kind of fortified guard post appears in documents as "*kuginuki*." See, for example, Fushiminamiya, *Kanmon nikki*, entry for Ōei 25 (1418)/6/2, vol. 1, 208 (also vol. 6, 122). Nakahara Yasutomi documents the need for permission to pass through a *kuginuki*. See Nakahara, *Yasutomiki*, vol. 2, 124.
45. For discussion and images, see Takahashi et al., eds., *Zushū Nihon toshi-shi*, 104–105.
46. On the buying and selling of land by commoners, see Seta, "Kinsei toshi seiritsu-shi josetsu," and Wakita, *Nihon chūsei toshi-ron*, esp. ch. 2.
47. On the early articulation of *suki* style, see Takahashi, *Rakuchū-rakugai*, part 2.

Chapter 7: Castle-Town Kyoto

1. For examples, see Schencking, "Catastrophe, Opportunism, Contestation"; and Reddaway, *The Rebuilding of London after the Great Fire*.
2. Hideyoshi's reconstruction of Kyoto has been explored in great detail in English by Mary Elizabeth Berry, first in her doctoral dissertation (Harvard, 1975) and then *Hideyoshi*, 193–203. The second section of this chapter draws liberally on Berry's writings, yet reaches several different conclusions due to findings made after her work was published.
3. On Kyoto as a castle-town, see Imatani, *Nazotoki chūsei-shi*, ch. 3 ("'Miyabi Kyōto' wa jōkaku toshi datta").
4. On the repairs to the Imperial Palace, see *KR* 4, ch. 1.
5. Nijō Castle appears most frequently in documents as "Nijō gosho" (Nijō Palace). The thirteenth shogun, Yoshiteru, had built a fortress at the same site a decade earlier. That structure, however, was much smaller and more short-lived. For a detailed examination, see Takahashi with Stavros, "Capitals in Kyoto at the Close of the Age of Warring States." The traditional centers of Ashikaga authority were at Muromachi and Sanjō-bōmon.
6. Yoshiteru's previous fortress in Kyoto has been called a "castle," even by the author. Recent research, however, has cast doubt on how well fortified that complex was. Yoshiaki's castle is sometimes called Kyū Nijō-jō (the former Nijō Castle) or Nijō-dai. This structure should not be confused with the Nijō

Castle that stands in Kyoto today, built almost half a century later by order of Tokugawa Ieyasu and considered in the epilogue. Records on Yoshiaki's Nijō Castle are reproduced in *DNS* 10:1, 903-, entries for Eiroku 12 (1569)/2/2.

7. The narrative presented here on Nijō-jō is covered in greater detail by Takahashi with Stavros in "Castles in Kyoto at the Close of the Age of Warring States." An account of early construction is in Yamashina, *Tokitsugu kyōki*, entry for Eiroku 12 (1569)/1/27, in *DNS* 10:1, 903-, entries for Eiroku 12 (1569)/2/2.
8. Yamashina, *Tokitsugu kyōki*, entry for Eiroku 12/2/14, and 3/17, in *DNS* 10:1, 903-, entries under Eiroku 12/2/2.
9. *Tamon'in nikki* refers, in particular, to "construction being done by tens of thousands of samurai." Entry for Eiroku 12/2/28, vol. 2, 114.
10. *Yasokai-shi Nihon tsūshin*, vol. 1, 435.
11. For discussion, see Takahashi with Stavros, "Capitals in Kyoto at the Close of the Age of Warring States," 59.
12. *Yasokai-shi Nihon tsūshin*, vol. 1, 433–434.
13. Yamashina, *Tokitsugu kyōki*, entry for Genki 1 (1570)/7/22: "Not having visited for some time, I called upon the shogun and got to see the three-storied, southwest tower (*tenshu*)."
14. Ōta, *Shinchō kōki*, vol. 2, "Kubō onkamae e go fushin no koto." Yamashina, *Tokitsugu kyōki*, entry for Eiroku 12 (1569)/4/2.
15. On Nobunaga, see, for example, *CHJ* 4, ch. 2.
16. On Nobunaga's burning of Kamigyō, see *KR* 4:88–91.
17. The pillage of Nijō Castle is recorded in Yoshida, *Kanemi kyōki*, entries for Genki 3 (1573)/7/12 and 13, vol. 1, 72. Yamashina, *Tokitsugu kyōki*, has the following: "Going to visit the site of the old shogunal castle, it seems as if the townspeople have taken the stones from the previously standing wall" (Tenshō 4 (1576)/9/14); and "Wanting to see the garden of the old shogunal palace, I went along as well. It appears as though townspeople have carried away all the garden stones" (Tenshō 4/9/18).
18. Yamashina, *Tokitsugu kyōki*, entries for Tenshō 4/9/14, vol. 1, 108 (*Dai Nihon kokiroku* edition).
19. Yamashina, *Tokitsugu kyōki*, entry for Tenshō 4/10/25, vol. 1, 110 (*Dai Nihon kokiroku* edition).
20. See Takahashi with Stavros, "Capitals in Kyoto at the Close of the Age of Warring States," 60.
21. These neighborhood names are known from inscriptions in several versions of *Rakuchū-rakugai chizu byōbu* and *Rakuchū ezu*.
22. Hideyoshi's so-called "great urban reconstruction" (*toshi dai-kaizō*) is explored in *KR* 4, ch. 3. Some of the key findings of that early research have since been revised and published, most recently, in Nihon-shi kenkyū-kai, ed., *Toyotomi Hideyoshi to Kyōto*.
23. *Jūroku-nana seiki Iezusukai Nihon hōkoku-shū*, vol. 3, 225. Also see additional documents on the proposed move in *DNS* 11:5, 69.
24. It was this second proposed move that inspired the invasion of Korea in that same year. See Berry, *Hideyoshi*, 206–217.

25. Mary Elizabeth Berry says Hideyoshi was, at best, a "peer" of Ieyasu during the years following Nobunaga's death. *Hideyoshi*, 80.
26. On Hideyoshi's "peace edicts," see Fujiki, *Toyotomi heiwa-rei to sengoku shakai*.
27. Adapted and abbreviated from a translation of Ōmura Yūko's *Tenshōki* by Berry, in *Hideyoshi*, 178.
28. Berry discusses the significance of these titles and the name Toyotomi in *Hideyoshi*, 179.
29. Adapted from the translation by Berry, in *Hideyoshi*, 195. Jurakudai is also often referred to in primary and secondary sources as "Jurakutei."
30. On Jurakudai's composition, see the essays by Morijima and Momose in Nihon-shi kenkyū-kai, ed., *Toyotomi Hideyoshi to Kyōto*.
31. For discussion, see Berry, *Hideyoshi*, 194–196.
32. The formal move (*ishi*) to Jurakudai took place in Tenshō 15 (1587)/9/13. See entries for that date in Yamashina, *Tokitsugu kyōki*, and Yoshida, *Kanemi kyōki*.
33. See Yokota, "Toyotomi seiken to shuto," 20–21.
34. There were three items to the oath. The first is not immediately relevant to this discussion. Adapted from the translation by Berry, in *Hideyoshi*, 143.
35. *Tamon'in nikki*, entry for Tenshō 17 (1589)/9/1, vol. 4, 194.
36. On the creation of a warrior enclave around Jurakudai, see Momose, "Jurakudai no chikujō to toshi no hatten," 137–138.
37. See *CHJ* 3:208.
38. For a translated document on the evictions, see Berry, *Hideyoshi*, 201. Further discussion on the creation of a warrior enclave is in Momose, "Jurakudai no chikujō to toshi no hatten," 137–138.
39. On Hideyoshi's creation of the three temple enclaves (as well as other things), see *KR*, ch. 3, part 3, and *SKR* 5:338–345.
40. See discussion in chapter 6.
41. For details on Agui, see Takahashi, *Kyōto chūsei toshi-shi kenkyū*, ch. 1.
42. The True Pure Land headquarters in Osaka appears in historical records as "Ishiyama Honganji." Ishiyama was the name of the location in Osaka where the temple stood. After the temple's fall, it was the site where Hideyoshi built his Osaka castle.
43. The retrospective character of the temple relocation project is discussed by Berry in *Hideyoshi*, 200–201.
44. Translation from Berry, *Hideyoshi*, 199.
45. On these policies, see Berry, *Hideyoshi*, 106–118.
46. This interpretation was first proposed by Niki in "'Odoi' e no michi."
47. True Pure Land had another headquarters at Yamashina. That too became a *jinai-machi* with significant defensive and martial capacity.
48. See Niki, "'Odoi' e no michi."
49. The neighborhood referred to here appears in documents as Rokuchō-chō. Occupied by high aristocrats since at least the early fifteenth century, Rokuchō-chō is explored in depth in Takahashi, *Kyōto chūsei toshi-shi kenkyū*, ch. 5. For Hideyoshi's policies toward the area, see *KR* 4:288–290.

50. Early research on Hideyoshi's "block splitting," such as that introduced in *KR* 4:299–300, recognized only a few areas in the city where such policies were carried out during Hideyoshi's time. Many more blocks were thought to have been split during the Tokugawa period. More recent findings have suggested, however, that many more blocks were split during Hideyoshi's time than previously thought. See Nakamura, "Toyotomi seiken no Kyōto toshi kaizō." What is introduced here comes mainly from Nakamura's work.
51. On this topic see *KR* 4:307–311 and for related documents, *SKR* 5:369–370, nos. 24–28.
52. The word used for "deliver" ("*kedo*") has a religious connotation, as if suggesting soteriological efficacy. The sword swipes are widely thought to have been inflicted during the Ikedaya incident of 1864.
53. Completed in 1595, Hōkōji was a grand monument to Hideyoshi's patronage of the Buddhist establishment. It included a "great Buddha" enclosed within a structure that was the largest built in Japanese history, and quite possibly the largest single wooden building ever created. See Berry, *Hideyoshi*, 196–198.
54. While a battle may, according to some records, have taken place on a bridge crossing the Kamo River in the twelfth century, a "Great Gojō Bridge" such as that eulogized in songs and folklore did not exist until the 1590s.

Epilogue: Bridge to the Modern

1. *Tokugawa jikki*, quoted in Heibon-sha, ed., *Kyōto-shi no chimei*, 814.
2. Ibid.
3. First explained by Nishi Kazuo in *Kenchiku gijutsu-shi no nazo o toku.*
4. Ieyasu was appointed shogun on 1603/2/12. He entered Nijō on 3/21, after which he held a grand *haiga* celebration to formally mark his investiture. See *SKR* 4:386–387, docs. 9–10.
5. See Takeda, "Hiroma no sōgon," 159–163.
6. Nijō's *tenshu* is pictured, for example, in the Ikeda and Funaki versions of *Rakuchū-rakugai-zu* folding screens. The latter is viewable on *e-Museum* (www.emuseum.jp).
7. On Tokugawa Masako and her *judai*, see Kubota, *Tokugawa Masako.* Masako was later to be called Tōfukumon-in. The procession from Nijō to the Imperial Palace is narrated visually in Mitsui Bunko's *Tōfukumon-in judai-zu*, pictured in Kubota, ed., *Shūkan Asahi hyakka: Nihon no kokuhō*, no. 062, 36–37. On this "Kan'ei expansion," see the entry for "Nijō-jō" in Heibon-sha, ed., *Kyōto-shi no chimei.*
8. Two new structures were built for Masako at the Imperial Palace (Nyōgo goten and Nyōgo osato goten). Together they reportedly rivaled the size of the emperor's residence.
9. The only other sites that might compete for this title are the Katsura and Shūgakuin detached palaces. The current Kyoto Imperial Palace also has several *shoin*-style structures of great historical and cultural value.
10. Major damage was sustained in 1660 (wind and rain), 1662 (storm), 1665 (earthquake), and 1701 (lightning). See the chronology in *KR*, vol. 10.

11. The main part of the Honmaru that stands at the site today was originally a structure at the Katsura detached palace, relocated in 1896.
12. Sixteen other sites in and around Kyoto were inducted along with Nijō Castle. On the (anachronistically named) "Historic Monuments of Ancient Kyoto (Kyoto, Uji and Otsu Cities)," see http://whc.unesco.org/en/list/688 (accessed November 4, 2013).
13. Berry, *Japan in Print*, 103. For leading scholarship on the early modern "noble village," see Toya, "Jinchū kara sōmon no uchi e," and "Kinsei ni okeru kuge-machi no keisei ni tsuite."
14. *Kyōdai ezu*, property of the International Research Center for Japanese Studies (Nichibunken). Viewable at http://tois.nichibun.ac.jp/chizu/santoshi_133.html (accessed November 4, 2013).
15. Major reconstructions and expansion took place in 1611 (first major Tokugawa patronage), 1619 (for Tokugawa Masako), 1641 (after a fire), 1708 (after a fire), 1788 (after the great Tenmei fire), 1854 (after a fire).
16. Takahashi et al., eds., *Zushū Nihon toshi-shi*, 188–189.
17. The only exception is the Reizei residence, which was probably preserved due to its being partially incorporated into the property of Dōshisha University.
18. *O-kanjōdokoro ate oboegaki*, cited in *KR* 4:547–549.
19. From *Hengaku kihan*, in *KR* 5:162.
20. For documents on urban development east of the Kamo River, see Kurokawa, *Yōshū fushi*, vol. 1, and the entry for "Kawahigashi Miyagawa-suji," in *Kyōmachi-kagami*, published in 1686. Both are cited and discussed in Takahashi, *Kyōto chūsei toshi-shi kenkyū*, 48.
21. Called *haibutsu-kishaku*, the Meiji-period campaign to persecute Buddhism is examined in English in Ketelaar, *Of Heretics and Martyrs in Meiji Japan*.

Character Glossary

Aburanokōji 油小路
aburaya 油屋
Agui 安居院
Amida 阿弥陀
Amidaji 阿弥陀寺
Aneyakōji 姉小路
ankokuji 安国寺
Antoku (emperor) 安徳
Arisugawa 有栖川
Ashikaga Tadayoshi 足利直義
Ashikaga Takauji 足利尊氏
Ashikaga Yoshiaki 足利義昭
Ashikaga Yoshiakira 足利義詮
Ashikaga Yoshihisa 足利義尚
Ashikaga Yoshikatsu 足利義勝
Ashikaga Yoshikazu 足利義量
Ashikaga Yoshimasa 足利義政
Ashikaga Yoshimitsu 足利義満
Ashikaga Yoshimochi 足利義持
Ashikaga Yoshinori 足利義教
Ashikaga Yoshiteru 足利義輝
Ashikaga Yoshitsugu 足利義嗣
Asukai 飛鳥井
Asuka-kyō 飛鳥京
Awataguchi 粟田口
Ayanokōji 綾小路
Azuchi 安土
Benkei 弁慶
bessō 別荘
betsugyō 別業
Biwa (-ko, lake) 琵琶(湖)
Biwako sosui 琵琶湖疎水
-bō 坊
Bōjō 坊城
bu 歩
Bueijin-chō 武衛陣町
buke-zukuri 武家造
Bunmei 文明
Buraku-in 豊楽院
bushi 武士
butsuden 仏殿
Byōdōin 平等院
chashitsu 茶室
chéng 城
chinjusha 鎮守社
Chion'in 知恩院
Chionji 知恩寺
Chiteiki 池亭記
chō 町
Chōan (Ch. Chang'an) 長安
Chōdō-in 朝堂院
chō-gumi 町組
Chōhōji 頂法寺
chūmon-rō 中門廊
Daidairi 大内裏
Daigoji 醍醐寺
Daigokuden 大極殿
Daikakuji 大覚寺

Daimon chō　大門町
daimyō　大名
Dairi　内裏
Dairizu　内裏図
Daitokuji　大徳寺
dajō daijin　太政大臣
Dajōkan　太政官
Dannoura　壇ノ浦
Dōshisha　同志社
dosō　土倉
Edo　江戸
eien no miyako　永遠の都（京）
Eiga monogatari　栄華物語
Ejiri　恵止
emaki　絵巻
Emishi　蝦夷
Engishiki　延喜式
Enryakuji　延暦寺
En'yū (emperor)　円融
fuchō　府庁
Fujiwara jidai　藤原時代
Fujiwara-kyō　藤原京
Fujiwara no Ason　藤原朝臣
Fujiwara no Kaneie　藤原兼家
Fujiwara no Kanemichi　藤原兼通
Fujiwara no Michinaga　藤原道長
Fujiwara no Morozane　藤原師実
Fujiwara no Munetada　藤原宗忠
Fujiwara no Nakako (Chūshi)　藤原仲子
Fujiwara no Shōshi　藤原璋子
Fujiwara no Teika　藤原定家
Fujiwara no Tsunefusa　藤原経房
Fujiwara no Yorimichi　藤原頼通
Fukudenji　福田寺
Fukuhara　福原
Funaki　舟木
furo　風呂
Fushimi　伏見
Fusōryakki　扶桑略記
fusuma-e　襖絵
gai-chō　外町
gekyō　下京
Genpei　源平
Ginkakuji　銀閣寺
Gion　祇園
Gion-sai　祇園祭
gissha　牛車
Godaigo (emperor)　後醍醐
Goen'yū (emperor)　後円融
Gohanazono (emperor)　後花園
Gojō　五条
Gojō-bōmon　五条坊門
Gokashiwabara (emperor)　後柏原
gokoku butsuji　護国仏事
Gokomatsu (emperor)　後小松
Gomizunoo (emperor)　後水尾
Gonara (emperor)　後奈良
gon-dainagon　権大納言
Goryō (shrine)　御霊
gosai-e　御斎会
Goshirakawa (emperor)　後白河
Gotoba (emperor)　後鳥羽
Gotsuchimikado (emperor)　後土御門
Goyōzei (emperor)　後陽成
Gozan　五山
Gukanshō　愚管抄
habakari　憚り
Hachijō　八条
haiga　拝賀
hare　晴
Harinokōji　針小路
hashinosunoko　端簀子
Heian Jingū　平安神宮
Heian-kyō　平安京
Heiji　平治
Heijō-kyō　平城京
Heike monogatari　平家物語
henchi　辺地
henushi　戸主
Hiei (-zan)　比叡(山)
Higashikyōgoku　東京極
Higashi no ichi　東市
Higashisanjō　東三条
Higashiyama　東山
Higashiyama-dono　東山殿
Hinokuchi　樋口
Hino Tadamitsu　日野忠光
hisashi　庇
hiwada-buki　檜皮葺
Hōgen　保元

Hōjōji 法成寺
Hōjōki 方丈記
Hōjō Tokiuji 北条時氏
Hōjō Yasutoki 北条泰時
Hōjūji 法住寺
Hōkanji 法観寺
Hokkai-mon 法界門
Hokke 法華
hoko 鉾
Hōkōgōin 法金剛院
Hōkōji 方広寺
hokumen no bushi 北面ノ武士
Honganji 本願寺
honjo 本所
Honkokuji 本国寺
Honmaru 本丸
Honnōji 本能寺
Honpōji 本法寺
Horikawa 堀川
Horikawain 堀川院
Horinouchi-chō 堀之内町
Hosokawa Masamoto 細川政元
Hosokawa Yoriyuki 細川頼之
Hosshōji 法勝寺
Hyakumanben 百万遍
Ichijō 一条
Ichijō Fuyuyoshi 一条冬良
Ichijōin 一条院
Ichijō Tsunetsugu 一条経嗣
ichi no hijiri 市の聖
Ikeda 池田
Ikkō-ikki 一向一揆
ima dairi 今内裏
Imadegawa 今出川
Imanokōji 今小路
Inabadō 因幡堂
Inokuma 猪熊
Insei-ki 院政期
Irie 入江
Ise 伊勢
Ishiyamachi 石屋町
Ishiyama Honganji 石山本願寺
izumi-dono 泉殿
-ji or *–tera* 寺
jibutsudō 持仏堂
Jien 慈円
jihō 寺法
Jimyōin 持明院殿
jinai-machi 寺内町
Jinchū 陣中
Jishōji 慈照寺
Jishū 時宗
Jōdoji 浄土寺
Jōdo Shinshū 浄土真宗
jōgai 城外
jōka-machi 城下町
Jōkyū 承久
Jōnanji 城南寺
jō-raku 上洛
Jōsai (-mon, gate) 上西門
Jōtō (-mon, gate) 上東門
jūbō 住坊
judai girei 入内儀礼
Jurakudai 聚楽第
Jurakudai-zu byōbu 聚楽第図屏風
Jurakutei 聚楽亭
jūyō bunka-zai 重要文化財
kabuki 歌舞伎
Kadenokōji 勘解由小路
kadomatsu 門松
kagariya 篝屋
kaisho 会所
Kajūji 勧修寺
Kamakura 鎌倉
Kameyama 亀山
Kamigyō 上京
kami-watari 上辺
Kamiyamachi 紙屋町
Kamo 鴨 or 加茂
Kamoi-dono 鴨井殿
Kamo no Chōmei 鴨長明
Kan'ei 寛永
Kangakuin 勧学院
Kanmu (emperor) 桓武
Kannon 観音
Kannon-den 観音殿
Kanō Tan'yū 狩野探幽
kanpaku 関白
Kanroji Chikanaga 甘露寺親長
kanshoku 官職
Kanshūji 勧修寺
kaō 花押

kara-hafu 唐破風
Karasuma (road) 烏丸
Karasumaru (family name) 烏丸
karei 家令
karei shokuin-ryō 家令職員令
kashiage 貸上
Kasuga 春日
Katsura 桂
Kawaramachi 河原町
kawara-nōryō 川原納涼
kawa-yuka 川床
Kayain 高陽院
ke 褻 or ケ
Keage 蹴上
kebiishi 検非違使
kedo 化度
ke-gosho 褻御所
keidai 境内
keishi 家司
kenmon 権門
Kenmu shikimoku 建武式目
Kenninji 建仁寺
keryō 家領
ki 気
Kikuchi 菊池
Kikutei 菊亭
kimi 君
Kinchū narabini kuge shohatto 禁中并公家諸法度
Kinkaku 金閣
Kinkakuji 金閣寺
Kinri 禁裏
Kitano 北野
Kita no dai 北第
kitanohe 北辺
Kitanokōji 北小路
Kitayama 北山
Kitayama-dono 北山殿
Kitsuji 木辻
Kiyamachi 木屋町
Kiyomizu 清水
kobashi 小橋
Kōdō 革堂
Kōfukuji 興福寺
Kōgi 公儀
Kogushi 小串
kōji 小路
Kōkamon 皇嘉門
kōke 公家
kokuhō 国宝
kōkyo 皇居
Konjaku-monogatari 今昔物語
Konoe 近衛
Konoe Nobutada 近衛信尹
Kōrokan 鴻臚館
kōsho 巷所
Kōya (-san) 高野(山)
kugai 公界
kuge 公家
Kuge-machi 公家町
kuginuki 釘貫
kugyō girei ni shitagaubeku 公卿儀礼可従
Kujō 九条
Kujō-bōmon 九条坊門
Kujō Hisatsune 九条尚経
Kūkai 空海
Kuni-kyō 恭仁京
kura 倉 or 蔵
kurai 位
kuriya-machi 厨町
Kurodani 黒谷
kurōdo-dokoro 蔵人所
kuruma-dome 車止
Kushige 櫛笥
Kusunoki Masashige 楠木正成
Kūya 空也
kyō 京
kyōchū 京中
kyōchū ashigaru 京中足軽
Kyōdai ezu 京大絵図
Kyōgoku 京極
Kyōgoku-dono 京極殿
Kyōhabutae 京羽二重
kyō no chi 京地
kyō no uchi 京内
Kyōōgokokuji 教王護国寺
kyōshiki 京職
Kyōsuzume 京雀
Kyōto 京都
Kyōto gyoen 京都御苑
Kyōwarabe 京童

machi 町
machi-gumi 町組
machishū 町衆
machiya 町家 or 町屋
Madenokōji 万里小路
mappō 末法
Marutamachi 丸太町
Masuda Nagamori 増田長盛
Matsubara 松原
Matsuura 松浦
Meigetsuki 明月記
Meiji 明治
Mibu 壬生
midō 御堂
Miidera 三井寺
mikoshi 御輿
mikura-machi 御倉町
Minami no dai 南第
Minamoto no Yoritomo 源頼朝
Minamoto no Yoshiie 源義家
Minamoto no Yoshitsuna 源義綱
Minamoto no Yoshitsune 源義経
Mino 美濃
Miyako 都 or 京
mokoshi 裳階
monzeki 門跡
monzeki satobō 門跡里坊
monzen 門前
monzen-machi 門前町
muen-jo 無縁所
Muromachi 室町
Muromachi-dono taikyō sashizu 室町殿大饗指図
Mushanokōji 武者小路
Myōhōin 妙法院
Myōkakuji 妙覚寺
Myōkenji 妙顕寺
Myōmanji 妙満寺
Myōshōgon-iki 妙荘厳域
Nagakute 長久手
Nagaoka-kyō 長岡京
naidaijin 内大臣
Nakahara Moronao 中原師直
Nakahara Moroshige 中原師茂
Nakamikado 中御門
Nakamikado Nobutane 中御門宣胤
Namu Amida Butsu 南無阿弥陀仏
Naniwa-kyō 難波京
Nanzenji 南禅寺
Nawa Nagatoshi 名和長年
nenjūgyōji 年中行事
Nenjūgyōji emaki 年中行事絵巻
Nichiren 日蓮
nie-dono 贄殿
Nijō 二条
Nijō-dai 二条第
Nijō gosho 二条御所
Nijō-jō 二条城
Nijō rikyū 二条離宮
Ninomaru 二の丸
Nishibōjō 西坊城
Nishi-Horikawa 西堀川
Nishikinokōji 錦小路
Nishi-Kushige 西櫛笥
Nishikyōgoku 西京極
Nishi no ichi 西市
Nishi no kyō 西京
nishi-no-tai 西対
Nishinotōin 西洞院
Nishi-Ōmiya 西大宮
Nishi-Yugei 西靭負
Nitta Hyōgo'nosuke 新田兵庫助
Nitta Sama'nosuke 新田左馬助
Nodera 野寺
noh 能
Nyōgo goten 女御御殿
Nyōgo osato goten 女御御里御殿
nyūkyō 入京
nyūraku 入洛
ō 王
Oda Nobunaga 織田信長
odō お堂
Odoi お土居
Ōdoneri 大舎人
Ōgimachi 正親町
Ōinomikado 大炊御門
ōji 大路
Ōmiya 大宮
Ōnin 応仁
Onjōji 園城寺
osame-dono 納殿
Oshinokōji 押小路

Ōtomo 大友
Ōtsu 大津
Parhae (Bohai, Bokkai) 渤海
Pontochō 先斗町
Rajōmon 羅城門
raku 洛
Rakuchū 洛中
Rakuchū-Rakugai 洛中洛外
Rakuchū-rakugai-zu byōbu 洛中洛外図屏風
Rakugai 洛外
Rakunai 洛内
Raku no uchi 洛内
Rakuyō 洛陽
Reizei 冷泉
Rekihaku kōbon 歴博甲本
Rengeōin 蓮華王院
Rikishōji 六勝寺
rishōtō 利生塔
Risshōji 六勝寺
Ritsuryō 律令
rō 廊
Rōjin zatsuwa 老人雑話
Rokkaku 六角
Rokkakudō 六角堂
Rokuhara 六波羅
Rokuhara Mitsuji 六波羅蜜寺
Rokuhara tandai (-fu) 六波羅探題(府)
Rokujō 六条
Rokujō-bōmon 六条坊門
Rokuonji 鹿苑寺
ryō 令
Ryūhonji 立本寺
Saga (emperor) 嵯峨
sagichō 左義長 or 三毬杖
Sai 道祖
Saichō 最澄
Saiji 西寺
Saionji 西園寺
Saionji Sanekane 西園寺実兼
sakaya 酒屋
sakumotsu-sho 作物所
sakura-mon 桜門
Sakura no baba-chō 桜馬場町
Sakyō 左京
Sameushi 左女牛
San'in 山陰
Sanjō 三条
Sanjō-bōmon 三条坊門
Sanjō-dono 三条殿
Sanjō Hachiman 三条八幡
Sanjō Kintada 三条公忠
Sanjō ōhashi 三条大橋
Sanjūsangendō 三十三間堂
sankin kōtai 参勤交代
sanmon 山門 or 三門
sato-dairi 里内裏
Seiganji 誓願寺
Seiryōden 清涼殿
seishi 制止
Seiwa Genji 清和源氏
Sekigahara 関ヶ原
sekkan-ki 摂関期
senkō 先皇
sentō-gosho 仙洞御所
Sen'yūji 泉涌寺
sesshō 摂政
shari-den 舎利殿
Shichijō 七条
Shichijō-bōmon 七条坊門
shigyō-hachimon 四行八門
shiin 私院
shijin sōō 四神相応
Shijō 四条
Shijō-bōmon 四条坊門
Shijō kawara yūryō 四条河原夕涼
shiki 職
Shimogamo 下鴨
Shimogyō 下京
shimo-watari 下辺
Shinano 信濃
Shinchō kōki 信長公記
shinden 神殿
shinden-zukuri 寝殿造
Shingon 真言
Shinmachi 新町
Shinsen'en 神泉苑
Shionokōji 塩小路
Shirakawa (emperor and district) 白河
Shirakawa (river) 白川

Shishinden 紫宸殿
shitaku tenjō 私宅点定
shitomido 蔀戸
shitsurai 室礼
shō 省
Shōbu 菖蒲
shōen 荘園
Shōgoin 聖護院
shō-gosho 小御所
shoin-zukuri 書院造
Shōkokuji 相国寺
shokunin 職人
Shōni 小弐
Shōren'in 青蓮院
shoshi-kuriya-machi 諸司厨町
Shūgakuin 修学院
shugo 守護
Shūi Miyako meisho zue 拾遺都名所図会
shukubō 宿坊
shukun 主君
shūri-sho 修理所
Silla 新羅
sōgamae 惣構
sōmon 総門 or 惣門
sōsō-rei 葬送令
soto-machi 外町
Sūkenmon-in 崇賢門院
suki 数奇 or 数寄
sukiwata-dono kairō 透渡殿回廊
Suminokura Ryōi 角倉了以
sumi-wake 住み分け
sunoko-en 簀子縁
Suzaku 朱雀
tacchū 塔頭
Tachiuri 立売
Taiheiki 太平記
Taihō 大宝
Taika 大化
Taikōki 太閤記
taikyō 大饗
tainoya 対屋
Taira no Ason 平の朝臣
Taira no Kiyomori 平清盛
Takakura 高倉
Takasegawa 高瀬川
Takatsuji 高辻
Takatsukasa 鷹司
Tamon'in nikki 多門院日記
Tendai 天台
tennō 天皇
Tenryūji 天竜寺
Tenshō 天正
Tenshōki 天正記
tenshu-kaku 天守閣
Teramachi 寺町
Teranouchi 寺ノ内
Toba (emperor and district) 鳥羽
Tōfukuji 東福寺
Tōfukumon-in 東福門院
Tōji 東寺
Tōjiji 等持寺
Tōjiji-ezu 等持寺絵図
tojō 都城
Tōkaidō 東海道
Tokugawa Hidetada 徳川秀忠
Tokugawa Iemitsu 徳川家光
Tokugawa Iemochi 徳川家茂
Tokugawa Ieyasu 徳川家康
Tokugawa Masako 徳川和子
Tokugawa Yoshinobu 徳川慶喜
Tōkyō-to 東京都
Tominokōji 富小路
toshi dai-kaizō 都市大改造
Toyotomi Hidetsugu 豊臣秀次
Toyotomi Hideyoshi 豊臣秀吉
Tsuchimikado 土御門
Tsūgenji 通玄寺
tsune-gosho 常御所
Uchino 内野
Uda (road) 宇多
Uesugi 上杉
Uji 宇治
Ukyō 右京
Umajiro 馬代
Umenokōji 梅小路
Uta (basin) 宇太 or 宇多
Utagawa Hiroshige 歌川広重
yagura 櫓
yama (float) 山
Yama (road) 山
Yamada Kunikazu 山田邦和

Yamamomo 楊梅
Yamana 山名
Yamashina Tokitsugu 山科言継
Yamashiro 山城
Yamashiro 山背
Yamashiro kokanshi 山城拒捍使
Yanagihara 柳原
Yanagita Kunio 柳田国男
Yasaka 八坂
Yodo 淀
Yōmei (-mon) 陽明(門)
Yōrō 養老
Yoshida 吉田
Yoshino 吉野
Yoshishige Yasutane 慶滋保胤
yotsu-ashi-mon 四足門 or 四脚門
zasu 座主
Zenchōji 善長寺
zōgū-shiki 造宮識
zuishin-sho 随身所
zuryō 受領
zushi 辻子

Bibliography

Abé, Ryūichi. *The Weaving of Mantra: Kūkai and the Construction of Esoteric Buddhist Discourse.* New York: Columbia University Press, 1999.

Adolphson, Mikael. *Gates of Power: Monks, Courtiers, and Warriors in Premodern Japan.* Honolulu: University of Hawai'i Press, 2000.

Akamatsu Toshihide and Kawakami Mitsugu. *Kinkaku to Ginkaku.* Tokyo: Tankō shinsha, 1964.

Akiyama Kunizō and Nakamura Ken. *Kyōto "machi" no kenkyū.* Tokyo: Hōsei daigaku shuppan-kyoku, 1975.

Amino Yoshihiko. *Igyō no ōken.* Tokyo: Heibon-sha (Heibon-sha raiburarii, no. 951), 1993.

———. *(Zōho) Muen—Kugai—Raku: Nihon chūsei no jiyū to heiwa.* Tokyo: Heibon-sha, 1978.

Ashikaga Kenryō, ed. *Kyōto rekishi atorasu.* Tokyo: Chūō kōrō-sha, 1994.

Ashikaga-ke kan'iki. In *GR* 4:270–281.

Azuma kagami (Shintei zōho). Edited by Kuroita Katsumi. 2 vols. Tokyo: Yoshikawa kōbun-kan, 2000.

Berry, Mary Elizabeth. *The Culture of Civil War in Kyoto.* Berkeley: University of California Press, 1997.

———. *Hideyoshi.* Cambridge, Mass.: Council on East Asian Studies, Harvard University, 1998.

———. *Japan in Print: Information and Nation in the Early Modern Period.* Berkeley: University of California Press, 2006.

Bowring, Richard. *The Religious Traditions of Japan, 500–1600.* Cambridge, UK: Cambridge University Press, 2005.

Buke nendaiki. In *(Zōho) Zoku shiryō taisei*, vol. 51, ed. Takeuchi Rizō. Kyoto: Rinsen shoten, 1979. Reprint 1998.

Cambridge History of Japan. Edited by Donald H. Shively and William H. McCullough. 6 vols. Cambridge, UK: Cambridge University Press, 1988–1999.

Coaldrake, William H. *Architecture and Authority in Japan.* London: Routledge, 1996.

Collcutt, Martin. *Five Mountains: The Rinzai Zen Monastic Institution in Medieval Japan.* Cambridge, Mass.: Council on East Asian Studies, Harvard University, 1981.

Conlan, Thomas. *From Sovereign to Symbol: An Age of Ritual Determinism in Fourteenth-Century Japan.* Oxford, UK: Oxford University Press, 2011.

Dai Nihon shiryō. Edited by Tōkyō daigaku shiryō hensanjo. Tokyo: Tōkyō daigaku shuppan-kai, 1922.

Fiévé, Nicolas, ed. *Atlas historique de Kyoto: Analyse spatiase des systèmes de mémoire d'une ville, de son architecture et de son paysage urbain.* Paris: UNESCO, 2008.

Fujii Manabu. "Saikoku o chūshin toshita Muromachi-ki Hokke kyōdan no hatten: Sono shakai kiban to Hokke ikki o chūshin to shite." *Bukkyō shi-gaku* (Jan. 1957): 1–21.

Fujiki Hisashi. *Toyotomi heiwa-rei to sengoku shakai.* Tokyo: Tōkyō daigaku shuppan-kai, 1985.

Fujiwara no Michinaga. *Midō kanpakuki*. 3 vols. In *Dai Nihon kokiroku*. Tokyo: Iwanami shoten, 1952–1954.

Fujiwara no Munetada. *Chūyūki*. 7 vols. In *Dai Nihon kokiroku*. Tokyo: Iwanami shoten, 1993–2011.

———. *Chūyūki*. 7 vols. In *(Zōho) Shiryō taisei*, vols. 9–15. Kyoto: Rinsen shoten, 2001.

Fujiwara no Sanetsuke. *Shōyūki*. 8 vols. In *Dai Nihon kokiroku*. Tokyo: Iwanami shoten, 1959–1976.

Fujiwara no Teika. *Meigetsuki*. 3 vols. Tokyo: Kokusho kankō-kai, 1969.

Fushiminomiya Sadafusa (Shinnō). *Kanmon nikki*. 6 vols. Tokyo: Kunai-chō shoryō-bu, 2002–2012. Page number citations in notes refer to numbers written in *kanji*, not Arabic numerals.

Gay, Suzanne. *The Moneylenders of Late Medieval Kyoto*. Honolulu: University of Hawai'i Press, 2001.

Goble, Andrew. *Kenmu: Go-daigo's Revolution*. Cambridge, Mass.: Council on East Asian Studies, Harvard University, 1996.

Gomi Fumihiko. "Shichō no kōsei to bakufu: 12–14 seiki no rakuchū shihai." *Rekishi-gaku kenkyū*, no. 392 (1973): 1–19.

Gotō Osamu. *Nihon kenchiku-shi*. Tokyo: Kyōritsu shuppan, 2003.

Grossberg, Kenneth. *Japan's Renaissance: The Politics of the Muromachi Bakufu*. Cambridge, Mass.: Council on East Asian Studies, Harvard University, 1981.

Grossberg, Kenneth A., and Kanamoto Nobuhisa, trans. *The Laws of the Muromachi Bakufu: Kemmu Shikimoku (1336) & Muromachi bakufu tsuikahō*. Tokyo: Monumenta Nipponica, 1981.

Gunma-ken-shi, shiryō hen. 37 vols. Maebashi: Gunma Prefecture, 1977–1992.

Gunsho ruijū. Edited by Hanawa Hokiichi. 530 vols. Tokyo: Zoku gunsho ruijū kansei-kai.

Hall, John W. "Kyoto as Historical Background." In *Medieval Japan: Essays in Institutional History*, ed. John W. Hall and Jeffrey Mass, 3–38. Stanford, Calif.: Stanford University Press, 1974.

Hall, John W., and Jeffrey P. Mass, eds. *Medieval Japan: Essays in Institutional History*. Stanford, Calif.: Stanford University Press, 1974.

Hanazono (Emperor). *Hanazono tennō shinki*. *(Zōho) shiryō taisei*, vols. 2–3. Kyoto: Rinsen shoten, 1965.

Hashimoto Fumio. *Architecture in the Shoin Style: Japanese Feudal Residences*. Tokyo: Kodansha International, 1981.

———, ed. *Shoin-zukuri*. Tokyo: Shibundō, 1972.

Hashimoto Yoshihiko. *Heian kizoku*. Tokyo: Heibon-sha, 1986.

Hayashiya Tatsusaburō. *Machishū: Kyōto ni okeru "shimin" keisei-shi*. Tokyo: Chūō kōron, 1964.

Hayashiya Tatsusaburō with George Elison. "Kyoto in the Muromachi Age." In *Japan in the Muromachi Age*, ed. John W. Hall and Toyoda Takeshi, 15–36. Berkeley: University of California Press, 1977.

Heian ibun. Edited by Takeuchi Rizō. 15 vols. Tokyo: Tōkyō-dō, 1947–1980.

Heibon-sha, ed. *Kyōto-shi no chimei*. Tokyo: Heibon-sha, 1979.

Heike monogatari. *Nihon koten bungaku taikei*, vols. 32–33. Tokyo: Iwanami shoten, 1959–1960.

Hongō Keiko. *Chūsei-jin no keizai kankaku*. Tokyo: Nippon hōsō shuppan kyōkai, 2004.

Hori Ichirō. *Kūya*. Tokyo: Yoshikawa kōbun-kan, 1963.

Horiuchi Akihiro. "Shirakawa gaiku ni okeru chiwari to sono rekishi-teki hensen." In *Insei-ki no dairi/Daidairi to in-gosho*, ed. Takahashi Masaaki, 309–342. Tokyo: Bunrikaku, 2006.

Horton, H. Mack, trans. *The Journal of Sōchō*. Stanford, Calif.: Stanford University Press, 2001.
Hosokawa Taketoshi. *Kyōto no jisha to Muromachi bakufu*. Tokyo: Yoshikawa kōbun-kan, 2010.
Hotate Michihisa. *Heian ōchō*. Tokyo: Iwanami shoten, 1996.
Hurst, G. Cameron III. "The Kōbu Polity: Court-Bakufu Relations in Kamakura Japan." In *Court and Bakufu in Japan: Essays in Kamakura History*, ed. Jeffrey Mass, 3–28. Stanford, Calif.: Stanford University Press, 1982.
———. "*Kugyō* and *Zuryō*: Center and Periphery in the Era of Fujiwara no Michinaga." In *Heian Japan: Centers and Peripheries*, ed. Mikael Adolphson, Edward Kamens, and Stacie Matsumoto, 66–101. Honolulu: University of Hawai'i Press, 2007.
———. "The Structure of the Heian Court." In *Medieval Japan: Essays in Institutional History*, ed. John W. Hall and Jeffrey Mass, 39–59. Stanford, Calif.: Stanford University Press, 1974.
Hyōhanki. In *(Zōho) shiryō taisei*, vols. 18–21. Kyoto: Rinsen shoten, 1965.
Ihara Kesao. *Nihon chūsei no kokusei to kasei*. Tokyo: Azekura shobō, 1995.
Iibuchi Kōichi. *Heian jidai kizoku jūtaku no kenkyū*. Tokyo: Chūō kōron bijitsu shuppan, 2002.
———. "Heian-ki shinden-zukuri ni okeru 'rei' oyobi 'hare' ni tsuite." *Nihon kenchiku gakkai keikaku-kei ronbun-shū*, no. 340 (1984): 149–158.
Imaeda Aishin. *Chūsei Zenshū-shi no kenkyū*. Tokyo: Tōkyō daigaku shuppan kai, 1970. Reissued 2001.
Imatani Akira. *Muromachi no ōken: Ashikaga Yoshimitsu no ōken sandatsu keikaku*. Tokyo: Chūkō shinsho (no. 978), 1990.
———. *Nazotoki chūsei-shi*. Tokyo: Yōsen-sha, 1997.
———. *Tenbun Hokke no ran: Busō suru machishū*. Tokyo: Heibon-sha, 1989.
Imatani Akira with Kozo Yamamura. "Not for Lack of Will or Wile." *The Journal of Japanese Studies* 18, no. 1 (Winter 1992): 45–78.
Inoue Mitsurō. "Insei-ki ni okeru shin-toshi no kaihatsu." In *Chūsei nihon no shosō (kami)*, ed. Yasuda Motohisa-sensei tainin kinen-kai, 339–365. Tokyo: Yoshikawa kōbunkan, 1989.
———. "Insei-ki no Kyōto: Toba to shirakawa." In *Kodai kara chūsei e (Chūsei toshi kenkyū 2)*, 132–150. Tokyo: Shinjin ōrai-sha, 1995.
Inryōken nichiroku. Edited by Tamamura Takeji and Katsuno Takanobu. 5 vols. Tokyo: Eitoku-sha, 1953–1954.
Itō Kiyoshi. *Nanbokuchō no dōran. Nihon no rekishi* series, vol. 8. Tokyo: Shūei-sha, 1992.
Itō Takeshi. *Toshi no kūkan-shi*. Tokyo: Yoshikawa kōbun-kan, 2003.
Itō Teiji with Paul Novograd. "The Development of *Shoin*-Style Architecture." In *Japan in the Muromachi Age*, ed. John W. Hall and Toyoda Takeshi, 227–310. Berkeley: University of California Press, 1977.
Jūroku-nana seiki Iezusukai Nihon hōkoku-shū. Edited by Matsuda Kiichi. 15 vols. Kyoto: Dōhō-sha, 1987–1998.
Kamo no Chōmei. *Hōjōki*. In *Shin Nihon koten bungaku taikei*, vol. 39. Tokyo: Iwanami shoten, 1989.
Kanroji Chikanaga. *Chikanaga kyōki*. 3 vols. In *(Zōho) shiryō taisei*, vols. 41–43. Kyoto: Rinsen shoten, 1955.
Kawakami Mitsugu. "Kinkaku to Ginkaku." In *Nihon bijutsu zenshū (Kitayama, Higashiyama no bijutsu)*, vol. 15, 134–145. Tokyo: Gakushū kenkyū-sha (Gakken), 1979.
———. *Nihon chūsei jūtaku no kenkyū*. Tokyo: Bokusui shobō, 1967. Reissued in 2003 by Chūō kōron bijutsu shuppan.
Kawamoto Shigeo. "Kizoku jūtaku." In *Emakimono no kenchiku o yomu*, ed. Koizumi Kazuko, Tamai Tetsuo, and Kuroda Hideo, 3–28. Tokyo: Tōkyō daigaku shuppan-kai, 1996.
———. *Shinden-zukuri no kūkan to gishiki*. Tokyo: Chūō kōron bijutsu shuppan, 2005.

Kawashima Masao. *Gion-matsuri: Shukusai no miyako.* Tokyo: Yoshikawa kōbun-kan, 2010.
Keene, Donald. *Yoshimasa and the Silver Pavilion: The Creation of the Soul of Japan.* New York: Columbia University Press, 2006.
Ketelaar, James Edward. *Of Heretics and Martyrs in Meiji Japan.* Princeton, N.J.: Princeton University Press, 1993.
Kitamura Masaki. *Heian-kyō: Sono rekishi to kōzō.* Tokyo: Yoshikawa kōbun-kan, 1995.
Kitayama-dono gyōkōki. In *GR* 3:523–567.
Kodera Takehisa. "Heian-kyō no kūkan-teki hensen ni kansuru kōsatsu: Gyōkō roji o chūshin toshite (1)" *Nihon kenchiku gakkai ronbun hōkoku-shū,* no. 165 (Nov. 1969): 93–100.
———. "Heian-kyō no kūkan-teki hensen ni kansuru kōsatsu: Gyōkō roji o chūshin toshite (2)" *Nihon kenchiku gakkai ronbun hōkoku-shū,* no. 166 (Dec. 1969): 65–74.
Koizumi Kazuko, Tamai Tetsuo, Kuroda Hideo, eds. *Emakimono no kenchiku o yomu.* Tokyo: Tōkyō daigaku shuppan-kai, 1996.
Kokushi taikei (Shintei zōho). Edited by Kuroita Katsumi. 60 vols. Tokyo: Yoshikawa kōbun-kan, 1929.
Konoe Michitsugu. *Goshinshin-in kanpakuki.* 2 vols. In *Dai Nihon kokiroku,* ed. Tōkyō daigaku shiryō hensan-jo. Tokyo: Iwanami shoten, 1999–2002.
Kostof, Spiro. *The City Shaped: Urban Patterns and Meanings through History.* Boston: Bulfinch Press, 1991.
Kubota Jun et al., eds. *Shūkan Asahi hyakka: Nihon no kokuhō,* no. 062 (Kyōto/Nijō-jō). Tokyo: Asahi Shinbun-sha, 1998.
Kubota Takako. *Tokugawa Masako.* Jinbutsu sōsho series, no. 252. Tokyo: Yoshikawa kōbun-kan, 2008.
Kuroda Jun'ichirō. "Nihon chūsei no kokka to tennō." *Rekishi hyōron,* no. 320 (1976): 1–14.
Kyoto Costume Museum (Fūzoku hakubutsu-kan), ed. *Genji monogatari Rokujō-in no seikatsu.* Kyoto: Seigensha, 1999.
Kyōto-shi, ed. *Kyōto no rekishi.* 10 vols. Tokyo: Gakugei shorin, 1968–1976.
———. *Shiryō Kyōto no rekishi.* 16 vols. Tokyo: Heibon-sha, 1979–1988.
———. *Yomigaeru Heian-kyō (Heian kento 1200 nen kinen).* Kyōto-shi, 1994.
Kyōto-shi maizo bunka-zai kenkyū-jo, ed. *Insei-ki no Kyōto: Shirakawa to Toba (tuke Hōkōgōin/Hōjūji-dono).* Kyoto: Kyōto maizo bunka-zai kenkyū-jo, 2007.
———. *Tokubetsu shiseki, tokubetsu meisho Rokuonji (Kinkakuji) teien, bōsai bōhan shisetsu kōji ni tomonau hakkutsu chōsa* (Kyōto-shi maizō bunkazai kenkyū-jo chōsa hōkoku, no. 15). Tokyo: Rokuonji Printing, 1997.
Mansai (Daigoji zasu). *Mansai jugō nikki.* 2 vols. Tokyo: Zoku gunsho ruijū kansei-kai, 1928.
Masuda Shigeo. "Heian no waka-shi de 'hare' to 'ke' towa nanika." *Kokubungaku: Kaishaku to kyōzai no kenkyū,* no. 11 (1977): 75–79.
McCullough, Helen C. *Ōkagami: The Great Mirror: Fujiwara Michinaga (966–1027) and His Times. A Study and Translation.* Tokyo: Tokyo University Press, and Princeton, N.J.: Princeton University Press, 1980.
McCullough, William H. "The Capital and Its Society." In *Cambridge History of Japan,* ed. Donald H. Shively and William H. McCullough. Vol. 2, *Heian Japan,* 97–182. Cambridge, UK: Cambridge University Press, 1999.
———. "Japanese Marriage Institutions in the Heian Period." *Harvard Journal of Asiatic Studies,* vol. 27 (1967): 103–167.
McCullough, William H., and Helen McCullough, trans. *A Tale of Flowering Fortunes: Annals of Japanese Aristocratic Life in the Heian Period.* 2 vols. Stanford, Calif.: Stanford University Press, 1980.
McKelway, Matthew. *Capitalscapes: Folding Screens and Political Imagination in Late Medieval Kyoto.* Honolulu: University of Hawai'i Press, 2006.

Mikawa Kei. "Toba-dono to insei." *Nihon-shi kenkyū*, no. 460 (2000): 61–67.

Momose Masatsune. "Jurakudai no chikujō to toshi no hatten." In *Toyotomi Hideyoshi to Kyōto: Jurakudai, Odoi, Fushimi-jō*, ed. Nihon-shi kenkyū-kai, 135–167. Kyoto: Bunrikaku, 2001.

Momozaki Yūichirō. *Chūsei Kyōto no kūkan-kōzō to reisetsu taikei*. Kyoto: Shibun-kaku shuppan, 2010.

———. "Chūsei sato-dairi jinchū no kōzō to kūkan-teki seishitsu ni tsuite." *Shigaku* 73, nos. 2 & 3 [a joint issue] (2004): 49–77.

———. "Chūsei sato-dairi no kūkan kōzō to 'jin.'" *Nihon rekishi*, no. 686 (2005): 17–33.

Mon'yōki. In *Taishō shinshū daizō-kyō, zuzō*, vols. 11–12. Tokyo: Taishō Daizōkyō shinshū kankō-kai, 1975–1978.

Mumford, Lewis. "City: Forms and Functions." In *International Encyclopaedia of the Social Sciences*, vol. 2, 447–455. New York: Macmillan Co. and the Free Press, 1968.

Museum of Kyoto, ed. *Kyōto: Gekidō no chūsei—mikado to shōgun to machishū to*. Kyoto: Kyōto bunka hakubutsu kan, 1996.

Nakahara Moromori. *Moromoriki*. 11 vols. Tokyo: Gunsho ruijū kansei-kai, 1968.

Nakahara Yasutomi. *Yasutomiki*. 4 vols. In *(Zōho) Shiryō taisei*, vols. 37–40. Kyoto: Rinsen shoten, 1965.

Nakamachi Mikako. "Heian jidai chūki no sato-dairi kūkan." *Shirin* 88, no. 4 (2005): 70–99.

Nakamikado Nobutane. *Nobutane kyōki*. 2 vols. In *(Zōho) shiryō taisei*, vols. 44–45. Kyoto: Rinsen shoten, 1955.

Nakamura Takeo. "Toyotomi seiken no Kyōto toshi kaizō." In *Toyotomi Hideyoshi to Kyōto: Jurakudai, Odoi, Fushimi-jō*, ed. Nihon-shi kenkyū-kai, 89–112. Kyoto: Bunrikaku, 2001.

Nakamura Toshinori. *Machiya no chashitsu*. Kyoto: Tankō-sha, 1981.

NHK Special. "Yomigaeru Heian-kyō: Aramata Hiroshi ga saguru 1200-nen no nazo." http://nhk.jp/chronicle/?B10001200999406050130083. Accessed March 1, 2013.

Nihon koten bungaku taikei. 100 vols. Tokyo: Iwanami shoten, 1958–1968.

Nihon-shi kenkyū-kai, ed. *Toyotomi Hideyoshi to Kyōto: Jurakudai, Odoi, Fushimi-jō*. Kyoto: Bunrikaku, 2001.

Niki Hiroshi. *Kūkan, ōyake, kyōdōtai: Chūsei toshi kara kinsei toshi e*. Tokyo: Aoki shoten, 1997.

———. "'Odoi' e no michi: Sengoku/shokuhō-ki ni okeru toshi no tenkai." In *Toyotomi Hideyoshi to Kyōto: Jurakudai, Odoi, Fushimi-jō*, ed. Nihon-shi kenkyū-kai, 43–60. Kyoto: Bunrikaku, 2001.

Nishi Kazuo. *Kenchiku gijutsu-shi no nazo o toku: Kōshō-tachi no chie to kufū*. Tokyo: Shōkoku-sha, 1986.

Nishi, Kazuo, and Kazuo Hozumi. *What Is Japanese Architecture? A Survey of Traditional Japanese Architecture*. Tokyo: Kodansha International, 1985.

Nishikawa Kōji and Takahashi Tōru. *Kyōto sen-nihyaku-nen, kami* (vol. 1). (No. 8 of series: *Nihon-jin wa dono yō ni kenzōbutsu o tsukutte kita ka*.) Tokyo: Sōshisha, 1997.

———. *Kyōto sen-nihyaku-nen, shimo* (vol. 2). (No. 9 of series: *Nihon-jin wa dono yō ni kenzōbutsu o tsukutte kita ka*.) Tokyo: Sōshisha, 1999.

Nochikagami. 4 vols. In *KST* (vols. 34–37).

Oboroya Hisashi. *Heian kizoku to teidai*. Tokyo: Yoshikawa kōbun-kan, 2000.

———. "Ōchō-ki no sumai: Sato dairi to kyō no fūkei." In *Genji monogatari to Heian-kyō: kōko, kenchiku, girei*, ed. Hinata Kazumasa, 124–159. Tokyo: Seikan-sha, 2008.

Ōta Gyūichi. *Shinchō kōki*. Full text and images available online through National Diet Library: http://dl.ndl.go.jp/info:ndljp/pid/2544599.

Ōta Seiroku. *Shinden-zukuri no kenkyū*. Tokyo: Yoshikawa kōbun-kan, 1987. Reissued in 2010.

Reddaway, Thomas F. *The Rebuilding of London after the Great Fire*. London: Arnold, 1951.
Rodrigues, João. *This Island of Japon: João Rodrigues' Account of 16th-Century Japan*. Translated by Michael Cooper. New York: Kodansha America, 1974.
Rokuonji, ed. *Rokuon*. Kyoto: Rokuonji, 1955.
Saionji Kinhira, *Kinhira kōki*. 4 vols. In *Shiryō sanshū*. Tokyo: Zoku gunsho ruijū kansei-kai, 1968–1979.
Sanbōin Kenshun. *Kenshun sōjō nikki*. Entries for Jōwa 2 (1346) and Bunna 4 (1355) transcribed by Hashimoto Hatsuko in Daigoji bunkazai kenkyū-jo, ed. *Kenkyū kiyō*, no. 12 (1992), and no. 13 (1993) respectively.
Sanjō Kindata. *Gogumaiki*. 4 vols. In *Dai Nihon kokiroku*. Tokyo: Iwanami shoten, 1980–1992.
Satō Shin'ichi. *Nanbokuchō no dōran. Nihon no rekishi series*, vol. 9. Tokyo: Chūō kōbun-sha, 1965.
Satō Shin'ichi and Ikeuchi Yoshisuke, eds. *Chūsei hōsei shiryō-shū, vol. 1, Kamakura bakufu-hō*. Tokyo: Iwanami shoten, 1993.
———, eds. *Chūsei hōsei shiryō-shū, vol. 2, Muromachi bakufu-hō*. Tokyo: Iwanami shoten, 1987.
Sawamura Jin et al. *Shin kenchiku-gaku taikei, vol. 2: Nihon Kenchiku-shi*. Tokyo: Shōkokusha, 1999.
Schencking, J. Charles. "Catastrophe, Opportunism, Contestation: The Fractured Politics of Reconstructing Tokyo following the Great Kantō Earthquake of 1923." *Japanese Studies* 29, no. 1 (May 2009): 111–129.
Seta Katsuya. "Kinsei toshi seiritsu-shi josetsu." In *Nihon shakai keizai-shi kenkyū* (Hōgetsu Keigo-sensei kanreki kinen-kai). Tokyo: Yoshikawa kōbun-kan, 1967.
———. *(Zōho) Rakuchū-rakugai no gunzō*. Tokyo: Heibon-sha (Heibon-sha raiburarii, no. 1700), 2009.
Shimizu Hiroshi, "Hōjōji no garan to sono seikaku." *Nihon kenchiku gakkai keikaku-kei ronbun hōkoku-shū*, no. 363 (May 1986): 158–167.
Shiryō sōran. Edited by Tōkyō daigaku shiryō hensanjo. 17 vols. Tokyo: Tōkyō daigaku shuppan-kai, 1963.
Shōyūki. See Fujiwara no Sanetsuke.
Stavros, Matthew. "Building Warrior Legitimacy in Medieval Kyoto." *East Asian History*, no. 31 (2006): 1–28.
———. "A Dis-Integrated Urban Landscape: Making Cities Medieval." *Nihon kodaigaku* 3 (March 2011): 71–101.
———. "Locational Pedigree and Warrior Status in Medieval Kyoto: The Residences of Ashikaga Yoshimitsu." *Japanese Studies* 29 (May 2009): 3–18.
———. "The Sanjō bōmon Temple-Palace Complex: The First Locus of Ashikaga Authority in Medieval Kyoto." *Japan Review*, issue 22 (July 2010): 3–29.
Steinhardt, Nancy Shatzman. *Chinese Imperial City Planning*. Honolulu: University of Hawai'i Press, 1990.
Suematsu Takeshi. "'Ōkagami' hōjōji shodō junkan ni miru ōidono Michinaga." *Shien* 139 (March 2002): 37–62.
Sukigara Toshio. *Chūsei Kyōto no kiseki*. Tokyo: Yuzankaku, 2008.
Taiheiki. Edited by Hasegawa Tadashi. In *Shinpen Nihon koten bungaku zenshū*, vols. 54–57. Tokyo: Shōgakukan, 1994–1998.
Takahashi Shin'ichirō. *Chūsei no toshi to bushi*. Tokyo: Yoshikawa kōbun-kan, 1996.
Takahashi Yasuo. "'Capitals' in Medieval East Asia." In *International Conference on East Asian Architectural Culture, Kyoto 2006*. Conference Proceedings (Discussion Panels), 2006.

———. "'Chōdō' to 'sentō' to hitobito." In *Kyō no rekishi to bunka: sengoku/Azuchi-momoyama jidai. Aya: Tenka-bito no tōjō* (vol. 4), ed. Murai Yasuhiko, 17–56. Tokyo: Kōdansha, 1994.

———. *Kyō machiya: Sennen no ayumi.* Tokyo: Gakugei shuppan-sha, 2001.

———. *Kyōto chūsei toshi-shi kenkyū.* Kyoto: Shibunkaku, 1983.

———. "Machi kara tōri e: Kyōto ni okeru kūkan ha'aku no hensen." In *Nihon toshi-shi nyūmon I: Kūkan*, ed. Takahashi Yasuo and Yoshida Nobuyuki, 238–239. Tokyo: Tōkyō daigaku shuppan-kai, 1986.

———. "Muromachi-ki Kyōto no toshi kūkan: Muromachi-dono to Shōkokuji to Tsuchimikado dairi." In *Seiken toshi (Chūsei toshi kenkyū 9)*, 56–94. Tokyo: Shinjin ōrai-sha, 2004.

———. *Rakuchū-rakugai: Kankyō bunka no chūsei-shi.* Tokyo: Heibon-sha, 1988.

Takahashi Yasuo with Matthew Stavros. "Castles in Kyoto at the Close of the Age of Warring States." In *Japanese Capitals in Historical Perspective: Power, Memory and Place in Kyoto, Edo and Tokyo*, 41–66. London: Curzon Press, 2003.

Takahashi Yasuo, Yoshida Nobuyuki, Miyamoto Masaaki, and Itō Takeshi, eds. *Zushū Nihon toshi-shi.* Tokyo: Tōkyō daigaku shuppan-kai, 1993.

Takeda Tsuneo. "Hiroma no sōgon." In *Nihon bijutsu zenshū (Kitayama, Higashiyama no bijutsu)*, vol. 18, 150–163. Tokyo: Gakushū kenkyū-sha (Gakken), 1979.

Tamon'in nikki. Edited by Tsuji Zennosuke. 6 vols. Tokyo: Kadokawa shoten, 1967.

Tasaka Yasuyuki. "Muromachi-ki Kyōto no toshi kūkan to bakufu." *Nihon-shi kenkyū*, no. 436 (Dec. 1998): 43–71.

Toby, Ronald. "Why Leave Nara?" *Monumenta Nipponica* 40, no. 3 (1985): 331–347.

Tōin Kinkata. *Entairyaku.* Vols. 1–4, Tokyo: Taiyō-sha, 1939. Vols. 5–7, Tokyo: Zoku gunsho ruijū kansei-kai, 1963.

Tōji ōdai-ki. In *Zoku gunsho ruijū*, vol. 29-shimo, 1–106. Edited by Hanawa Hokiichi. 1185 vols. Tokyo: Zoku gunsho ruijū kansei-kai.

Tomishima Yoshiyuki. "Hosshōji garan keitai to sono tokuchō." *Nihon kenchiku gakkai keikaku-kei ronbun-shū*, no. 516 (1999): 243–249.

———. "Hosshōji hakkaku kyūjū no tō no fukugen ni tsuite." In *Kyōto-shinai iseki hakkutsu chōsa hōkoku.* Kyoto: Kyōto-shi bunka shimin-kyoku, 2011.

———. "Insei-ki ni okeru Hosshōji kondō no igi ni tsuite." *Nihon-gaku kenkyū* (Kanazawa kōgyō daigaku Nihon-gaku kenkyū-jo), no. 4 (2001): 23–56.

———. "Shōkokuji shichi-jū no tō: Anchi Butsu to kuyō-e no kūkan kara mita konryū no igi." *Nihon shūkyō bunka kenkyū* 5, no. 1 (2001): 37–66.

———. "Tōjiji butsuden to Shōkokuji hakkō-dō, Kenmitsu Bukkyō kūkan toshite no hyōka ni tsuite." *Bukkyō geijutsu*, no. 273 (March 2004): 33–60.

Toya Nobuhiro. "Jinchū kara sōmon no uchi e: Kuge-machi no seiritsu to sono kūkan-teki tokuchitsu." In *Nenpō toshi-shi kenkyū*, 41–60. Tokyo: Yamakawa shuppan-sha, 2012.

———. "Kinsei ni okeru kuge-machi no keisei ni tsuite." *Kenchiku-shi-gaku*, no. 55 (2010): 2–18.

Tsunoda Bun'ei, ed. *Heian-kyō teiyō.* Tokyo: Kadokawa shoten, 1994.

———. *Ōchō no eizō: Heian jidai-shi no kenkyū.* Tokyo: Tōkyō-dō shuppan, 1970.

Umada Ayako. "Tōji-ryō kōsho: Shōen ryōshu ni yoru toshi-shihai no ichi kōsatsu." *Nihon-shi kenkyū*, no. 159 (1975): 62–86.

Uwayokote Masataka, "*Taiheiki* no shakai." In *Taiheiki no sekai: Henkau no jidai o yomu*, ed. Nagazumi Yasuaki, Uwayokote Masataka, and Sakurai Yoshirō, 181–257. Tokyo: Nippon hōsō shuppan kyōkai, 1987.

Van Goethem, Ellen. "The Four Directional Animals in East Asia: A Comparative Analysis." *Asien- und Afrika-Studien der Humboldt-Universitat zu Berlin* 38 (2011): 201–216.

. *Nagaoka: Japan's Forgotten Capital.* Leiden: Brill, 2008.
Varley, H. Paul. "Ashikaga Yoshimitsu and the World of Kitayama: Social Change and Shogunal Patronage in Early Muromachi Japan." In *Japan in the Muromachi Age*, ed. John W. Hall and Toyoda Takeshi, 193–204. Berkeley: University of California Press, 1977.
———. "Cultural Life in Medieval Japan." In *CHJ* 3:447–499.
———. *Imperial Restoration in Medieval Japan.* New York: Columbia University Press, 1971.
von Verschuer, Charlotte. *Across the Perilous Sea: Japanese Trade with China and Korea from the Seventh to the Sixteenth Centuries.* Ithaca, N.Y.: Cornell University East Asia Series, 2006.
Wakita Haruko. *Nihon chūsei toshi-ron.* Tokyo: Tōkyō daigaku shuppan-kai, 1981.
Watanabe Takashi and Gomi Fumihiko, eds. *Tochi shoyū-shi.* Tokyo: Yamakawa shuppansha, 2002.
Watson, Burton. *Four Huts: Asian Writings on the Simple Life.* Boston: Shambala Publications, 1994.
Yamada Kunikazu. *Kyōto toshi-shi no kenkyū.* Tokyo: Yoshikawa Kōbun-kan, 2009.
———. *Nihon chūsei no shuto to ōken toshi: Kyōto, Saga, Fukuhara.* Tokyo: Bunrikaku, 2012.
Yamashina Noritoki. *Noritoki kyōki.* 3 vols. In *Shiryō sanshū.* Tokyo: Zoku gunsho ruijū kansei-kai, 1970–1974.
Yamashina Tokitsugu. *Tokitsugu kyōki.* 17 vols. In *Dai Nihon kokiroku.* Tokyo: Iwanami shoten, 1959–1991.
———. *Tokitsugu kyōki.* 6 vols. Tokyo: Zoku-gusho ruiju kansei-kai, 1966.
Yanagita Kunio, ed. *Minzokugaku jiten.* Tokyo: Tōkyō-dō shuppan, 1951.
———. *Shokumotsu to shinzō.* In *Yanagita Kunio zenshū*, vol. 10. Tokyo: Tsukuma shobō, 1997.
Yasokai-shi Nihon tsūshin. Edited by Murakami Naojirō. 2 vols. Tokyo: Takubundō, 1943–1944.
Yokoi Kiyoshi. *Higashiyama bunka: Sono haikei to kisō.* Tokyo: Hanbai kyōikusha Sābisu, 1979.
Yokota Fuyuhiko. "Toyotomi seiken to shuto." In *Toyotomi Hideyoshi to Kyōto: Jurakudai, Odoi, Fushimi-jō*, ed. Nihon-shi kenkyū-kai, 18–42. Kyoto: Bunrikaku, 2001.
Yoshida Kanemi, *Kanemi kyōki.* 2 vols. Tokyo: Zoku gunsho ruijū kansei-kai, 1971.
Yoshie Akio. "Chūsei zenki no toshi to bunka." In *Kōza Nihon rekishi 3, chūsei, vol. 1*, 207–252. Tokyo: Tōkyō daigaku shuppan-kai, 1984.
Yoshishige Yasutane. *Chiteiki.* In *Nihon koten bungaku taikei*, vol. 69, 417–436. Tokyo: Iwanami shoten, 1964.
Zoku gunsho ruijū. Edited by Hanawa Hokiichi. 1185 vols. Tokyo: Zoku gunsho ruijū kansei-kai.

Index

Page numbers in **boldface** refer to illustrations.

About the Author

Matthew Stavros is a historian of early Japan at the University of Sydney. He trained in architectural and urban history at Kyoto University and read history at Princeton University, where he earned a PhD in East Asian Studies. He teaches on all periods of Japanese history and historiography, research methods in Asian Studies, classical Japanese, and more broadly on the histories and cultures of East Asia.